STRATEGIES TO HELP SOLVE OUR SCHOOL DROPOUT PROBLEM

Franklin Schargel
Jay Smink

EYE ON EDUCATION
6 Depot Way West, Suite 106
Larchmont, N.Y. 10538

Library of Congress Cataloging-in-Publication Data

Schargel, Franklin P.
    Strategies to help solve our school dropout problem / by
    Franklin P. Schargel, Jay Smink.
        p. cm.
    Includes bibliographical references.
    ISBN 1-930556-14-4
        1. Dropouts—United States—Prevention. 2. School
    improvement programs—United States. 3. Educational
    change—United States. I. Smink, Jay. II. Title.

LC143 .S22 2001
371.2'913'0973—dc21   00-067718

Production services provided by:
ComManagement
1211 Courtland Drive
Raleigh, NC 27604
919.833.3350

Also available from Eye On Education

The Directory of Programs for Students at Risk
By Thomas Williams

Beyond Vocational Education:
Career Majors, Tech Prep, Schools Within Schools,
Magnet Schools, and Academies
By David Pucel

Coaching and Mentoring First-Year and Student Teachers
India Podsen and Vicki Denmark

Collaborative Learning in Middle and Secondary Schools:
Applications and Assessments
Dawn Snodgrass and Mary Bevevino

Data Analysis for Comprehensive Schoolwide Improvement
Victoria Bernhardt

Measurement and Evaluation:
Strategies for School Improvement
James McNamara, David Erlandson, and Maryanne McNamara

Motivating and Inspiring Teachers:
The Educational Leader's Guide for Building Staff Morale
Todd Whitaker, Beth Whitaker, and Dale Lumpa

Performance Assessment and Standards-Based Curricula:
The Achievement Cycle
Allan Glatthorn, et al.

Performance Standards and Authentic Learning
Allan Glatthorn

The School Portfolio: A Comprehensive Framework
For School Improvement, Second Edition
Victoria Bernhardt

Staff Development: Practices That Promote
Leadership in Learning Communities
Sally Zepeda

FOREWORD

Lowering the student dropout rate in America is one of the most significant challenges facing educators today. Without a good education, today's students will be ill prepared to meet the challenges of the new economy and contribute fully to American society. Our children will be able to fulfill the promise of tomorrow only if we enable them to overcome the obstacles of today. Keeping our kids in school, introducing them to the joy of learning, and providing them with an opportunity to truly enjoy their education is paramount to their future success.

I first became interested in solving the problem of student dropouts because of the struggles of the students in my home state of Nevada, which has one of the highest dropout rates in the country. As a member of the Nevada University and Community College System Board of Regents, I worked to keep higher education in Nevada affordable and accessible to all students, so they could continue their education *after* high school. When I became a Member of Congress, I pledged to continue that work and take it a step further by fighting to ensure that students have every opportunity to finish high school.

In my work to keep kids in school, I have talked to students, educators, and parents. I have listened to their struggles and I have learned a great deal from each and every one of them. Local and community involvement in dropout prevention is absolutely vital. Changes at the local level *do* have a positive impact on the graduation rates of students. That's why this book and the strategies for improvement it discusses are so important.

First, the authors call attention to the student dropout problem, a critical issue in the American education system. Second, they offer hope and suggestions on how to resolve this devastating problem using effective strategies taken from research and personal observations gleaned from highly successful dropout prevention programs in many school settings across America. In Congress, I have introduced student dropout legislation that encompasses the strategies discussed in this book. We know that viable solutions *are* available and these proven solutions can offer guidelines for other schools and communities to study and adapt to their own unique conditions. A significant increase in the high school graduation rate is within our reach.

The rapidly changing times of this new millennium require that schools, communities, businesses, and governments become fully committed partners to address this issue. Together, they can reach out to every parent and youth and demonstrate what needs to be done to improve the learning process, increase achievement levels, and increase the graduation rate. The public has made it clear that schools must be improved and held accountable for teaching all students and providing each student with the skills to succeed in life and in the workforce. This book gives insight on how best to address the school improvement issue and offers recommendations to educational leaders at all levels.

After you have read this book, I urge you to join hands with other partners in your sphere of influence and work to provide each child with the best education your community can provide. We have a golden opportunity in this country to make a difference in the lives of millions of children. If we can spark their interest in learning and keep them in school, we will have gone a long way toward ensuring not only our children's future, but also the future of our country. It is essential that the nation as a whole accept the responsibility to resolve the school dropout problem.

The Honorable Shelley Berkley
U.S. House of Representatives
First District, Nevada

ABOUT THE AUTHORS

Franklin P. Schargel is a graduate of the University of the City of New York. He also holds Master's Degrees in secondary education from City University and in school administration and supervision from Pace University, New York. His career spans thirty-three years of classroom teaching and eight years of supervision and administration as an assistant principal.

Franklin served on the Guidelines Development Committee for the Malcolm Baldrige National Quality Award in Education and was for two years an examiner for the Baldrige Award. In addition, he was a judge for the Secretary of the Air Force Quality Award and is now a judge for the USA Today/RIT Quality Cup. He currently serves as vice chair of the American Society of Quality's Education Division.

As president of his training firm, The Schargel Consulting Group, Franklin has presented countless workshops for educational, community, and business groups throughout the United States, Europe, Canada, and Latin America, teaching people how to transform their educational systems into world-class organizations.

The author of the book *Transforming Education Through Total Quality Management: A Practitioner's Guide* and of many articles in leading educational journals and business magazines, Franklin lives in Albuquerque, New Mexico.

Franklin would be interested in hearing from the readers of this book at franklin@schargel.com.

Jay Smink has been the executive director of the National Dropout Prevention Center, located at Clemson University, Clemson, SC, since 1988. He is a professor of education in the College of Health, Education, and Human Development and serves as the executive director of the National Dropout Prevention Network. Dr. Smink earned his M.Ed. in industrial education and Ed.D. in educational administration from Penn State.

His B.S. is in industrial arts from Millersville State College, Pennsylvania.

Dr. Smink was formerly director of marketing and dissemination at the National Center for Research in Vocational Education at The Ohio State University. He served in the Pennsylvania Department of Education as director of the Bureau of Research and Evaluation and as director of the Research Coordinating Unit for Vocational Education. Dr. Smink was the Pennsylvania director of a major nationwide school improvement project that featured the utilization of new curriculum and research products in local schools, and he has conducted many national and regional workshops for administrators, teachers, and community leaders on a wide range of key educational issues. Dr. Smink was a teacher in the Halifax Area School District (Pennsylvania) and also owned and operated a computer micrographics business.

A frequent guest on television and radio talk shows, Dr. Smink is recognized as a national leader and authority on dropout prevention, school reform, mentoring, service learning, alternative schools, school-to-work, project evaluation and accountability, educational marketing, dissemination, and program management.

Dr. Smink would like to hear from the readers of this book at sjay@clemson.edu.

About the National Dropout Prevention Center and Network

The National Dropout Prevention Center (NDPC) is a partnership of concerned leaders—representing business, educational and policy interests, and Clemson University—created to reduce significantly America's dropout rate. NDPC is committed to meeting the needs of youth in at-risk situations by reshaping school and community environments to ensure that all youth will receive the quality education and services to which they are entitled.

Both influenced by and seeking to influence research, practice, policy, and perceptions, NDPC provides technical assistance to develop, demonstrate, and evaluate dropout prevention efforts; conducts action research; and collects, analyzes, and disseminates information about efforts to improve the schooling process.

The National Dropout Prevention Network is a membership organization of more than 3,000 teachers, counselors, school administrators, state department of education staff, and business and community leaders who are concerned with dropout issues. The Network is guided by an Executive Board of national leaders representing educators; policymakers; community, business and labor groups; parents; and other concerned persons. Membership benefits in the Network include free subscriptions to the quarterly *National Dropout Prevention Newsletter* and *The Journal of At-Risk Issues*; complimentary research publications each year; participation in regional institutes and national conferences; and access to special databases and Internet chat lines. Dr. Jay Smink serves as the Executive Director of the National Dropout Prevention Network.

CAVEATS

In this book, we have focused on the problem of dropouts from primary and secondary schools. Although we believe this is far more critical to our nation than the post-secondary school dropout problem, the latter is also a serious concern. Colleges and universities accept the better graduates of our nation's public and private schools, yet they manage to retain only 45 to 50 percent of these students. In totality, only about 25 percent of our school-aged population now graduates from post-secondary schools. In an increasingly brain-dependent society, this should be of great concern.

In Chapter 19, we look briefly at the issue of school dropouts around the world. For most industrialized nations, the causes of the dropout problem are similar to those in the United States. We believe that in these countries, the fifteen strategies we recommend will yield results as dramatic as those to be attained in our own schools. In developing nations, the reasons students leave school vary from region to region; therefore, strategies must be tailored to address the particular causes of the problem in each region.

Many of the programs described in this book cannot be duplicated exactly. Schools vary in so many factors (size, community, culture, location, staff, faculty, and administration, to name a few) that "copy cat" duplication will not work. Nevertheless, the programs can serve as models of effective strategies in action, to be adapted or customized to fit individual schools, teachers, educational leaders, and communities.

The fact that we list programs and schools using the fifteen most effective strategies for dropout prevention is not intended as an endorsement. We merely wish to identify some schools and programs that are putting these strategies to work. The schools and programs listed here have provided contact information for publication here. We gratefully acknowledge their support and cooperation.

CONTRIBUTING AUTHORS

This book is a collaborative effort. The ideas for the book were created and initiated by Franklin Schargel and Jay Smink, and, as principal authors, they bear the responsibility for any errors or omissions. As the early research and format of the book began to develop, it became increasingly clear that, since senior staff at the National Dropout Prevention Center were involved in the research and identification process to list the 15 most effective strategies for dropout prevention, they should become significant contributors to the book.

It made perfect sense to capture the unique expertise of each Center staff member and have her contribute to the book by writing about the strategies that she had researched. Therefore, a special acknowledgment goes to each of the senior staff at the National Dropout Prevention Center who served as contributing authors for nine of the chapters as follows:

♦ Marty Duckenfield—Chapter 8, "Service Learning."

♦ Patricia Cloud Duttweiler—Chapter 10, "Out-of-School Enhancement"; Chapter 11, "Professional Development: An Investment in Quality"; and Chapter 15, "Systemic Renewal."

♦ Cheryl Lane—Chapter 14, "Individualized Learning."

♦ Marilyn Madden—Chapter 4, "Family Involvement" and Chapter 18, "Violence Prevention and Conflict Resolution."

♦ Linda Shirley—Chapter 12, "Diverse Learning Styles and Multiple Intelligences."

• Jan Wright—Chapter 5, "Early Childhood Education."

ACKNOWLEDGMENTS

The authors recognize that many other individuals have made important contributions towards the creation of this publication.

In addition to the input of the National Dropout Prevention Center senior staff, hundreds of other educational, community, and business leaders across the nation have given vision and direction to successful dropout prevention programs in local schools. Although we cannot name them all, several appear as contact persons in the section describing effective strategies. The involvement of these innovative schools in numerous National Dropout Prevention Center and Network activities afforded the Center's staff the opportunity to witness the success of different strategies with students in at-risk situations. As local school staff engaged in research, demonstration projects, and professional development activities, the Center's staff and the authors studied the strategies compiled here. On behalf of the school leaders and policymakers who we hope will use this book as a guide in developing their own school improvement plans, we thank them.

We extend a special note of gratitude to Peg Chrestman of the National Dropout Prevention Center for her tireless word processing assistance and for editing the initial drafts. We also wish to thank Susie Turbeville of the Center who provided assistance in reviewing and critiquing several sections of the book.

We are grateful to our editors, Celia Bohanon and Robert Sinclair, who made our multiple voices sound more like one, and to our publisher, Robert Sickles, who understood the vision, supported it, and made it a reality.

Franklin extends thanks to Sandy Schargel—Franklin's intellectual partner, first reader, inspiration and critic—for her faith and understanding.

Finally, our gratitude to David S. and Kelly G. who supplied the inspiration by explaining that being at risk need not be debilitating.

TABLE OF CONTENTS

PART I IDENTIFYING THE PROBLEM 1

1 INTRODUCTION 3

    DROPOUTS—A NATIONAL PROBLEM 3

    HOW IS THE EDUCATIONAL ARENA CHANGING? 5

        AN AGING POPULATION 5

        NEW PATTERNS OF IMMIGRATION 5

        MOVEMENT WITHIN THE COUNTRY 6

        CHANGING FAMILY STRUCTURES 7

        POVERTY 8

        TEENAGE SEX AND PREGNANCY 8

        DRUGS 8

        VIOLENCE AND CRIME 9

    WHAT CAN WE DO ABOUT DROPOUTS? 10

        THE NEED FOR SYSTEMIC RENEWAL 11

    CONCLUSION 12

    REFERENCES 12

    END NOTES 13

2 WHO DROPS OUT AND WHY 14

    INTRODUCTION 14

    DEFINING THE DROPOUT 14

    TYPES OF DROPOUT RATES 16

        EVENT DROPOUT RATES 16

        STATUS DROPOUT RATES 17

        COHORT DROPOUT RATES 18

        HIGH SCHOOL COMPLETION RATES 18

    WHY STUDENTS DROP OUT 20

        FACTORS LINKED TO HIGH DROPOUT RATES 21

PREDICTING DROPOUTS ISN'T THAT SIMPLE 23

WHAT DROPOUTS SAY 24

DROPOUTS ARE A SYSTEMIC PROBLEM 25

CONCLUSION 27

REFERENCES 27

END NOTES 28

PART II STRATEGIES FOR SUCCESS 29

3 IDENTIFYING EFFECTIVE STRATEGIES FOR DROPOUT
PREVENTION 31

INTRODUCTION 31

STATE AND FEDERAL INITIATIVES 31

REVIEW AND ACCOUNTABILITY 33

HALLMARKS OF SUCCESSFUL REFORM 34

A COMPREHENSIVE SCHOOL IMPROVEMENT PLAN 37

FIVE STEPS OF A COMPREHENSIVE SCHOOL
IMPROVEMENT PLAN 38

THE FIFTEEN MOST EFFECTIVE STRATEGIES FOR DROPOUT
PREVENTION 39

EARLY INTERVENTIONS 40

THE BASIC CORE STRATEGIES 41

MAKING THE MOST OF INSTRUCTION 42

MAKING THE MOST OF THE WIDER COMMUNITY 43

CONCLUSION 44

REFERENCES 44

PART III EARLY INTERVENTIONS 45

4 FAMILY INVOLVEMENT 47

INTRODUCTION 47

FAMILY INVOLVEMENT 47

FAMILY INVOLVEMENT DEFINED 48

HOW CAN SCHOOLS SUPPORT FAMILY
INVOLVEMENT? 50

HOW CAN FAMILIES PROMOTE FAMILY
INVOLVEMENT? 51
RELATED RESEARCH AND RESOURCES 52
GUIDELINES FOR EFFECTIVENESS IN FAMILY
INVOLVEMENT 52
EFFECTIVE PROGRAMS AND PRACTICES 56
CONCLUSION 57
REFERENCES 58

5   EARLY CHILDHOOD EDUCATION 60
NATURE VERSUS NURTURE 60
IT'S BEEN PROVEN 61
APPROACHES 63
IT DOESN'T STOP AT PRESCHOOL:
THE EARLY GRADES 66
BEYOND THE EARLY GRADES 69
QUALITY COUNTS 69
CONCLUSION 70
REFERENCES 72

6   READING AND WRITING..................................... 74
CONCLUSION 75

PART IV   THE BASIC CORE STRATEGIES 77

7   MENTORING 79
INTRODUCTION 79
WHY ADOLESCENTS NEED MENTORS 80
STRUCTURED MENTORING PROGRAMS 82
GOALS AND EXPECTED BENEFITS OF MENTORING 84
THE IMPACT OF MENTORING 85
KEY COMPONENTS OF A MENTORING PROGRAM 88
PLANNING A MENTORING PROGRAM 90
LIMITS OF AND CONCERNS ABOUT
MENTORING PROGRAMS 93

PROGRAM EVALUATION 94

EFFECTIVE PROGRAMS AND PRACTICES 95

CONCLUSION 98

REFERENCES 99

8 SERVICE LEARNING 100

INTRODUCTION 100

THE ROOTS OF SERVICE LEARNING 100

WHY SERVICE LEARNING IS EFFECTIVE 102

IMPACT ON ACADEMICS 102

IMPACT ON SOCIAL SKILLS 103

EFFECTIVE PROGRAMS AND PRACTICES 105

CONCLUSION 109

REFERENCES 109

9 ALTERNATIVE SCHOOLING 110

INTRODUCTION 110

THE NEED FOR ALTERNATIVE SCHOOLING
OPPORTUNITIES 111

ALTERNATIVE SCHOOLING FOR STUDENTS AT RISK 113

BEST PRACTICES AND DESIGN RECOMMENDATIONS FOR
ALTERNATIVE SCHOOLS 116

PROGRAM EVALUATION, STANDARDS, AND IMPACT 117

EFFECTIVE PROGRAMS AND PRACTICES 119

CONCLUSION 124

REFERENCES 124

10 OUT-OF-SCHOOL ENHANCEMENT 126

INTRODUCTION 126

WHAT DOES OUT-OF-SCHOOL ENHANCEMENT DO? 127

RESEARCH ON OUT-OF-SCHOOL PROGRAMS 128

CHARACTERISTICS OF QUALITY OUT-OF-SCHOOL
PROGRAMS 129

IMPLEMENTING EFFECTIVE OUT-OF-SCHOOL
PROGRAMS 131

EFFECTIVE PROGRAMS AND PRACTICES 132

LANGUAGE ARTS AFTER-SCHOOL PROGRAMS 132

ACADEMICALLY-ORIENTED AFTER-SCHOOL
PROGRAMS IN OTHER FIELDS 134

RELATED RESOURCES 136

CONCLUSION 137

REFERENCES 137

PART V MAKING THE MOST OF INSTRUCTION 139

11 PROFESSIONAL DEVELOPMENT: AN INVESTMENT IN
QUALITY 141

INTRODUCTION 141

LINKING TEACHER QUALITY AND STUDENT
ACHIEVEMENT 142

HIGH-QUALITY TEACHING 143

INEFFECTIVE PROFESSIONAL DEVELOPMENT PRACTICES 145

COMPONENTS OF EFFECTIVE PROFESSIONAL
DEVELOPMENT 147

EFFECTIVE PROGRAMS AND PRACTICES 149

CONCLUSION 150

REFERENCES 151

12 DIVERSE LEARNING STYLES AND
MULTIPLE INTELLIGENCES 152

INTRODUCTION 152

THE THEORY OF MULTIPLE INTELLIGENCES 153

THE EIGHT INTELLIGENCES 153

BENEFITS OF THE THEORY OF MULTIPLE
INTELLIGENCES 154

INCORPORATING THE THEORY OF MULTIPLE
INTELLIGENCES INTO CLASSROOM PRACTICES 155

EFFECTIVE PROGRAMS AND PRACTICES 155
CONCLUSION 161
REFERENCES 162

13 INSTRUCTIONAL TECHNOLOGIES 163
INTRODUCTION 163
THE DIGITAL DIVIDE 164
THE POTENTIAL OF TECHNOLOGY 166
FORMS OF TECHNOLOGY 166
RESISTANCE TO TECHNOLOGY 167
EFFECTIVE PROGRAMS AND PRACTICES 168
CONCLUSION 169
REFERENCES 169

14 INDIVIDUALIZED LEARNING 171
INTRODUCTION 171
LEARNING FROM THE IEP (INDIVIDUALIZED EDUCATION
    PROGRAM) 172
STRATEGIES FOR INDIVIDUALIZING STUDENTS'
    LEARNING EXPERIENCES 173
EFFECTIVE PROGRAMS AND PRACTICES 174
    INDIVIDUALIZATION IN THE REGULAR CLASSROOM 174
EFFECTIVE PROGRAMS IN ALTERNATIVE SCHOOLS 177
CONCLUSION 178
REFERENCES 179

PART VI MAKING THE MOST OF THE WIDER SCHOOL
    COMMUNITY 181

15 SYSTEMIC RENEWAL 183
INTRODUCTION 183
THE PROBLEM 183
THE SOLUTION: SYSTEMIC RENEWAL 188
EFFECTIVE PROGRAMS AND PRACTICES 188

CONCLUSION 190

REFERENCES 191

16 COMMUNITY COLLABORATION 193

INTRODUCTION 193

COMMUNITY COLLABORATION IS A MUST 193

WHAT ARE COMMUNITY COLLABORATIONS? 194

BASIC COMPONENTS OF COMMUNITY
    COLLABORATIONS 198

IMPACT AND INFLUENCE OF COMMUNITY
    COLLABORATIONS 201

NEW AND FUTURE COMMUNITY COLLABORATIONS 203

EFFECTIVE PROGRAMS AND PRACTICES 203

CONCLUSION 205

REFERENCES 205

17 CAREER EDUCATION AND WORKFORCE READINESS 207

INTRODUCTION 207

THE NEED FOR WORKFORCE READINESS 208

NEW FORMS OF CAREER EDUCATION 209

COMPREHENSIVE CAREER DEVELOPMENT PROGRAMS 210

SCHOOL-TO-WORK OPPORTUNITIES 211

BENEFITS FOR DROPOUT PREVENTION 213

EFFECTIVE PROGRAMS AND PRACTICES 214

CONCLUSION 215

REFERENCES 216

18 VIOLENCE PREVENTION AND CONFLICT RESOLUTION 217

INTRODUCTION 217

THE NEED FOR VIOLENCE PREVENTION PROGRAMS 217

VIOLENCE PREVENTION AND CONFLICT RESOLUTION 220

COMPONENTS OF THE STRATEGY 221

EVIDENCE OF IMPACT 222

EFFECTIVE PROGRAMS AND PRACTICES 224

CONCLUSION 225
REFERENCES 225

PART VII PERSPECTIVES AND PRESCRIPTIONS 227

19 THE GLOBAL PERSPECTIVE 229
INTRODUCTION 229
EUROPE 230
CANADA 232
DEVELOPING NATIONS 234
ARAB NATIONS 235
LATIN AMERICA AND THE CARIBBEAN 236
ASIA 236
SOUTHWEST ASIA 237
CONCLUSION 239
REFERENCES 239

20 A PRESCRIPTION FOR AMERICA 241
INTRODUCTION 241
SCHOOLS 243
STUDENTS 245
PARENTS 245
TEACHERS 246
GOVERNMENT LEADERS 247
THE BUSINESS COMMUNITY 248
THE MEDIA 250
THE REST OF US 250
REFERENCES 252

PART I

IDENTIFYING THE PROBLEM

There is no question that a school dropout problem exists, that it is serious, and that we must make a concerted effort to address the problem. In the next two chapters, we examine this problem in the context of American society and the educational arena in the twenty-first century. We focus on the statistics that add detail and clarity to our image of the students who drop out of school and the reasons they leave. Based on these facts, we outline the essential features of an effective response.

1

INTRODUCTION

*No country has succeeded without educating its people;
education is key to sustaining growth and reducing poverty.*

James D. Wolfensohn, President, The World Bank

In this chapter, we look at the school dropout problem in the context of American society today. We outline demographic and societal trends that influence the educational arena in the twenty-first century. Finally, we identify the need for a concerted effort to address the school dropout problem and set forth the fundamental components of a successful reform initiative.

DROPOUTS—A NATIONAL PROBLEM

Each year, hundreds of thousands of young adults leave school without successfully completing a high school program. As these numbers accumulate year by year, they mount into the millions. "In October 1998, there were 3.9 million 16- through 24-year-olds who were not enrolled in a high school program and had not completed high school"—a figure that represents 11.8 percent of the total population in this age group (Dropout Rates in the United States: 1998).

America's dropout problem is costly to the individual, to business, and to society. Because high school graduates earn 70 percent more than dropouts (Carnevale, 1998), each dropout means losses of gainful employment and tax revenue. Furthermore, dropouts today are more likely to be single parents, be on welfare, commit crimes, and go to prison (82 percent of America's prisoners are high school dropouts (U.S. Dept. of Justice, 1998)

3

Forty-five percent of all the people who earn the minimum wage are high school dropouts, but only 3 percent of college graduates work at minimum wage (U.S. Dept. of Labor, *Time*, 1999)

Our dropout problem is not new; at the beginning of the twentieth century, it was estimated that the United States had a 90 percent high school dropout rate (Dropouts, 1998). But until 1945, school dropouts could be absorbed by our economy or our military. As the American economy moved from a brawn-based to a brain-based economy, the absence of a high school diploma became a major deterrent to employability. Within the United States, the bulk of employment (78 percent) is in service industries (Roberts, 1995). Most of these jobs require knowledge, skills, and in all probability, the use of technology.

Today, only 60 percent of dropouts have been able to find work one year after leaving school (OERI, 1991), and if they can't work today, there is little likelihood that they will be working tomorrow. "In any given year, the likelihood of slipping into poverty is about three times higher for high school dropouts than for those who finished high school" (Casey Foundation, 1998, p. 22). In the twenty-first century, lacking a high school diploma virtually guarantees, at best, low-level employment; at worst, poverty or unemployment. Furthermore, American workers now compete for jobs in a global economy. Domestic and multinational producers of goods and services are no longer limited by national borders. They can look to schools worldwide for knowledgeable graduates with a broad range of specialized skills in foreign languages, computer literacy, and technical knowledge.

In the future, the wealth of nations will be more clearly linked to knowledge than to a nation's raw material. As economist Lester Thurow noted, "In the 21st century, the education and skills of the workforce [will] end up being the dominant competitive weapon." (Thurow, 1992)

Department of Education statistics indicate that the national dropout rate is now 14 percent.[1] Although the rate is falling, this is deplorably high for an industrialized nation like the United States. No society can afford to waste 14 percent of its human resources in this way.

How Is the Educational Arena Changing?

Data furnished by the Bureau of the Census, the Bureau of Labor Statistics, and the Departments of Labor, Education and Correction show several trends in the United States that will have a dramatic effect on education in the twenty-first century.[2] These include demographic changes (an aging population, new immigration patterns, movement within the country, a changing family structure) and societal changes (increased poverty, teenage sex and pregnancy, drug use, crime and violence).[3]

An Aging Population

America is graying at a rapid rate, and this will continue into the twenty-first century. Children are becoming a declining part of the population while an expanding proportion of the population is becoming elderly. As our population ages, we will become more dependent on fewer workers (and on the schools that educate those workers). Further, as today's white, non-Latino workers age, they will be replaced in the workforce by minority groups—groups that traditionally have greater difficulty in school and a higher dropout rate (*U.S. News*, August 14, 1995, p. 11).

Our aging population will require more government services—not only health and social services, but also other forms of public assistance (such as an expanded public transportation system). Local, state, and federal budgets will feel the pressure. Public schools are expensive to build and to operate. As our population continues to age, there will be an increased demand for a visible return on this educational investment. The elderly already tend to resist funding for schools.[4] In years to come, it will be essential to convince these voters that money spent on schools represents a long-term investment in individuals with a potential for huge returns to the country.

New Patterns of Immigration

We are now quite visibly a nation of immigrants. Most of the "old immigrants" (1492–1965) came from Europe; the societies they left had well-established governments, defined infrastructures, and structured school systems, with trained teachers, organized curriculum, and a tradition of compulsory schooling.

Today, many immigrant students come from nations without compulsory education. Some have never attended school; some are illiterate in their native language as well as in English; many have severe reading limitations. In the United States, school placement is based on age; a five-year-old enters kindergarten, a fourteen-year-old is in the seventh or eighth grade. But placing a student who has never been in school or who has limited school experience in a middle school puts the child in a vulnerable position. The added burden of having to learn English increases the odds that the child will fail or be retained (held back). In addition, today's immigration patterns are leading to a more culturally and ethnically diverse population. More and more teachers are encountering the challenge of teaching classes containing students with a wide mix of native languages and cultural backgrounds. "While there is enormous variance, today's immigrant on average has less education, is more likely to drop out of high school and has an income that does not seem to be catching up with those of native-born Americans" (U.S. Bureau of the Census, Population Profile of the United States: 1995). Helping these new immigrants, many of whom will become citizens, to catch up requires a sustained investment of both time and energy.

MOVEMENT WITHIN THE COUNTRY

Not only are people moving into the United States, they are moving within the country as well. One in six Americans moves each year; the "average American" makes 11.7 moves in a lifetime (Current Population Reports, pp. 20–481). While most moves are local—from one residence to another within the same county—almost 8 million people annually move between counties, and almost 7 million people move to another state (Roberts, 1995). The U.S. Constitution places public education in the hands of the states. Curricula, standards, and the quality of public education vary dramatically from state to state, and even from district to district within a state. A student who moves from a school with high educational standards to a less demanding school loses in one way. But a student who moves to a more challenging school may fall far behind, become discouraged, and possibly even drop out.

CHANGING FAMILY STRUCTURES

In the past century, families have changed radically. Large households are becoming less common, as are households headed by a married couple, and the number of married child-less couples is greater than the number of couples with children. The fastest growing family group is the single-parent household. One-third of all family groups are headed by one parent, including 23 percent of all-white, 61 percent of black, and 33 percent of Hispanic family groups. Single mothers represent 86 percent of all single parents (Day, 1993). According to the Census Bureau, the number of single-parent homes grew from 3.8 million in 1970 to 11.4 million in 1994 (Day, 1993). Divorce has become more common, and it affects the economic well-being of newly-single mothers and their children. Half of the black single mothers and one-third of the white single mothers who were not poor while they were married were likely to be living in poverty within a year after divorce (Day, 1993).

Men and women are marrying later than ever before; increasingly, women are choosing careers, delaying marriage and childbirth. Almost two-thirds of all families now have a mother in the workforce. Even in two-parent families, it is not unusual to have both parents working at two or more jobs (Day, 1993).

These changes in family structures and lifestyles are changing schools as well. Schools now provide meals and extended-day childcare services; they also take a direct role in teaching skills that were traditionally within the domain of the family or church—from driver's education to sex education, from swimming to personal hygiene. Teachers act as supportive adults in order to help learning to take place, but also—often uncomfortably—as surrogate parents dealing with matters beyond their traditional scope or formal training. For many youngsters, the primary adult they speak to during the week is a teacher.

POVERTY

Contrary to popular belief, the largest group living in poverty is not the elderly but the young. Some 15.7 million children are poor. There are more poor American children now than at any other time in the past three decades (U.S. Bureau of the Census, 1995, Population Profile, p. 2). The Department of Labor estimates that one out of four children lives in poverty. Approximately 7.6 million school-age children, more than 17 percent of the total student population, live in poverty (General Accounting Office, 1993). Children bring the problems of poverty into the nation's schools and classrooms. Students who are hungry have difficulty concentrating in class; students who lack adequate medical care may fail to thrive academically; students who have been abused can't function as they should.

TEENAGE SEX AND PREGNANCY

Teenagers are having sex younger than ever before—according to one survey, as early as age 14 (Casey Foundation, 1998). A Kaiser Family Foundation Study of more than 1,500 teens, ages 12 to 18, found that at least 73% of boys and 55% of girls are sexually active by 18 (*USA Today*, June 25, 1996, p. D1). Even though there is an increased awareness and use of birth control devices, the pregnancy rate of sexually active teenagers is still above 20% (Casey Foundation, 1998). More than two thirds of the teenagers who had babies in 1996 were unmarried; among black teenagers having babies, only 10 percent were married. (Casey Foundation, 1998). Furthermore, almost 80 percent of the unmarried women who had a child before finishing high school are living in poverty (compared to 8 percent of those who finish high school, marry, and have a baby after the age of 20) (*New York Times*, March 22, 1994, p. B6).

DRUGS

The acceptance and the use of drugs have grown since the 1960s. "The number of teenagers using marijuana has nearly doubled, according to the Substance Abuse and Mental Health Services Administration, which conducted 22,181 interviews.

Among teenagers 7.3% said they had smoked marijuana in the preceding month, up from 4% in 1992" (*New York Times*, September 13, 1995).

The use of drugs is not just an inner-city problem. For example: "Twenty-four percent of students in New York State have used marijuana at least once, compared with 19% in New York City. Four percent of those in New York State have tried crack as opposed to 2% in New York City. Twelve percent in New York State have tried cocaine as opposed to 9% nationally. White students used drugs more than Hispanic or black" (*New York Times*, December, 1993). Students who use drugs not only lower the quality of their own learning, but frequently disrupt the classroom and interfere with the learning of others.

VIOLENCE AND CRIME

Violence and crime play a large part in the lives of today's children. Children are both victims and perpetrators of violent crime. They face violence in the media, in their homes, and even at school. The American Psychological Association reports that the average child is exposed to 8,000 television murders and more than 100,000 other acts of violence before entering seventh grade (*New York Times*, March 3, 1992 and *USA Today*, Kim Painter, July 10, 1996). The availability of guns and the glorification of violence in films and television has made the use of weapons to settle disputes acceptable. Children have come to see violence as a way to resolve problems.

Jeffrey Grogger, an economist at the University of California at Los Angeles, found that minor levels of violence lowered the chance of students graduating from high school by about one percentage point and their chance of going to a four-year college by four percentage points. Moderate levels of violence reduced the likelihood of high school graduation by about five percentage points and of college attendance by seven percentage points (*Business Week*, August 11, 1997, p. 24).

Disaffected, frequently violent youth, or at-risk children have potentially negative effects on the attitudes, behavior, and achievement of other students. Many schools address the antagonistic, estranged or indifferent youngster by retaining them in a grade. Studies show that this increases the chances of dropping out.

WHAT CAN WE DO ABOUT DROPOUTS?

Schools are succeeding in what they have always done well—preparing highly motivated young people for post-secondary schools and careers. These students learn under almost any conditions. Schools continue to fail where they have always failed—with students with low expectations, students with otherwise committed parents, students with physical and mental handicaps, students who are not interested in the present educational environment. *And that number is growing.*

Seeking to be globally competitive, states have been raising standards and adding new assessments. Other voices call for national standards and national assessments. Yet as a nation, we frequently ignore the students who cannot meet *today's* standards. Some even say that a dropout rate of 1 or 2 percent may be acceptable. But for a child who leaves school, the dropout rate is 100 percent. For the nation, the costs are frequently unknown and unknowable. Could a potential dropout, kept in school, become a skilled surgeon, a creative inventor, a passionate high school teacher?

A great deal has been written on dropout prevention and at-risk children. Much of this literature has focused on placing the blame, rather than remedying the situation or preventing its occurrence. Some blame the dropout problem on the parents; others blame society; still others blame the children. Some choose a short-term, quick-fix solution to this complex problem; when that fails, they try another. Many a proposed remedy addresses the symptoms rather than the causes. Few programs—far too few—focus on systemic reform.

A significant decrease in the number of dropouts cannot possibly come from placing blame, or from inspection-based activities such as tests or higher standards. Rather, it requires fundamental changes in curriculum design processes, work-flow design, and staff training; it demands creative technology use and the development of partnerships with key stakeholders. We need to build dropout prevention into all existing and newly created programs. If we don't, our whole nation will be the loser.

THE NEED FOR SYSTEMIC RENEWAL

We are in the midst of a period of major educational reform. Most of these efforts will not succeed. They will fail for a variety of reasons. The three most prevalent are that the attempted reforms are episodic, that they address symptoms rather than causes, and that they are not systemic.

Reforms Are Episodic. First of all, many reform efforts follow a pattern of starts and stops, spurts and pauses. A movement may begin with rapid growth, spurred by a champion or a group with a passion for its success. At some point, it reaches a plateau; its leaders pause, perhaps seeking new allies, perhaps—as they should—measuring and assessing their progress. Meanwhile, those who resist change (for whatever reason) muster their forces to oppose the reform. At this juncture, the movement will gather strength, fade, or fail.

Schools believe that goals, once achieved, are stopping points. The reality is they are merely plateaus. Once a goal is reached, a new plan must be developed and deployed, actions taken, and the results measured. The cycle is continual.

Reforms Address Symptoms Rather Than Causes. Secondly, most organizations address symptoms rather than the causes of a problem. For one thing, this seems easier, because the symptoms are usually apparent and visible. In addition, as a society we are highly reactive. Rather than taking preventive measures, we wait for a problem to develop. Because we spend most of our time, energy, and resources putting out fires, we have little to devote to correcting the underlying causes.

Reforms Are Not Systemic. The third and most significant reason for failure is the absence of systemic renewal. Educational organizations—indeed, all organizations—are like jigsaw puzzles, composed of interrelated, interconnected pieces. Changing one piece changes and may well distort the entire puzzle. In an organization, changing just one element will not necessarily improve the whole. A district that introduces a new technology or science program without preparing the parents, staff, and teachers in earlier or subsequent grades and schools may be setting the program up for failure. (This is one of the primary reasons why "new math" failed.) Reformers who neglect to look at the whole picture are doomed to fail.

Those who seek a single cure for the complex ills of education—who believe that eliminating one problem will supply the needed remedy—are destined for disillusionment. By contrast, systemic renewal focuses on discovering the root causes, directing efforts to remove them, and preventing their recurrence.

CONCLUSION

Among the most enduring educational problems is that of the student dropout rate. Its ramifications are woven into the fabric of today's American society, an older society whose family structures differ from those of decades past. Elements such as poverty, new patterns of immigration, and other societal shifts make it imperative that our implementation of educational reform include systemic redress of the dropout problem.

REFERENCES

The Annie E. Casey Foundation. (1998). Kids Count Data Book.

Barkley, Bob. NEA National Center for Innovation. Conversation, August 21, 1996.

Business Week, August 11, 1997.

Carnevale, A.P. (1998). Education and Training for America's Future. Washington, DC: The Manufacturing Institute.

Current Population Reports, pp. 20–481, Geographic Mobility: March 1992 to March 1993.

Day, Jennifer Cheeseman. (1993). Population Projections of the United States, by Age, Sex, Race, and Hispanic Origin: 1993 to 2050. U.S. Bureau of the Census, Current Population Reports, Series P25-1104. U.S. Government Printing Office, Washington, DC.

Dropout Rates in the United States: 1998, "Status Dropout Rates."

General Accounting Office, 1993.

New York Times, March 3, 1992.

New York Times, December, 1993.

New York Times, March 22, 1994.

New York Times, September 13, 1995.

OERI. (1991). Youth Indicators 1991: Trends in the Well-being of American Youth. Washington, DC: Office of Educational Research and Improvement, U.S. Department of Education.

Roberts, S. (1995). Who We Are: A Portrait of America Based on the Latest U.S. Census, New York *USA*

Thurow, L. (1992). *Head to Head.* New York, p. 51.

USA Today, Kim Painter, July 10, 1996.

U.S. Bureau of the Census. (1995) Current Population Reports. Series P23-189, Population Profile of the United States: 1995. U.S. Government Printing Office, Washington, DC.

U.S. Bureau of the Census (1995). Statistical Abstract (115th Edition). Washington, DC.

U.S. Department of Justice, Juvenile Justice Bulletin, April 1998.

U.S. Department of Labor, Bureau of Labor Statistics. Reported in *Time* Magazine, November 22, 1999.

U.S. News, Aug. 14, 1995.

U.S. Bureau of the Census, Profile of the Nation.

USA Today, June 25, 1996.

END NOTES

[1] See Chapter 2 for a description of the variety of ways to count dropouts. The percentage used here is a conservative count.

[2] The U.S. Bureau of the Census collects data and issues 43 reports during the course of the ten years between censuses. A number of them have been used in gathering information for this book, including Current Population Reports, Series P23-189, *Population Profile of the United States: 1995*, U.S. Government Printing Office, Washington, DC, 1995. Day, Jennifer Cheeseman. *Population Projections of the United States, by Age, Sex, Race, and Hispanic Origin: 1993 to 2050,* U.S. Bureau of the Census, Current Population Reports, Series P25-1104, U.S. Government Printing Office, Washington, DC, 1993. *Statistical Abstract,* U.S. Bureau of the Census, 1995 (115th Edition), Washington, DC, 1995.

[3] Readers will recognize that the demographic and social factors described here are not uniquely American. Such changes are occurring to a greater or lesser extent within most industrialized societies.

[4] "The elderly systematically vote against education levies when they have a chance. The elderly establish segregated restricted retirement communities for themselves where the young are not allowed to live so that they do not have to pay for schools." Bob Barkley, NEA National Center for Innovation.

2

WHO DROPS OUT AND WHY

A country should be judged by how it cares for its most vulnerable citizens.

Benjamin Netanyahu, Former Prime Minister of Israel

INTRODUCTION

The first step to resolving our school dropout problem is to define the nature of the problem. In this chapter, we describe the various criteria by which dropout rates are measured. We take a closer look at the factors linked to high dropout rates and the characteristics of students who drop out of school. The statistics lead us to the conclusion that the dropout problem can be addressed effectively only by a systemic approach.

DEFINING THE DROPOUT

Trying to determine who drops out, why they drop out, and even the number of dropouts is a complicated process. States differ in their definition of dropouts; they use different time periods during the school year when dropout data are collected, different data collection methods, different ways of tracking youth no longer in school, and different methods of calculating the dropout rate. Some states subtract students who return to school from the dropout total; others do not. Some districts count students enrolled in high school equivalency programs as drop-

14

outs; others do not. Some states count as dropouts those who register early for college without obtaining a high school diploma, enter the military, or enter correctional or mental institutions; others do not. States allow students to leave school at different ages. (See chart, Compulsory Age Requirements.)

"Some states do not report students who receive a certificate of attendance or other alternative certificate, and some do not report the number of students 19 or younger who are awarded a diploma on the basis of the General Education Development (GED) test. Students who completed high school with some credential other than a regular diploma can account for a sizable proportion of the high school completers. For example, in Florida, Louisiana, Oklahoma, and Tennessee, 19 percent or more of the completers received an alternative credential" (U.S. Dept. of Education, Key Statistics, p. 31).

Educators, school boards, and elected officials respond to different pressures in computing statistics on school attendance. Some school districts, seeking additional educational services, carry phantom students on the school records even after they have dropped out.[1] Some states now label districts with a "low performance rating" for having too many dropouts. There, it is in administrators' best interest to embrace a calculation method that makes their rate appear low. In other cases, inflating the rate of dropouts attracts additional funding for at-risk students.

Forty-six states and the District of Columbia "usually report" (National Educational Goals Panel Monthly, p. 2) dropout data through the Common Core of Data Survey to the National Center for Education Statistics. but only twenty-two of them and the District of Columbia were using a common dropout definition adopted by the National Center for Education Statistics (NCES) According to this definition, a dropout is an individual who

- ♦ was enrolled in school at some time during the previous school year and was not enrolled on October 1 of the current school year, or
- ♦ was not enrolled on October 1 of the previous school year although expected to be (e.g., was not reported as a dropout the year before), and

+ was not graduated from high school or completed state- or district-approved educational program, and

+ does not meet any of the following exclusionary conditions:

+ transfer to another public school district, private school, or state- or district-approved educational program,

+ temporary school-recognized absence due to suspension or illness, or

+ death.

Dropout statistics have implications beyond the schoolhouse. The success/failure rate of local schools (frequently measured by graduation rates and post-secondary school attendance rates) helps determine the resale value of homes and is frequently used to influence businesses to move into an area. On the other hand, those who want to shock the public have a motivation to use the methods indicating a high dropout rate. The reality is that as a nation, we do not have a standardized operational definition of who is a dropout, nor do we have a standard method for counting and reporting dropouts. Nevertheless, some useful statistics are available.

TYPES OF DROPOUT RATES

The U.S. Department of Education uses a variety of ways to calculate dropout rates. Each type provides a different perspective of the student dropout population and reveals different ways of viewing the issue. The National Center for Education Statistics presents definitions and data for all four types of dropout rates in order to provide a more complete profile of the dropout problem in the United States.

EVENT DROPOUT RATES

Event dropout rates describe the proportion of students who leave school each year without completing a high school program. For example, event dropout rates for 1997 describe the proportion of youths ages 15 through 24 years who dropped out of grades 10 to 12 in the year preceding October 1997. This annual measure of recent dropout occurrences provides important information about how effective educators are in keeping students enrolled in school.

Demographic data collected in the Current Population Survey (CPS) permit event dropout rates to be calculated across a variety of individual characteristics, including race, sex, region of residence, and income level.

About five out of every 100 young adults enrolled in high school in 1996 left school before October of 1997 without successfully completing a high school program. Students who remained in high school longer than the majority of their age cohort dropped out at higher rates than their younger peers did. Hispanic students were more likely than white and black students to drop out (Headden,1997). Event dropout rates were not significantly different between white and black students.

STATUS DROPOUT RATES

Status rates provide cumulative data on dropouts among all young adults within a specified age range. Specifically, status dropout rates represent the proportion of young adults ages 16 through 24 who are out of school and who have not earned a high school credential. Status rates are higher than event rates because they include all dropouts, regardless of when they last attended school. Since status rates reveal the extent of the dropout problem in the population, this rate also can be used to estimate the need for further education and training designed to help dropouts participate fully in the economy and life of the nation.

Over the last decade, between 300,000 and 500,000 tenth-through twelfth-grade students left school each year without successfully completing a high school program. (Each year some of these young adults return to school or an alternative certification program, and others age out of this group.) In October of 1997, some 3.6 million young adults were not enrolled in a high school program and had not completed high school. These youths accounted for 11 percent of the 33 million 16- through 24-year-olds in the United States in 1997. Like the event rate, this estimate is consistent with those reported over the last 10 years, but lower than in the early 1970s.

Status dropout rates of whites remain lower than for blacks, but over the past quarter century the difference between blacks and whites has narrowed. Hispanic young adults in the United States continue to have higher status dropout rates than either whites or blacks.[2]

COHORT DROPOUT RATES

Cohort rates measure what happens to a group of students from a single age group or specific grade over a period of time. "If a group of students were followed over time, the annual event dropout rates would add up to a larger cohort dropout rate. For example, if 4 percent of students dropped out each year beginning with grade 9, by the end of grade 12 this would add up to a cohort rate of about 15 percent. A cohort rate gives an estimate of how many students eventually fail to complete high school" (U.S. Dept. of Education Key Statistics, p. 32).

HIGH SCHOOL COMPLETION RATES

The high school completion rate represents the proportion of 18- to 24-year-olds who have completed a high school diploma or an equivalent credential, including a General Educational Development (GED) degree. The high school completion rate has increased for white and black young adults since the early 1970s, with 1997 rates of 90.5 percent for whites and 82 percent for blacks. Hispanic young adults have not shared in this improvement, with 66.7 percent reported as having completed high school in 1997.

The majority of students complete a regular diploma and graduate from high school; others complete high school by an alternative route, such as passing the GED exam. During the 1990s the percent of young adults who were not enrolled in school but held a high school credential remained relatively unchanged. However the percentage holding an alternative certification increased from 4.9 percent in 1990 to 9.1 percent in 1997 (and the percentage holding regular diplomas decreased by a similar amount) (The Condition of Education, 1999).

Goal #2 of the National Educational Goals states: By the Year 2000, the high school graduation rate will increase to at least 90 percent. According to the National Education Goals Panel, in 1997 (the last year for which data were available) 18- to 24-year olds in 17 (out of 51) states had already achieved a 90 percent high school completion rate (National Educational Goals Panel, available on line at www.negp.gov/p3-1.htm). Data supplied by the Office of Juvenile Justice and Delinquency Prevention of the Department of Justice are different because they use a three-year average rather than a single year. Below is the percentage rate of high school graduation by state (including Washington, D.C).

STATE	1991–1993	1994–1996	1996 Rank
Connecticut	90.9	96.1	1
Minnesota	91.7	95.3	2
Maryland	91	93.4	3
Nebraska	92.5	93.3	4
North Dakota	95.7	93	5
Hawaii	92.8	92.6	6
Wisconsin	92.4	92.5	7
Massachusetts	90.5	92	8
Maine	93.4	91.8	9
Iowa	94	91.6	10
Kansas	91.4	91.6	10
Utah	94.6	91.3	11
New York	87.6	90.9	12
Montana	91.6	89.8	13
Pennsylvania	90.5	89.6	14
South Dakota	91.2	89.6	14
Wyoming	92.1	89.4	16
Illinois	86	89.3	17
West Virginia	84.6	89.3	17
Missouri	88.3	89.1	19
Delaware	90.3	88.8	20
South Carolina	85.5	88.7	21
Indiana	87.4	88.3	22
Michigan	88.3	88	23

Colorado	87.2	87.9	24
D.C.	87.2	87.8	25
Alaska	89	87.8	25
New Hampshire	89	87.7	27
Ohio	89.7	87.7	27
Rhode Island	90.4	87.5	29
North Carolina	84.2	87.2	31
New Jersey	89.8	87	32
Vermont	89.6	87	32
Oklahoma	81.8	87	32
Alabama	81	86.8	35
Washington	89.2	86.8	35
Arkansas	87.7	86.7	37
Virginia	89.8	86.6	38
UNITED STATES (AVERAGE)	85.7	85.8	39
Arizona	81.1	85.8	39
Idaho	89	85.2	40
Mississippi	88.6	83.9	41
Tennessee	77.5	83.3	42
New Mexico	84.3	82.7	43
Kentucky	82.6	82.2	44
Louisiana	82.5	82.2	44
Nevada	83.3	81.4	46
Georgia	81.9	81.3	47
Oregon	85.5	81.1	48
Florida	84.5	80.1	49
Texas	81.2	79.3	50
California	78.2	78.6	51

(Adapted from Synder and Sickmund, 1999.)

WHY STUDENTS DROP OUT

Would it be useful to draw a profile of the typical dropout? Those who favor such a profile believe that defining those predictors would facilitate early identification and intervention for those most likely to drop out. Those who oppose developing a profile argue that labeling students as likely dropouts would lead educators to expect less of those students.

FACTORS LINKED TO HIGH DROPOUT RATES

Is it possible to draw a profile of the typical dropout? One way to attempt this is to look at the data about who drops out. What factors are linked to high dropout rates?

Student Retention. Poor academic performance linked to retention in one grade is the single strongest school-related predictor of dropping out. One report indicated that out of every ten dropouts, nine had been retained at least one year. Slavin (1991) noted that retention does not improve achievement. "[P]romoted students perform better than non-promoted students in the next year on measures of academic achievement, personal adjustment, self-concept and attitudes toward school... [Further, a] widely quoted finding from the Youth in Transition Study is that one grade retention increases the risk of dropping out by 40 to 50 percent, and more than one by 90 percent" (Slavin, pp. 104–105).

Poverty. "Students from low-income families are three times as likely to drop out of school as those from more affluent homes" (Casey Foundation, 1993, p.11). Female students who come from families in the lowest SES quartile drop out of school at five times the rate of females from the highest quartile. Male students in the lowest quartile drop out at two and a half times the rate of those in the highest quartile (Casey Foundation, 1993).

In 1997, young adults living in families with incomes in the lowest 20 percent of all family incomes were nearly seven times as likely as their peers from families in the top 20 percent of the income distribution to drop out of high school (U.S. Dept. of Education, Dropout, 1993)

Ethnicity. According to the 1999 Goals Panel Report, about 85 percent of all 18- through 24-year-olds who were not enrolled in school had completed high school (a slight increase since the early 1970s). "The rate of school completion exceeds 85 percent for Asians and whites and is about 80 percent for Blacks.... [D]uring the past 12 years the overall national dropout rate for 16- to 24-year-olds has fallen from 14.1 percent to 11 percent"

(U.S. Dept. of Education, Reaching The Goals, p. 1). The bad news is that the graduation and completion rates for Hispanic students have not been rising. This is particularly troubling since there is a growing number of Hispanics in the population and a high number of young Hispanics (Day, 1993).

Limited English Proficiency. In 1995, of those 16- to 24-year-olds who spoke a language other than English at home, the dropout rate was 44 percent of those who had difficulty speaking English, substantially higher than that of those who did not have difficulty speaking English (12 percent) (U.S. Dept. of Education, The Condition of Education, 1997).

Young people from non–English-language backgrounds are one and a half times more likely to leave school than those from English-language backgrounds. So while high school dropout rates have been declining, the trend for Hispanic students is the opposite. In 1992, roughly 50 percent of Hispanics ages 16 to 24 dropped out of high school, up from 30 percent in 1990. The higher Hispanic dropout rate should be coupled with the fact that one-third of the Hispanic immigrant group who came to the United States by 1995 without a high school diploma had not entered an American school (Day, 1993). The dropout rate for Hispanics who do not speak English is between three and four times higher than the rate for those who do (Day, 1993). The large increase in the number of foreign-born Hispanic immigrants with little or no English language skills may help explain the current high dropout rates among this group.

Pregnancy. Teenagers who get pregnant tend to drop out of high school. It has been estimated that between 30 and 40 percent of female teenage dropouts are mothers (Casey Foundation, 1998).

Tracking. Statistics indicate that most dropouts are either from special education or the non–college-bound track.

"Special education" used to indicate predominantly physical disability. Increasingly, it is used to label those unable to function in a traditional school or classroom. These students are often labeled "learning disabled." Minority students generally comprise the majority of learning-disabled special education students.

One study found that 36.4 percent of special education students with physical disabilities dropped out before completing a diploma or receiving a certificate of attendance.

Geographic Location. The dropout rate is higher in the inner cities than in suburbs and non-metropolitan areas. In some districts, it is double the national average.

The dropout rate is higher in the southern and western states than in the mid-Atlantic and New England states. "In 1998, status dropout rates in the Midwest (8 percent) and Northeast (9.4 percent) were significantly lower than dropout rates in the South (13.1 percent) and West (15.3 percent)" (U.S. Dept. of Education, Dropouts, 1998, p.14). Approximately 88 percent of the young adults in the Northeast and Midwest have completed high school, compared to a completion rate of 83.4 percent in the South and 80.4 percent in the West.

PREDICTING DROPOUTS ISN'T THAT SIMPLE

Although certain social, economic, ethnic or racial characteristics increase the statistical likelihood that students will drop out, nobody can predict with any degree of certainty that particular students who have these characteristics will drop out, or that others who do not fit the profile will not. In one 1988 study, the U.S. Department of Education examined information on six commonly used indicators of "at risk" students. These factors included:

- ◆ single-parent family
- ◆ family income of less than $15,000
- ◆ home alone more than three hours a day
- ◆ parents have no high school diploma
- ◆ sibling dropped out
- ◆ limited English proficiency

Over half (53 percent) of the students who dropped out had none of these risk factors, 27 percent had one, and 20 percent had two or more (National Education Longitudinal Study of 1988: A Profile).

The national profile of dropouts from the sophomore class of 1980 shows:

- 66 percent were white
- 87 percent had an English-language home background
- 68 percent came from two-parent families
- 42 percent attended suburban high schools
- 80 percent had neither children nor spouses
- 60 percent had C averages or better
- 71 percent never repeated a grade[3]

Literature from the Goals 2000 campaign confirms this: "It remains true that the majority of dropouts are not those who seem to be most at risk. That is, although the dropout rate for blacks is 50 percent higher than for whites, and twice as high for Hispanics, 66 percent of the actual dropouts are white, while just 17 percent are black and 13 percent are Hispanic. Moreover, most dropouts are not from broken homes, not poor and not pregnant. Consequently, if our graduation rate is to climb to 90 percent, it will have to be achieved by putting greater emphasis on retaining students whose background and behavior are not generally thought of as the defining characteristics of students who drop out" (U.S. Dept. of Education, Reaching the Goals, p. 1).

WHAT DROPOUTS SAY

These mainstream dropouts raise the question of why a large number of seemingly advantaged students leave school. In 1990, tenth-grade dropouts were asked to identify the reasons they left school. The reasons they gave are listed below:

Reasons	Total	Male	Female
School-related:			
Did not like school	51.2	57.8	44.2
Could not get along with teachers	35.0	51.6	17.2
Could not get along with students	20.1	18.3	21.9
Was suspended too often	16.1	19.2	12.7
Did not feel safe at school	12.1	11.5	12.8
Was expelled	13.4	17.6	8.9
Felt I didn't belong	23.2	31.5	14.4
Could not keep up with school work	31.3	37.6	24.7
Was failing school	39.9	46.2	33.1
Changed school, didn't like new one	13.2	10.8	15.8
Job-related:			
Couldn't work and go to school at same time	14.1	20.0	7.8
Had to get a job	15.3	14.7	16.0
Found a job	15.3	18.6	11.8
Family-related:			
Had to support family	9.2	4.8	14.0
Wanted to have family	6.2	4.2	8.4
Was pregnant	31.0	——	31.0
Became parent	13.6	5.1	22.6
Got married	13.1	3.4	23.6
Had to care for family member	8.3	4.6	12.2
Other:			
Wanted to travel	2.1	2.5	1.7
Friends dropped out	14.1	16.8	11.3

(U.S. Department of Education, National Center for Education Statistics, National Education Longitudinal Study of 1988 – First Follow-up Study, 1990.)

DROPOUTS ARE A SYSTEMIC PROBLEM

Some view dropping out as an occurrence. Educators realize it is a process. Frequently the process begins in primary school. As students go through school, an accumulation of negative experiences increases the likelihood that they will drop out. Since students cannot physically leave school in the primary grades, the dropout problem first surfaces in middle or high school. However, there is a growing perception that the needs of at-risk students can and should be addressed in primary school.

The dropout problem begins long before the actual event of leaving school adds another number to the statistics. Furthermore, the dropouts reflected in the statistics do not represent the full extent and complexity of the problem. We can distinguish three types of dropouts:

♦ Dropouts—students who are leaving or have left school.

♦ Tune-outs—students who stay in school but disengage from learning.

♦ Force-outs—those who are suspended or expelled.

The first group is highly visible—easy to identify and measure. These students are the ones most frequently addressed in prevention, retention and recovery programs.

The second category is less readily apparent. These students may attend school regularly, or not. Some pass their classes, earn credits, are promoted, even get relatively good grades. School may be easy for them; it may be boring; it may not meet their needs at all. Unless they cause problems or disrupt classes, they are tolerated, even ignored. Some may eventually drop out. But even if these students complete high school, does the diploma stand for something of value?

The third group contains the troublesome students—those who refuse to follow school rules, or who are involved in crimes either inside or outside school. Rebellious, disruptive, alienated, these students don't fit the system, and they are encouraged—or told—to leave. The school's problem is solved; the student's problem, and our society's problem, is not.

It's time to recognize that the dropout problem is a systemic problem that can be addressed effectively only by a systemic approach. We must look at everything we do in schools with a fresh eye. Our primary goal is not simply to keep students in our classrooms until they graduate, but to provide them with an education that prepares them for a full and productive life beyond the classroom. Each one of our nation's children is a unique and valuable resource. What can we do in schools to make the most of this potential national treasure?

CONCLUSION

The foregoing chapter asked that, before addressing the problem of dropouts, we take a long, hard look at the characteristics of this segment of the population. As we do this, several aspects of the issue come to light which were not necessarily part of our initial belief system. Not only do we find that the identity of dropouts differs from the predictable, but also we encounter an array of varying criteria for measuring the problem. Indeed, the more we study dropouts, the more complicated the research becomes.

REFERENCES

The Annie E. Casey Foundation, Kids Count Data Book, 1993.

The Condition of Education. (1999). National Center for Education Statistics, NCES 1999-022. Washington, DC: U.S. Government Printing Office.

Day, J, *Population Projections of the United States, by Age, Sex, Race, and Hispanic Origin: 1993 to 2050*, U.S. Bureau of the Census, Current Population Reports, Series P25-1104, U.S. Government Printing Office, Washington, D.C., 1993.

Headden, S. (1997). The Hispanic Dropout Mystery. *U.S. News & World Report*, pp. 64-65.

National Educational Goals Panel, available on line at www.negp.gov/p3-1.htm

National Educational Goals Panel Monthly, Vol. 2, No. 19, August 2000.

National Education Longitudinal Study of 1988: A Profile of the American Eighth Grader.

New York Times, December 16, 1999, p. A30

Slavin, R. (1986). Effective Classroom Programs for Students at Risk.

Synder, H., and Sickmund, M. (1999). Juvenile Offenders and Victims, 1999 National Report. Washington, DC: Office of Juvenile Justice and Delinquency Prevention.

U.S. Department of Education. Dropout Rates in the United States: 1998. Office of Educational Research and Improvement.

U.S. Department of Education. Dropout Rates in the United States: 1993. Office of Educational Research and Improvement.

U.S. Department of Education. Key Statistics on Public Elementary and Secondary Schools and Agencies: School Year 1995–96. U.S. Department of Education, Office of Educational Research and Improvement.

U.S. Department of Education. Reaching the Goals: Goal 2 High School Completion. U.S. Department of Education, Office of Educational Research and Improvement.

U.S. Department of Education. (1997). The Condition of Education 1997: The Social Context of Education. U.S. Department of Education.

U.S. Department of Education. (1989). National Center for Education Statistics, High School and Beyond Survey, Sophomore Cohort.

U.S. Department of Education, National Center for Education Statistics, National Education Longitudinal Study of 1988 – First Follow-up Study, 1990.

END NOTES

[1] In New York State, dead students were counted as present and even received report cards with passing grades. *New York Times*, December 16, 1999, p. A30.

[2] High Hispanic dropout rates are partly attributable to counting the foreign-born Hispanics. ". . . [T]he status dropout rate of 44.4 percent for Hispanic 16- through 24-year-olds born outside the 50 states or the District of Columbia was at least double the rate of 20.5 percent for Hispanic youths born in the United States." (Dropout Rates in the United States: 1998. U.S. Department of Education, Office of Educational Research and Improvement, p. 12.)

[3] U.S. Department of Education, National Center for Education Statistics, High School and Beyond Survey, Sophomore Cohort (1989). High School and Beyond is a national longitudinal survey of 1980 high school sophomores and seniors in 1980. The base year survey was a sample of 1,015 high schools with a target number of 36 seniors and 36 sophomores in each of the schools. A total of 58,210 students participated in the base-year survey. The first follow-up activities took place in the spring of 1982. The second survey was done in the spring of 1986. While the data are dated, later studies confirm the information.

PART II

STRATEGIES FOR SUCCESS

Educators, community leaders, business leaders, and policymakers at the local, state, and national level have worked for many years to increase student achievement levels and graduation rates. Though these efforts have not eliminated the school dropout problem, they provide an instructive foundation for future school reform initiatives. We can identify the hallmarks of effective school improvement measures. Even more significantly, we can identify a set of fundamental strategies for dropout prevention.

In the next chapter, we draw on observation and research to identify strategies for dropout prevention. Based largely on the work of the National Dropout Prevention Center, we list fifteen effective strategies for dropout prevention and begin to explore them in detail.

3

IDENTIFYING EFFECTIVE STRATEGIES FOR DROPOUT PREVENTION

We were born to succeed, not to fail.

Henry David Thoreau

INTRODUCTION

We begin this chapter with an overview of school reform initiatives in the United States: How have schools attempted to increase student achievement levels and graduation rates? Next, we examine the outcome of these efforts: What are the hallmarks of effective school improvement measures? Finally, we turn to the question at the heart of this book: What are the most effective strategies for dropout prevention?

STATE AND FEDERAL INITIATIVES

Since 1983, when the report *A Nation at Risk* called for action to raise student achievement levels and high school graduation rates in the United States, many different federal and state agencies have initiated school reforms and social service programs targeted to children and families in at-risk situations. In 1987, the Education Commission of the States conducted a survey of state initiatives for youth at risk (Isenhart and Bechard, 1987) to see how states were responding to the problem of school dropouts. The most common measures were add-on programs tailored to specific problems, needs, and community resources. Many schools introduced preschool programs; Arkansas, for example, chose the Home Instruction Program for Preschool Youngsters (HIPPY), providing guidance for parents who care for their children at home.

Another common state strategy was to introduce pilot projects involving a systemic change in the way services were provided. The underlying belief was that structures that worked most effectively for at-risk children would also benefit all children. For example, Illinois and New York provided funds to set up alternative programs or schools for disruptive students. Florida began a major effort to experiment with full-service schools, allowing multiple social service agencies to interact more freely with local schools, serving both students and families on the school campus.

During the last decade, most states have also designed their own statewide initiatives to help low-performing schools increase achievement levels and reduce dropout rates. Each state has taken its own approach, targeting different student groups, parents, or professional educators. For example, Texas introduced district accountability ratings, based on a combined analysis of attendance rates, dropout rates, and student group performances on the Texas Assessment of Academic Skills (TAAS). North Carolina launched its Early Start Program, Florida and Washington offered full-service schools, and Maryland integrated service learning strategies into its schools.

Many schools and communities have benefited from these programs, yet schools and individual student achievement levels and graduation rates have remained less than satisfactory, as have other social indicators, including neighborhood crime, teenage pregnancies, and families at or below poverty level.

These school- and community-based issues have attracted federal attention as well. For example, just in the last decade the U.S. Congress allowed schools to organize themselves so that those with student poverty rates as low as 50 percent could use Title I funds to improve the entire school. In 1997, Congress authorized additional funding to help low-performing schools seek new programs to raise student achievement. Another major initiative was the U.S. Department of Education's School Dropout Demonstration Assistance Program (SDDAP), which funded 85 dropout-prevention programs from 1991 to 1996. The SDDAP grants, designed to reduce the dropout rates, were awarded to school districts, nonprofit community-based organizations, and educational partnerships. With wide latitude in how they served students, these three-year projects yielded a range of innovative options for addressing the dropout problem.

Although some programs were effective, most SDDAP programs had almost no impact in preventing dropping out (Dynarski and Gleason, 1999). However, the overall evaluation did identify several successful programs offering support to students who had already dropped out and were seeking GED certificates. Alternative schools also showed some successes. But no single program managed to improve all the major objectives examined, including attendance, test scores, and grades.

REVIEW AND ACCOUNTABILITY

There is a need for the federal, state and local governments to recognize the need to search for best practices and identify proven school reform models. As evidence of the multitude of school reform models under study, the Office of Educational Research and Improvement (OERI), U.S. Department of Education, in 1998 published a list of 27 models that they have supported at some time in their development (Talley and Martinez, 1998). A recent review of 24 schoolwide models of school reform, including 18 models from the OERI list, illustrates how many different approaches can be designed and promoted. The report, completed by the American Institutes for Research (Herman, 1999), provided a snapshot of the approaches' relative strengths in three areas: (1) evidence of positive effects on student achievement; (2) support that developers provide schools as they adopt the approaches; and (3) first-year adoption costs. It is interesting to note that only three of these programs showed strong evidence of positive effects on student achievement.

Nearly all state education agencies have also initiated accountability systems directed to local districts and schools to increase their student achievement levels and graduation rates. Many states have targeted the low-performing schools and have been willing to offer them additional technical assistance to improve curriculum and instructional practices. North Carolina and Texas are among the most aggressive states, where principals and teachers can lose their jobs if student achievement levels and other program results do not meet state standards.

Other states have established additional priorities focused on the goals of meeting new state standards and raising student achievement levels compared to other states or to indicators common in the international community. Several of these initiatives—including Florida's full-service schools, Kentucky's overall school reform measures, and Arizona's charter schools—show notable promise.

At the local level, many school districts are designing their own program improvement plans. Some plans are comprehensive, encompassing dramatic administrative and instructional changes across the entire school system. However, most locally developed educational changes tend to address a relatively small segment of the educational system—a new reading program, a new library system, a new charter school or vouchers. Many local districts react to fads or to the availability of new funding sources, such as those that have recently encouraged the creation of after-school homework centers or the development of alternative schools. Furthermore, as districts embrace new programs supported by federal or state agencies, they often encounter an overwhelming flood of mandates and regulations and lose sight of the mission and goals at the local school level. Finally, many local school leaders are not equipped to provide overall guidance and leadership to major school reform initiatives. Thus, despite federal, state, and local initiatives, too often student achievement levels and graduation rates have not appreciably improved.

HALLMARKS OF SUCCESSFUL REFORM

What can responsible school or community leaders do with all the demographic, economic, and education information presented in the previous chapters (or available from many other sources)? How can our schools and communities deliver a more effective educational experience to America's children? What are the characteristics of school reform programs that have succeeded?

Surveying research about the causes of and remedies for disaffected students in the United States, Australia, Europe, and Canada, Reva Klein (1999) posed similar questions. Klein also pondered how the mass of information and the accumulated experience of good practices could be consolidated so that educational leaders are not constantly reinventing wheels, then claiming that the newest and shiniest wheel is the best. She found no easy answers, no quick fixes to reduce the school dropout rate. However, Klein identified proven school improvement processes, successful approaches to working with "disaffected youth" or "students in at-risk situations," and numerous models of excellence that could easily be adapted to other schools and communities.

Samuel C. Stringfield, an educational researcher at Johns Hopkins University, suggests that the keys to success in local programs include readiness for change and the way new programs are implemented. Other researchers have noted different components of effective reform. A recent article in *Education Week* (Olson, 1999) discussed these issues, listing nine key ingredients that help in school reform:

1. Schools are allowed to make a free, informed choice to select the design, based on a decision by its faculty, often through a secret ballot.

2. Faculty members who do not support the design can "transfer with dignity."

3. The principal and other administrators must provide strong leadership at the school site.

4. The design is clear and specific, and the developers must clearly explain how it is supposed to work.

5. Money and time are available for everyone in the school to participate in professional development, planning, and collaboration.

6. The design team must provide structured materials and long-term, targeted technical assistance.

7. A designated person in the school is responsible for managing the reform process.

8. The school participates in a network of like-minded schools and colleagues.

9. The district has stable leadership that supports the design, has a culture of trust between schools and the central office, provides schools with some autonomy over budgets and hiring, and commits resources for professional development and planning.

No single or specific model or process will be the best model for every school and community. However, several guiding principles apply to all. The U.S. Office of Education (Pechman) offers these principles as reminders to local planners:

1. Strong leadership enhances the prospect of successful reforms.

2. Reform goals should be based on a shared vision that includes the active support of a range of stakeholders.

3. School reform takes time and involves risk.

4. Reform participants must have training before they implement reform.

5. Reform strategies should be flexible enough to accommodate several solutions to a given problem.

6. Reform may require redesigning organizational infrastructure.

7. Reform is not cost-free. Prospects for reform improve whenever resources are available to support the new, emerging system.

8. Reform is an ongoing process that requires continuous self-assessment.

A COMPREHENSIVE SCHOOL IMPROVEMENT PLAN

Well-designed and well-implemented school improvement programs appear in every type of community and in every region across the nation, but no two school improvement plans look exactly alike. In general, however, the most successful school improvement programs are comprehensive, reflecting the vision and philosophy of the entire school and all the constituents involved in the learning process. A comprehensive improvement plan usually engages the entire breadth of the curriculum, including a review and revision of the content of each subject, how it is delivered and assessed, and how it is integrated with all other facets of the school environment.

The need to develop and implement a comprehensive school improvement plan is not a new concept to school leaders. What is new, however, is the recognition that such a plan must have broad-based support and involvement, reflect community collaborations, involve educators in its development, be fiscally responsible, include accountability measures, and be designed to improve student achievement and increase the graduation rate.

Total school renewal calls for a comprehensive school improvement plan that outlines a new or revised educational vision, sets priorities, defines administrative and governing structures, and assigns resources and time lines for school and student expectations. Among the basic planning issues are management questions such as:

- Who should take the lead in developing and implementing the plan?
- What are the specific issues that need to be resolved?
- What resources are available?
- What time frame is realistic?
- What are the expected results and consequences?
- What are the results to be measured?
- How are the results to be measured, and by whom?

Five Steps of a Comprehensive School Improvement Plan

Though it is beyond the scope of this book to explore the details of implementing a comprehensive school improvement plan, a brief outline may be useful. These are the five basic steps in a school improvement planning process:

1. Identify district, school, and program priorities

   ♦ Establish consensus of all parties on district vision and priorities

   ♦ Determine program goals and expectations

   ♦ Affirm district commitment to participate and support the process

2. Assess needs of current program

   ♦ Define programs and target problem areas requiring needs assessment data

   ♦ Develop data collection plan, and collect data from multiple sources

   ♦ Organize and analyze information

   ♦ Determine strengths and weaknesses of current policies and practices

   ♦ Prioritize program improvement areas to be addressed

3. Select program improvements

   ♦ Create selection criteria for proposed new program improvement products or practices

   ♦ Identify and study the merits of new or revised policies, products, or practices

   ♦ Prioritize and select the program improvements to be implemented

4. Implement changes

   ♦ Develop an implementation plan reflecting facilities, equipment, and personnel needs

- ◆ Establish costs, time lines, and persons responsible for specific implementation tasks
- ◆ Initiate new program improvements and provide maintenance and monitoring procedures to ensure success

5. Monitor and evaluate processes and programs

- ◆ Develop an evaluation plan for existing and new program improvements
- ◆ Initiate evaluation design and data collection procedures
- ◆ Analyze formative evaluation data of ongoing program revisions
- ◆ Analyze summative data for program impact data
- ◆ Prepare report for decision makers and other groups interested in the effectiveness of the new program improvements
- ◆ Continue the school improvement planning process

In summary, a comprehensive school improvement plan developed for a given time period is part of an ongoing cycle that should become part of the culture of a successful school. Educational leaders seeking to keep students in school, to improve academic performance, and increase graduation rates, must master this planning process.

THE FIFTEEN MOST EFFECTIVE STRATEGIES FOR DROPOUT PREVENTION

How do local educational leaders determine which of the multitude reform models, curriculum initiatives, administrative structures, or other school improvement practices are the very best for their local needs? We recommend that local leadership teams, with the assistance of outside resource organizations, thoroughly review as much information as possible from many different sources and then make program improvement decisions based on local priorities and the resources available.

One valuable resource organization is the National Dropout Prevention Center, which has been studying the issue of school dropouts since 1986. The Center has focused on identifying model dropout prevention programs and successful practices in representative schools and communities from across the nation.

From experiences with demonstration projects in all types of schools across the nation, the Center has observed a close relationship among model programs, outstanding schools, good administrative leadership, excellent teaching practices, and effective strategies for dropout prevention programs. They all seem to add up to higher student achievement levels and increased high school graduation rates. Hence, effective strategies for dropout prevention programs become basic components of a comprehensive school improvement program, and vice versa.

Based on this research, we have identified fifteen effective strategies that have the most positive impact on the dropout rate. These strategies, although apparently discrete, work well together and frequently overlap. They produce good results as stand-alone programs (for example, mentoring or family involvement projects), but when school districts develop a program improvement plan that encompasses most or all of these strategies, the benefits are more than additive. The greater the number of these strategies the school improvement plan incorporates, the greater the likelihood of an increased graduation rate. These strategies have yielded success in rural, suburban, and urban schools and at all school levels from kindergarten to twelfth grade.

These fifteen strategies lie at the heart of efforts to solve our school dropout problem. We offer a brief overview here. In the following chapters, we describe the individual strategies in greater detail, provide examples of programs that have implemented them successfully, and list resources and references for further information and assistance.

EARLY INTERVENTIONS

A thorough review of needs assessments and comprehensive planning processes in local schools indicates that most school improvement programs should begin with a comprehensive family involvement initiative, a solid early childhood education program, and a strong reading and writing program. When this common core of program strategies is in place, particularly at the elementary level, districts can go on to determine the need for additional strategies.

Family Involvement. Research consistently finds that family involvement has a direct, positive effect on children's achievement and is the most accurate predictor of a student's success in school.

Early Childhood Education. Birth-to-three interventions demonstrate that providing a child additional enrichment can modify IQ. The most effective way to reduce the number of children who will ultimately drop out is to provide the best possible classroom instruction from the beginning of their school experience.

Reading and Writing Programs. Because reading and writing are the foundation for effective learning in almost every subject taught in school, programs to help low-achieving students improve their reading and writing skills yield benefits that support all other strategies for dropout prevention.

THE BASIC CORE STRATEGIES

Four key strategies complement and supplement the common-core programs. Each of these strategies has the capacity to enhance relevancy and generate excitement in the learning process, both within and beyond the normal school environment. These strategies promote opportunities for the student to form bonding relationships with adult role models and to engage in learning opportunities that extend beyond the school day and the normal 180-day school year. Individually or collectively, these four potent strategies will have a significant impact with the low-performing students who are so often difficult to engage within the normal school setting or in typical classroom activities.

Mentoring/Tutoring. Mentoring is a one-to-one caring, supportive relationship between a mentor and a mentee that is based on trust. Tutoring, also a one-to-one activity, focuses on academics and is an effective way to address specific needs such as reading, writing, or math competencies.

Service Learning. Service learning connects meaningful community service experiences with academic learning. This teaching/learning method promotes personal and social growth, career development, and civic responsibility and can be a powerful vehicle for effective school reform at all grade levels.

Alternative Schooling. Alternative schooling provides potential dropouts a variety of options that can lead to graduation, with programs paying special attention to the students' individual social needs and the academic requirements for a high school diploma.

Out-of-School Enhancement. Many schools provide afterschool and summer enhancement programs that eliminate information loss and inspire interest in a variety of areas. Such experiences are especially important for students at risk of school failure.

MAKING THE MOST OF INSTRUCTION

No sustained and comprehensive effort to keep students in school can afford to ignore what happens in the classroom. Strategies that produce better teachers, expand teaching methods to accommodate a range of learning styles, take advantage of today's cornucopia of technological resources, and meet the individual needs of each student can yield substantial benefits.

Professional Development. Teachers who work with youth at high risk of academic failure need to feel supported and need to have an avenue by which they continue to develop skills and techniques, and learn about innovative strategies.

Openness to Diverse Learning Styles and Multiple Intelligences. When educators show students that there are different ways to learn, students find new and creative ways to solve problems, achieve success, and become lifelong learners.

Instructional Technologies. Technology offers some of the best opportunities for delivering instruction that engages students in authentic learning, addresses multiple intelligences, and adapts to students' learning styles.

Individualized Learning. A customized individual learning program for each student allows teachers flexibility with the instructional program and extracurricular activities.

MAKING THE MOST OF THE WIDER COMMUNITY

Students who come to school bring traces of a wider community; when students leave school, either before or after graduation, they return to that community. It's impossible to isolate "school" within the walls of the school building. Effective efforts to keep students in school take advantage of these links with the wider community.

Systemic Renewal. Systemic renewal calls for a continuing process of evaluating goals and objectives related to school policies, practices, and organizational structures as they impact a diverse group of learners.

Community Collaboration. When all groups in a community provide collective support to the school, a strong infrastructure sustains a caring environment where youth can thrive and achieve.

Career Education and Workforce Readiness. A quality guidance program is essential for all students. School-to-work programs recognize that youth need specific skills to prepare them for the larger demands of today's workplace.

Conflict Resolution and Violence Prevention. A comprehensive violence prevention plan, including conflict resolution, must deal with potential violence as well as crisis management. Violence prevention means providing daily experiences at all grade levels that enhance positive social attitudes and effective inter-personal skills in all students.

CONCLUSION

Professional educators and community leaders who work with children and youth have long recognized the need for effective strategies for dropout prevention. Business leaders and policymakers at the local, state, and national level bring another perspective to the problem. Many years of observation and research have yielded a solid list of strategies that work. When thoughtfully implemented in a comprehensive school improvement plan, these fifteen strategies can help to solve our school dropout problem.

REFERENCES

Boesel, D., and Fredland, E. (1999). *College for All* ? U.S. Department of Education, Office of Educational Research and Improvement.

Dynarski, M., and Gleason, P. (1999). *How Can We Help?* Princeton, NJ: Mathematica Policy Research, Inc.

Herman, R. (Project Director). (1999). *An Educator's Guide to Schoolwide Reform.* Arlington, VA: Educational Research Service.

Isenhart, L. and Bechard, S. (1987). *The ECS Survey of State Initiatives for Youth at Risk.* Denver, CO: Education Commission of the States.

Klein, R. (1999). *Defying Disaffection.* England: Staffordshire. Trentham Books Limited.

Olson, L. (1999, April 14). Following the Plan. Washington, DC: *Education Week.*

Pechman, E. (Study Director). (1998). *An Idea Book on Planning,* Vol. 1. U.S. Department of Education, Office of Educational Research and Improvement.

Talley, S. and Martinez, D.H. (Eds.). 1998. *Tools for Schools.* U.S. Department of Education, Office of Educational Research and Improvement.

PART III

EARLY INTERVENTIONS

Evidence has shown that there is a need to identify those early factors in a child's life that place a child at risk. Although focus on family involvement, early childhood education, and reading and writing begins when children are young, they continue throughout a student's development.

4

FAMILY INVOLVEMENT

American taxpayers reach deep into their pocket[s] to meet the costs, both direct and indirect, of policies that are based on remediation rather than prevention.

Carnegie Corporation (1994, p. 9)

INTRODUCTION

Research and experience show that a comprehensive effort to keep students in school depends on three fundamental components: strong family involvement, good early childhood education, and the development of solid reading and writing skills. This common core of strategies establishes the framework on which all other initiatives build. When they are in place, other programs can move forward strongly. When they are lacking, other strategies falter. Schools and communities that seek to reduce the number of students who drop out of school must start here.

FAMILY INVOLVEMENT

Efforts to get families involved in schools are not new. Research dating back some 35 years consistently finds that parent/family involvement has a direct, positive effect on children's achievement.

A recent seminar at Harvard University addressed research findings from six commissioned papers regarding successful youth in high-risk environments. Two crucial findings from the seminar were that (1) regardless of class, race, and socioeconomic background, most parents share the same aspirations and expectations for their children; and (2) despite the similarities, parents' access to social supports—resources that facilitate achievement of these goals—varies dramatically across neighborhoods (Harvard, 1999).

The public school system of America is open to all students, regardless of family background. Yet some parents send their children to school as if there were an unbridgeable gap between school and home. The teacher's lament, "I never see the parents that I need to see," is often a red flag, warning that children are at risk of failing, of dropping out, of having what in today's world amounts to no future at all (Balster, 1991).

How has this gap been created? Is the parent unwilling, or is the school uninviting? It is essential that schools recognize these critical questions and begin to bridge the gap, reaching out so that all students feel a part of the learning community. As Joyce Epstein (1987a) points out, family-like schools make students feel part of a "school family," where they receive individual attention that improves motivation.

FAMILY INVOLVEMENT DEFINED

Various authors have described the range of family involvement in schooling (Anderson, 1983; Comer, 1986; Conoley, 1987; Davies, 1987; Epstein, 1987b, 1988; Loven, 1978). We prefer the continuum developed by Adelman, listing measures that endeavor to help both the individual and the system.

- ♦ Meeting basic obligations to the student; helping caretakers meet their own basic needs
- ♦ Communicating about matters essential to the student
- ♦ Making essential decisions about the student
- ♦ Supporting the student's basic learning and development at home
- ♦ Solving problems and providing support at home and at school related to the student's special needs
- ♦ Working for a classroom's or school's improvement

♦ Working for improvement of all schools (Adelman, 1994)

Family involvement in schools requires a partnership. Successful partnerships view student achievement as a shared responsibility, and all stakeholders—including parents, administrators, teachers, and community leaders—play important roles in supporting children's learning (Funkhouser and Gonzales, 1996).

Job and family demands leave many parents with little free time. Single-parent families and those with two working parents have become the norm. The parents who stay away tend to be members of racial and ethnic minorities, have less income, and are less at ease with the English language—often just those whose children are more at risk of failing in school (Smith et al., 1995). Schools bear the responsibility to reach out to families, especially those whose children are at risk of failing or dropping out. We know that parental involvement decreases as children become older—a time when young people face peer pressure, drugs, and gangs, and need their parents more than ever. James P. Comer, after working for eighteen years with at-risk youth and striving to involve their parents in their education, drew the conclusion that "the failure to bridge the social and cultural gap between home and school may lie at the root of the poor academic performance" (Comer et al., 1996). For decades, federal programs such as Head Start, Follow Through, Chapter One/Title One, and Special Education have mandated that parents or family be closely involved. In addition, hundreds of schools and thousands of teachers are successfully involving the families of students who are not in federally funded programs.

Many schools and teachers, however, have not made significant progress in reaching out to families. While some parents are informed about some things some of the time by some teachers in some schools, most families still feel "lucky" to be informed about or asked to participate in activities with their children. Often schools and communities do not fully understand the problems parents and families encounter and the importance of reaching out to them in order to build the kind of relationships that engage parents as true, active partners early in their children's education.

Schools and school systems that involve families successfully began by responding to the qualities, characteristics, and needs of the parents in order to overcome the barriers that interfere with communication. These barriers include parents' level of literacy; the language preferred for reading, listening, speaking, and writing; daily commitments and responsibilities that may affect the time, energy, and attention available to devote to school; and level of comfort in becoming involved in their children's education.

HOW CAN SCHOOLS SUPPORT FAMILY INVOLVEMENT?

Overcome Barriers. The most important step for schools is to be welcoming and inviting to all families. Start by involving teachers in diversity training. Students today come from many ethnic backgrounds; teachers who understand and appreciate this will communicate better with the diverse families they serve. Diversity training will also help create a climate that accepts students' different ability levels and learning styles. Students have the right to the same resources and equal treatment, regardless of their ability or culture.

Respect Educational Backgrounds of Family Members. Often parents and caregivers feel alienated from school because of their own negative experiences. Some have had personal difficulties with school; others may have dropped out, or never connected with school in the first place. It is important for the school to recognize and overcome such barriers.

Encourage Active Participation with Extended Hours. Schools can encourage family participation by asking parents when they can attend meetings, rather than simply announcing times that suit the school. They can involve parents in decision making by extending school hours into the weekend and evenings, giving parents an opportunity to "show up" and be heard. More ambitiously, they can develop lifelong education programs for the entire community. Adult education, childcare, after-school care, vocational programs, and even leisure activities can be very appealing to families.

Visit Families in Their Homes. Provide for a home-visit liaison. Home visits show families that they are important to the school. They also provide an opportunity to identify families that engage in high-risk behavior and to initiate discussions about community services that can assist.

Increase and Broaden Communication through the Use of Technology. Schools that bridge the digital divide creatively can support families better. Not all homes have computers; some homes do not have telephones. Provide a service where families can get in touch with the school easily. Some people cannot read, so the use of audio and video communication is important.

Develop a Strong Home–School–Community Base. Reach beyond parents and families into the community by using service learning projects that take students out of the classroom and into local businesses, hospitals, restaurants, and the like.

How Can Families Promote Family Involvement?

Show an Interest in School Policies. Parents should be aware of school policies and help their children understand them. Families can take time to go to the school, meet the teachers and the principal, and touch base occasionally between more formal meetings.

Participate in School Functions. School activities allow families and school faculty to join together in the spirit of fun and the celebration of education. When planned events are not on the horizon, family members may be able to go to lunch with their children or participate in recess activities.

Provide a Home Where Education Is Important. Families that value education in words and actions instill in their children the belief that graduation from high school is a worthwhile and attainable goal.

Volunteer in the School as Often as Possible. Schools are happy to have family members help out in classrooms, in the cafeteria, in the library, in the office, on the playground—just about anywhere they are needed. A short course provided by the school district is often mandatory. Volunteering is a win-win for both students and volunteers.

RELATED RESEARCH AND RESOURCES

The most comprehensive and ongoing survey of the research is a series of publications developed by Anne Henderson: *The Evidence Grows* (1981), *The Evidence Continues to Grow* (1987), and *A New Generation of Evidence: The Family Is Critical to Student Achievement* (Henderson and Berla, 1995). Citing more than 85 studies, these publications document the profound and comprehensive benefits for students, families, and schools when parents and family members become participants in their children's education and their lives. The evidence is now beyond dispute: "When parents are involved in their children's education at home their children do better in school" (Henderson and Berla, 1995).

GUIDELINES FOR EFFECTIVENESS IN FAMILY INVOLVEMENT

The following is taken from the National Parent Teacher Association's review of the literature on the effectiveness of family involvement in education (National PTA, 1998):

Parent and Family Involvement and Student Success

- ◆ When parents are involved, students achieve more, regardless of socioeconomic status, ethnic/racial background, or the parents' education level.
- ◆ The more extensive the parent involvement, the higher the student achievement.
- ◆ When parents are involved in their students' education, those students have higher grades and test scores, better attendance, and complete homework more consistently.

♦ When parents are involved, students exhibit more positive attitudes and behavior.

♦ Students whose parents are involved in their lives have higher graduation rates and greater enrollment rates in post-secondary education.

♦ Different types of parent/family involvement produce different gains. To have long-lasting gains for students, parent involvement activities must be well planned, inclusive, and comprehensive.

♦ Educators hold higher expectations of students whose parents collaborate with the teacher. They also hold higher opinions of those parents.

♦ In programs that are designed to involve parents in full partnerships, student achievement for disadvantaged children not only improves, it can reach levels that are standard for middle-class children. In addition, the children who are farthest behind make the greatest gains.

♦ Children from diverse cultural backgrounds tend to do better when parents and professionals collaborate to bridge the gap between the culture at home and the learning institution.

♦ Student behaviors such as alcohol use, violence, and antisocial behavior decrease as parent involvement increases.

♦ Students are more likely to fall behind in academic performance if their parents do not participate in school events, develop a working relationship with their child's educators, or keep up with what is happening in their child's school.

♦ The benefits of involving parents are not confined to the early years; there are significant gains at all ages and grade levels.

♦ Junior and senior high school students whose parents remain involved make better transitions, maintain the quality of their work, and develop realistic plans for their future.

♦ Students whose parents are not involved, on the other hand, are more likely to drop out of school.

♦ The most accurate predictor of a student's achievement in school is not income or social status, but the extent to which that student's family is able to (1) create a home environment that encourages learning; (2) communicate high, yet reasonable, expectations for their children's achievement and future careers; and (3) become involved in their children's education at school and in the community.

Parent and Family Involvement and School Quality

♦ Schools that work well with families have improved teacher morale and higher ratings of teachers by parents.

♦ Schools where parents are involved have more support from families and better reputations in the community.

♦ School programs that involve parents outperform identical programs without parent and family involvement.

♦ Schools where children are failing improve dramatically when parents are enabled to become effective partners in their child's education.

♦ The school's practices to inform and involve parents are stronger determinants of whether inner-city parents will be involved with their children's education than are parent education, family size, marital status, and even student grade level.

Parent and Family Involvement and Program Design

♦ The more the relationship between parents and educators approaches a comprehensive, well-planned partnership, the higher the student achievement.

- For low-income families, programs offering home visits are more successful in involving parents than programs that require parents to visit the school. However, when parents become involved at school, their children make even greater gains.

- When parents receive frequent and effective communication from the school or program, their involvement increases, their overall evaluation of educators improves, and their attitudes toward the program are more positive.

- Parents are much more likely to become involved when educators encourage and assist parents in helping their children with their schoolwork.

- Effective programs are led by a team of administrators, educators, and parents, and have access to financial resources.

- When they are treated as partners and given relevant information by people with whom they are comfortable, parents put into practice the involvement strategies they already know are effective, but have been hesitant to contribute.

- One of the most significant challenges to conducting an effective program is the lack of instruction on parent and family involvement that educators and administrators receive in their professional training.

- Collaboration with families is an essential component of a reform strategy, but it is not a substitute for high-quality education programs or comprehensive school improvement.

Most of these positive findings come out of the elementary level and not the middle school or high levels of public education. Most of the research from the middle and high school level surveys reveals that families are trying to guide their children, but with limited assistance from the schools (Catsambis and Garland, 1997). It is important for parent involvement programs to move from activities that merely focus on informing parents about school programs to activities that offer parents opportunities for broader levels of involvement.

EFFECTIVE PROGRAMS AND PRACTICES

Head Start has been especially successful in enlisting families as partners in the education of preschoolers. Even Start—a two-generational program that links the education of under-achieving parents with the education of their children (ages one through seven)—has been implemented to increase the literacy skills of parents so that their children can succeed in school. Through Even Start, parents are helped to improve the preschool activities of their children and to understand their role in their children's education.

The Minnesota Department of Education's Early Childhood Family Education Program (ECFE) offers parents various involvement opportunities through centers based in housing projects, low-income apartments, storefronts, and elementary schools. Each center has a parent advisory board that is involved in deciding program content as well as fund-raising strategies. Regular parent group meetings include parent-guided discussions about topics ranging from educational concerns to nutrition, child and spouse abuse, chemical addictions, child development, and discipline. ECFE also employs parents as classroom and community aides.

To be ready for school, children must live in an environment where language and behavior standards promote learning. Many children, however, come from situations where parents do not read to them and sometimes do not even talk to them. Avance, a program begun in 1973 in San Antonio, Texas, teaches parents the fundamentals of caring for their children—child growth and development, health, nutrition, cleanliness, and patience. It also develops self-esteem, helping poor women to achieve their dreams. Women are encouraged to complete the requirements for high school graduation and to seek additional education. Sixty percent of the mothers who started the program went on to complete the requirements for a GED.

The national PTA is the largest volunteer child advocacy organization in the United States. A not-for-profit association of parents, educators, students and other citizens active in their schools and communities. Parent involvement is the foundation that has guided the work of National PTA for 103 years. One of their most successful programs is *Building Successful Partnerships*. It is a multifaceted, national initiative that focuses on the importance of parent involvement in education. The goals of the program are:

♦ to increase awareness of the *National Standards for Parent/Family Involvement Programs*

♦ to promote the use of *Building Successful Partnerships: A Guide for Developing Parent and Family Involvement programs*, an Implementation guide to the National Standards

♦ to present instructional workshops on all facets of parent involvement to facilitate meaningful discussion among parents, administrators, teachers, and other key stakeholders.

Related Organizations

National Parent Teachers Association (PTA)
330 N. Wabash Avenue, Suite 2100
Chicago, IL 60611-3690
312-670-6782
www.pta.org

The National Coalition for Parent Involvement in Education (NCPIE)
1201 16th Street NW, Box 39
Washington, DC 20036
202-822-8405
www.ncpie.org

The Partnership for Family Involvement in Education
U.S. Department of Education
400 Maryland Avenue, SW
Washington, DC 20202-8173
800-872-5327
www.pfie.ed.gov

CONCLUSION

Family involvement significantly enhances learning opportunities for all students and is crucial for those students in at-
risk situations. Unfortunately, the parents of at-risk students are
often the most reluctant to become involved in school. Therefore, schools and communities must systemically seek effective
strategies that will work to involve the families of youth who
are struggling academically and socially.

REFERENCES

Adelman, H. S. (1994). Intervening to Enhance Home Involvement in
Schooling. *Intervention in School and Clinic, 29*, 5, 276–287.

Anderson, C. (1983). An Ecological Developmental Model for a Family
Orientation in School Psychology. *Journal of School Psychology, 21*, 179–189.

Balster, L. (1991). *Involving At-Risk Families in Their Children's Education.*
Eugene, OR: ERIC Digest Series Number EA 58.

Carnegie Corporation. (1994*). Starting Points: Meeting the Needs of Our
Youngest Children.*

[on-line] http://www.carnegie.org/startingpoints/startpt1.html.

Catsambis S., and Garland, J. E., (1997*). Parental Involvement in Students'
Education During Middle School and High School.* Baltimore, MD: Office of Educational Research and Improvement, U. S. Department of Education, Center
for Research on the Education of Students Placed at Risk.

Comer, J. P. (1986). Parent Participation in the Schools. *Phi Delta Kappan.
67*, 442–446.

Comer, J. P., Haynes, N. M., Joyner, E. T., and Ben-Avie, M., (Eds.). (1996*)
Rallying the Whole Village: The Comer Process for Reforming Education.* New York:
Teachers College Press.

Conoley, J. C. (1987). Schools and Families: Theoretical and Practical
Bridges. *Professional School Psychology, 2*, 191–203.

Davies, D. (1987). Parent Involvement in the Public Schools: Opportunities for Administrators. *Education and Urban Society, 19*, 147–163.

Epstein, J. L. (1987). *Toward a Theory of Family-School Connections: Teacher
Practices and Parent Involvement across the School Years.* Berlin, NY: Aldine
DeGruyter.

Epstein, J. L. (1988). How Do We Improve Programs for Parent Involvement? *Educational Horizons, 66*, 58–59.

Funkhouser, J. E., and Gonzales M. R., (1996). *Family Involvement in Children's Education: Successful Local Approaches, An Idea Book*. Washington, DC: U. S. Department of Education, Office of Education Research and Improvement.

Harvard University, John F. Kennedy School of Government. (1999). Successful Youth in High-Risk Environments. A report from the Urban Seminar Series on Children's Health and Safety. Cambridge, MA: Author.

Henderson, A. T. and Berla, N., (1995). *A New Generation of Evidence: The Family Is Critical to Student Achievement*. Washington, DC: Center for Law and Education.

Loven, M. (1978). Four Alternative Approaches to the Family/School Liaison Role. *Psychology in the Schools, 15*, 553–559.

National PTA. (1998). *National Standards For Parent/Family Involvement Programs*. Chicago, IL.

Smith, T. M., M. Perie, N. Alsalam, R. P. Mahoney, B. Yupin, and B. A. Young. (1995). *The Condition Of Education 1995*. Washington DC: Office of Educational Research and Improvement, U.S. Department of Education, National Center for Education Statistics.

5

EARLY CHILDHOOD EDUCATION

*The direction in which education starts a man
will determine his future life.*

Plato

When people think about dropout prevention, their thoughts generally focus on high school students who may not graduate. But very few dropouts sail through school with few problems until they reach high school. Most were at risk for dropping out long before then—some even before they were born.

NATURE VERSUS NURTURE

Current research shows that while nature—heredity—certainly plays a role in brain development, nurture—environment—has a profound impact. Prenatal and early brain development is rapid and extensive. In fact, the vast majority of synapses—the connections between brain cells—are produced during the first three years of life. As a child interacts with the environment, these synapses are "activated" (Wells, 1990). Synapses that are frequently activated become permanent; those that are not tend to disappear. Experiences affect not only the number of brain cells and the number of connections, but also the way these connections are wired. Thus, the influence of early environment on brain development is long-lasting (Carnegie Corporation, 1994; Education Commission of the States, 1996).

Brain development depends not only on the number of experiences, but also on the type of experiences. A child's early environment is critical. Poverty and economic stability are two of the most powerful predictors of children's later success (National Governors' Association, 1992). In 1995, 24 percent of America's children under the age of three lived in poverty (Wells, 1990). Students from low-income families are 2.4 times more likely to drop out than children from middle-income families and 10.5 times more likely than students from high-income families (NCES, 1994). Children living in poverty are more likely to be exposed to one or more of these risk factors:

♦ inadequate nutrition, which can cause social withdrawal, delayed motor skills, and delayed physical growth (Brown and Pollitt, 1996)

♦ prenatal exposure to substance abuse, which can cause stunted neurons and a lack of brain cells (Mayes, 1996)

♦ maternal depression, which can cause children to be more withdrawn, be less active, and have shorter attention spans (Belle, 1990)

♦ inadequate attachments to others (Brookes-Gunn et.al., 1995);

♦ limited access to medical care

♦ an unsafe or unpredictable physical environment

♦ a high level of stress in the home

♦ poor quality of daycare

The good news is that effective prevention and intervention can make a difference. The type of early care children receive affects their development. If a child forms a secure attachment to a nurturing caregiver in a safe, stimulating environment, the synapses will be effectively developed. Furthermore, research shows that timely, intensive intervention can alter the brain, helping to compensate for earlier deficiencies (Wells, 1990).

IT'S BEEN PROVEN

Prevention and intervention focused on early childhood

education can take several forms. The most conventional are formal early childhood education programs—daycare, preschool, and nursery school.

Perhaps one of the best-known and longest-standing research projects on early childhood programs is the study of the Perry Preschool Project. In the mid-1960s, 123 African-American three- and four-year-olds were identified as being at high risk of failing school, with indicators that included being born into poverty. Half of the children received two years of a high-quality preschool program based on High/Scope's active learning approach; the other half received no preschool. Follow-up studies were done at ages five, eight, fifteen, nineteen, and twenty-six. Various psychological and "real-world" factors were considered, such as intellectual development, school achievement patterns, social maturity/behavior, family attitudes, job training and employment, pregnancy rates, patterns of crime, and use of welfare assistance. A cost-benefit analysis was also conducted. The findings showed immediate, positive effects on intellectual performance; a reduced incidence, time spent in, and level of special education services; and a higher graduation rate. Those who attended the preschool program also had a lower rate of delinquency as youths and a reduced incidence of arrests in general, and specifically for dealing drugs, as adults. As adults, these youth had a higher rate of employment, a lower rate of welfare assistance, fewer out-of-wedlock births, a higher average salary, and were more often homeowners (Barnett, 1996; Barnett et al., 1984; Schweinhart, Barnes, and Weikart, 1993). Barnett, in his 1984 study of the Perry Preschool participants, stated that "a successful preschool experience can permanently alter the success/failure trajectory of a person's life in significant and very positive ways" (Barnett et al., 1984, p.107), and that "over the lifetimes of the participants, preschool is estimated to yield economic benefits with an estimated present value that is over seven times the cost of one year of the program" (Barnett et al., 1984, p.107).

Quality of childcare is a major issue in the arena of early childhood education. One of the largest studies of formal childcare was conducted by the National Center for Early Development and Learning at the University of North Carolina-Chapel Hill (Peisner et al., 1999). The Cost, Quality, and

Outcomes Study looked at more than 800 seven-year-olds who had been in childcare from the age of three. Data were collected based on the quality of the childcare experience and its effect on language, academic, and social skills at age five. The study showed that children who experienced higher-quality childcare (a low child-adult ratio, the caregivers specifically trained, and the children in a safe and stimulating environment) showed higher levels of language, academic, and social skills through kindergarten, with the effects carrying over through second grade in the academic and social areas ((Peisner et al., 1999).

The National Institute of Child Health and Human Development has been involved in collecting data on over 1,000 children from all over the United States since they were born in 1991. The Study of Early Childcare and Youth Development is slated to follow these youth through sixth grade, possibly even tracking them through their transition into high school. The initial findings were released in 1997. The researchers' preliminary conclusions at the end of the children's third-grade year were that higher-quality childcare is associated with better outcomes, including less problem behavior and higher cognitive and language skills. They went on to say that in terms of the cognitive and language skills, children in high-quality childcare fared better than those cared for exclusively by their mothers, but exclusive care by mothers was found to be better than low-quality care (Jacobson, 2000).

APPROACHES

The many possible approaches (or combinations of approaches) to early childhood education can be broadly categorized into "in-home" and "out-of-home" strategies.

In-Home Strategies. Because parents are a child's first teachers, it is imperative that they understand the importance of their role in their child's development. Examples of in-home programs include:

- ◆ Hawaii's Healthy Start, which serves families identified through screening at birth as highly stressed and/ or at-risk for child abuse

- ♦ Healthy Families America (HFA), a child-abuse prevention program that evolved from Hawaii's Healthy Start and is now the subject of a pioneering multi-site research network

- ♦ The Nurse Home Visitation Program (NHVP), a university-based demonstration program developed in Elmira, New York, which expanded to Memphis and Denver and now is being replicated nationally

- ♦ Parents as Teachers (PAT), promoting the development of children from birth to three years, which began in Missouri and now operates at more than 2,000 sites across the country

- ♦ The Home Instruction Program for Preschool Youngsters (HIPPY), which seeks to prepare three- to five-year-olds for kindergarten and first grade, a demonstration program that worked with poor families in 24 sites to promote children's development, parents' ability to parent, and family self-sufficiency

- ♦ Infant Health and Development Program, which provided interventions such as home-based parent training, child development, and parenting classes for 1,000 babies at eight sites for three years

The report *Home Visiting: Recent Program Evaluations* presents a review of a number of these programs. The generalized findings were that the programs produced some benefit in parenting or in the prevention of neglect and child abuse; that the parents were hungry for information and support; that program outcomes may be affected by staff skills, training, and turnover, as well as by the extent to which curricula are delivered to families as intended by the program model; that the key elements that would predict which families will benefit from a home visiting model, or which program site will succeed, have not been identified; and that adaptations of existing programs, to improve these services and results, should be tried. In other words, more studies are needed to determine what type of program will be of benefit to whom (Packard Foundation, 1999). However, it seems obvious that more direct services to new parents are warranted.

For additional information:

Home Instruction Program for Preschool Youngsters (HIPPY)
220 East 23rd Street, Suite 300
New York, NY 10010
212-532-7730
http://www.c3pg.com/hippy.htm

Out-of-Home Strategies. Out-of-home programs, usually in the form of childcare or preschool, are much more common than in-home programs. Head Start, a federally funded program for four-year-olds from low-income families, has provided early childhood education for more than thirty years. Private programs, in the form of daycare or preschool, are the other option.

For additional information:

Head Start, Administration for Children and Families
U.S. Department of Health and Human Services
National Head Start Association
1651 Prince Street
Alexandria, VA 22314
703-739-0875
http://www.nhsa.org

Other out-of-home care programs include prenatal and young-child health care. In *Every Child Ready for School: Report of the Action Team on School Readiness* (National Governors' Association, 1992), the authors concluded that "health and education are inextricably linked in enabling children to be ready to learn to lead productive lives" (p.18). They went on to say that "each federal dollar invested in WIC prenatal benefits returns about $3.50 over eighteen years in inflation-adjusted present value," and that "medical costs for children participating in Medicaid's Early and Periodic Screening, Diagnostic, and Treatment program were nearly 13% lower than those for nonparticipating Medicaid-eligible children" (p.19).

It Doesn't Stop at Preschool: The Early Grades

A full consideration of early childhood education must go beyond preschool to include kindergarten through third grade in the traditional school. There was a time when kindergarten focused on a child's introduction to school—allowing learning through play, academic readiness skills, and social development. However, as more children attend preschool, many schools have moved elements of the traditional first-grade curriculum into the kindergarten year. This frequently involves a more concentrated use of books and workbooks. Are these children really ready for that? Are all first-grade children really ready for that? What makes for a good primary grade program?

In 1990, Carolyn Cummings synthesized research on what is appropriate for young children in the public schools (Cummings, 1990). Among her conclusions:

- The curriculum must be responsive to the children's developmental needs. An inflexible, highly structured, teacher-directed curriculum with many paper/pencil tasks is not developmentally appropriate.

- The content must be integrated and relevant, incorporating hands-on learning, and should not place emphasis on skills taught in isolation.

- Parents must be involved.

- The community must be involved.

- Kindergarten entrance ages should not exclude children on the assumption that they are "not ready." The school should be ready for the child, not the other way around.

- Children should not be assigned to differentiated kindergarten and transitional first-grade programs based on an invalid screening instrument.

- The use of widespread retention or remediation classes if expectations aren't met is not effective in the long term, and may even be detrimental.

Katz (1987) stated that learning and development are best served in the long term by learning through interaction and by projects that help make sense of the child's own experiences. She goes on to say that when reading skills are taught in isolation, they lack relevance, undermine interest, and can make a child who is not developmentally ready feel incompetent. Kostelnik (1993) states that children must be treated as individuals, not as a group; we must see and plan for each child as distinct from other children. McClellan and Katz (1993) cite evidence that a child who does not have minimal social competence by age six has a high probability of being at risk throughout life.

How can public and private schools meet young children's individual developmental needs—intellectual and social? Two effective strategies for schools are mixed-age grouping and smaller class size.

Mixed-Age Grouping. A mixed-age group usually includes children spanning three years, but the span can be as few as two years or as many as five. Mixed-age grouping seeks to capitalize on the differences in experience, knowledge, and abilities of the children involved. Mixed-age grouping mirrors society in general more closely than the traditional grade level concept. Because the children are of different ages, teachers tend to address individual differences more readily, rather than assume that all children of the same age will function at the same level. An additional advantage is that older children are available to help the younger ones. The older students learn through teaching, which validates their worth and usefulness; the younger children benefit from increased attention and the presence of role models. The older children generally respond positively to the expectations that are inherent in being role models (Katz, 1995). In a 1989 ERIC digest, Evangelou (1989) reported that mixed-age grouping elicits pro-social behaviors in both the older and the younger students and that students show increased cognitive learning and internalizing of new understandings.

Smaller Class Size. While studies on smaller class size have been conducted since the 1950s, conclusive evidence based on large numbers of children was not available until after the early 1980s, when states began passing legislation and providing funds to help districts reduce class size in the early grades.

In early 1999, the U.S. Department of Education released a report showing that when class size is reduced to 15–20 students, reading and math achievement is higher; disadvantaged and minority students experience the greatest benefits. The benefits are both short-term and long-term. At the end of fifth grade, students who had been in smaller class sizes for grades one through three were about five months ahead of those who had been in larger classes. High-school students who had been in the smaller classes in grades one through three were less likely to be retained or suspended, were making better grades, and were taking more advanced courses. The results also showed that teachers of smaller classes spend more time on instruction, spend less time on discipline problems, know their students better, and provide more individualized instruction based on where each child is in the learning process. Smaller class size contributed to more special help for students who needed it, increased student participation, and improved student behavior (U.S. Department of Education, 1999).

Based on this research, the U.S. Department of Education initiated the Class Size Reduction Program, an initiative to help communities hire 100,000 qualified teachers over seven years. The goal is to reduce class size in grades one through three to a national average of eighteen students. Some twenty states, including Indiana, Tennessee, and Wisconsin, now have class size reduction initiatives in place (U.S. Department of Education, 1999).

For additional information:

Indiana Department of Education
Center for School Improvement and Performance
Division of PRIME TIME
Room 229, State House
Indianapolis, IN 46204
317-232-9152
www.doe.state.in.us/primetime/welcome.html

BEYOND THE EARLY GRADES

Finally, out-of-home programs for early childhood education include parenting classes for teens—both those who are already parents and those who are not. Such programs give young people early exposure to information about the impact of environment on child development, help them develop an understanding of their responsibility as parents, and provide links to the resources available in the community.

For additional information:

**The Success by Six Learning Center
Clark County School District
2832 East Flamingo Road
Las Vegas, NV 89121
702-799-5477**

QUALITY COUNTS

Early childhood programs alone, however, are not enough. As demonstrated in the Cost, Quality, and Outcomes Study (Peisner et al., 1999), and the Study of Early Child Care and Youth Development, they must be quality programs. The quality of childcare is related to the quality of outcomes (National Association for the Education of Young Children, 1998).

In *Promising Strategies for At-Risk Youth*, Baas (1991) listed the following components of effective programs for at-risk youth:

♦ aggressive school leadership

♦ parental involvement

♦ school-based solutions

♦ high, but attainable standards

♦ alternative strategies for learning

♦ continued professional development for staff

♦ smaller class size

♦ community involvement, including integrated school-community services

The National Association for the Education of Young Children provides one of the most comprehensive guides for quality standards (1998). These accreditation criteria cover interactions among teachers and children, the curriculum, relationships among teachers and families, staff qualifications and professional development, administration, staffing, the physical environment, health and safety, nutrition and food service, and evaluation. NAEYC endorses small class size, qualified staff with ongoing staff development, curriculum and supporting materials that are appropriate for varying developmental needs and are relevant and meaningful, encouragement of emotional and social as well as intellectual development, and strong parent/family involvement, among others.

CONCLUSION

It seems clear that more effort needs to be put into true prevention and intervention in the early years. The National Governors' Association advanced this conclusion in their 1992 report, stating:

> Investment in the youngest, most at-risk individuals will provide the largest returns. Many of the studies on prenatal care and child development preschool programs reflect that those who benefited the most were individuals who were considered the most at risk—the poor, uninsured, and economically disadvantaged. The success of many prevention programs relies on their intensiveness and quality.
>
> Early investment in services for children and families has beneficial short- and long-term results—not only for the individual, but also for society.
>
> Services provided to one individual often help other family members. Not only are the lives of those receiving help improved immediately through preventive initiatives, but these programs and services also diminish the chance of future crises, thus helping to break the intergenerational cycle of poverty.

Prevention cannot start too early. We must:

♦ offer multiple approaches, paying particular attention to the economically disadvantaged;

♦ continue to work to break the cycle through **quality** programs;

♦ expend our resources where they will do the most good, have the greatest impact, in both the short term and the long term. In other words, we must focus more resources on early childhood education.

Related Organizations

Association for Supervision and Curriculum Development
1703 North Beauregard Street
Alexandria, VA 22311-1714
703-578-9600 or 1-800-933-ASCD
http://www.ascd.org

Frank Porter Graham Child Development Center
University of North Carolina at Chapel Hill
CB # 8180
105 Smith Level Road
Chapel Hill, NC 27599
919-966-7168
http://www.fpg.unc.edu

Intercultural Development Research Association
5835 Callaghan Road, Suite, 350
San Antonio, TX 78228-1190
210-444-1710
www.idra.org

National Association for the Education of Young Children
1509 16th Street, NW
Washington, DC 20036
202-232-8777 or 1-800-424-2460
http://www.naeyc.org

National Institute on Early Childhood Development and
Education
Office of Educational Research and Improvement

U.S. Department of Education
555 New Jersey Avenue, NW
Washington, DC 20208
202-219-1935
http://www.ed.gov/offices/OERI/ECI/index.html

Parents as Teachers National Center
10176 Corporate Square Drive, Suite 230
St. Louis, MO 63132
314-432-4330
http://www.partnc.org

REFERENCES

Baas, Alan. (1991). *Promising Strategies for At-Risk Youth*. ED 328958. Eugene, OR: ERIC Clearinghouse on Educational Management.

Barnett, W. S. (1996). *Lives in the Balance: Age-27 Benefit-Cost Analysis of the High/Scope Perry Preschool Program*. Monographs of the High/Scope Educational Research Foundation, 11. Ypsilanti, MI: High/Scope Press.

Barnett, W. S., Berrueta-Clement, J. R., Schweinhart, L. J., Epstein, A. S., and Weikart, D. P. (1984). *Changed Lives: The Effects of the Perry Preschool Program on Youths through Age 19*. Monographs of the High/Scope Educational Research Foundation, 8. Ypsilanti, MI: High/Scope Press.

Belle, D. (1990). Poverty and Women's Mental Health. *American Psychologist, 45*(3), 385–389.

Brookes-Gunn, J., Klebanov, P., Liaw, F., and Dincan, G. (1995). Toward an Understanding of the Effects of Poverty upon Children. In Fitzgerald, H.E. Lester, B.M., and Zuckerman, B. (Eds.). *Children of Poverty: Research, Health, and Policy Issues*. New York: Garland Publishing.

Brown, L. and Pollitt, E., (1996). Malnutrition, Poverty, and Intellectual Development. *Scientific American, 274*(2), 38–43.

Carnegie Corporation. (1994*). Starting Points: Meeting the Needs of Our Youngest Children*. [on-line] http://www.carnegie.org/starting-points/startpt1.html.

Cummings, Carolyn. (1990) *Appropriate Public School Programs for Young Children*. ED 321890, ERIC Clearinghouse on Elementary and Early Childhood Education, Urbana, IL.

The David and Lucile Packard Foundation. (1999). *Home Visiting: Recent Program Evaluations*. The Future of Children 9(1). The David and Lucile Packard Foundation. Los Altos, CA.

Education Commission of the States. (1996). *Brain Research and Education: Bridging the Gap between Neuroscience and Education*. Publication no. SI-96-7.

Evangelou, Demetra. (1989) *Mixed-Age Groups in Early Childhood Education*. ED 308990, ERIC Clearinghouse on Elementary and Early Childhood Education, Urbana, IL.

Jacobson, Linda. (2000). On Assignment: Research Lessons from Life: Long-Term Study of Child Development Seen as Growing 'National Treasure.' *Education Week*, July 12, 2000, pp. 42–45.

Katz, Lillian. (1987). *What Should Young Children Be Learning?* ED 290554, ERIC Clearinghouse on Elementary and Early Childhood Education, Urbana, IL.

Katz, Lillian. (1995). The Benefits of Mixed-Age Grouping. ED 38411, ERIC Clearinghouse on Elementary and Early Childhood Education, Urbana, IL.

Kostelnick, Marhorie. (1993). *Developmentally Approriate Programs*. ED 356101, ERIC Clearinghouse on Elementary and Early Childhood Education, Urbana, IL

Mayes, L. (1996). *Early Experience and the Developing Brain: The Model of Prenatal Cocaine Exposure*. Paper presented at the invitational conference: "Brain Development in Young Children: New Frontiers for Research, Policy, and Practice," University of Chicago, June 12–14, 1996.

McClellan, Diane E. and Katz, Lillian G. (1993). *Young Children's Social Development: A Checklist*. ED 356100, ERIC Clearinghouse on Elementary and Early Childhood Education, Urbana, IL.

U.S. Department of Education. (1999). *Local Success Stories: Reducing Class Size*. http://www.ed.gov.offices/OESE/ClassSize/localsuccess.html.

National Association for the Education of Young Children. (1998). *Accreditation Criteria and Procedures of the National Association for the Education of Young Children*. Washington, DC, 17–66.

National Governors' Association. (1992). *Every Child Ready for School: Report of the Action Team on School Readiness*, 7.

NCES. (1994). *Dropout Rates in the United States: 1993*. Washington, DC: National Center for Education Statistics, U.S. Department of Education.

Peisner, E., Burchinal, P., Clifford, D., Culkin, M., Howes, C., and Kagan, S. L. (1999). *Cost, Quality and Outcomes Study*. National Center for Early Development and Learning, Frank Porter Graham Child Development Center, UNC-Charlotte. http://www.fpg.unc.edu/~ncedl, 1999.

Schweinhart, L .J., Barnes, H. V., and Weikart, D. P. (1993). *Significant Benefits: The High/Scope Perry Preschool Study through Age 27*. Monographs of the High/Scope Educational Research Foundation, 10. Ypsilanti, MI: High/Scope Press.

Wells, S. E. (1990). *At-Risk Youth: Identification, Programs, and Recommendations*. Englewood, CP: Teacher Idea Press.

6

READING AND WRITING

Reading maketh a full man, conference a ready man,
and writing an exact man.

Francis Bacon

Among the fifteen effective strategies for dropout prevention, the one basic program unquestionably found in one form or another in every school building in America is a reading and writing program. Although reading and writing as such may be emphasized more in elementary and middle schools than in high schools, these skills should remain a point of emphasis in secondary schools, particularly for those students at risk of academic failure.

Because reading and writing skills are fundamental to effective learning in almost every subject taught in school, they have received the thoughtful attention of the educational community for decades, even centuries. Today's educators can choose from a vast number of programs and a broad range of possible approaches. Not surprisingly, many reading specialists and researchers still argue about the best way to teach these basic skills, particularly when students have academic problems. The federal government alone has promoted many different reading and writing approaches in the Head Start program over the past three decades.

Clearly, a comprehensive listing of reading and writing programs is beyond the scope of this book. Even a partial listing of selected programs might err by omission. For the most part, individual schools and school districts are in the best position to identify their specific needs and find an approach or program that works for them.

Regardless of the approach taken, however, a strategy for promoting strong reading and writing skills is an essential component—perhaps the most important component—of any effort to keep at-risk students in school. All of the other strategies for dropout prevention must link to, support, and build on this keystone.

CONCLUSION

Investment in programs that promote family involvement in schools, support child development in the early years, and develop strong reading and writing skills for students at all grade levels will yield substantial rewards. These core strategies form the foundation for the initiatives to be explored in the chapters to come.

Specifically, the strategies discussed in Part III , Chapters 4 through 6, aim to make the most of each student's potential. What better way than to start each schoolchild off with appropriate early education? In Part IV, Chapters 7 through 10, we address those strategies that form the underpinnings of all dropout prevention programs. The strategies addressed in Part V, Chapters 11 through 14, seek to make the most of classroom instruction. What better way than to establish good reading and writing skills? Finally, the strategies outlined in Part VI, Chapters 15 through 18, strive to make the most of the assets found in the wider school community. What better way than to encourage all families to be involved with their children's education? Building on these key components, schools and communities can find ways to keep their students in school.

PART IV

THE BASIC CORE STRATEGIES

Research and experience show that four key strategies—mentoring, service learning, alternative schooling, and out-of-school enhancement—have the greatest power to make a significant impact on the school dropout problem. These student-centered strategies engage potential dropouts in dynamic and meaningful learning opportunities within and beyond the classroom walls. When students are at risk of dropping out because they are performing poorly in traditional classroom activities or in the normal school setting, one or a combination of these key strategies can make a difference. In the following chapters, we describe each of these potent strategies for dropout prevention and show how they can work to make the most of the students in America's schools.

7

MENTORING

I wish every mountaineer a big brother, a man to inspire love and respect, to keep an eye on you roping up, to take an almost tender care of you while introducing you to that tough and arduous life.

Gaston Rebuffat

INTRODUCTION

Ask a student, "Why did you drop out of school?" The typical reply is, "No one cared if I stayed or left!" Students who lack strong personal support from a parent, a friend, a teacher—anyone who cares—are at risk of dropping out of school and possibly the community as well. In years past, two-parent families, nearby grandparents and other relatives, and close-knit neighborhoods offered more of the support and guidance that young people need. As this chapter will show, mentoring has resurfaced as an effective strategy for working with youth who need role models and a positive support system in today's world as well.

Mentoring has a long and proven history. The early Greeks practiced mentoring; today, it is as common in business and politics as it is in schools. A mentor is simply a wise and trusted friend with a commitment to provide guidance and support. Though many mentoring relationships involve tutoring in academic subjects, this is certainly not always the case. Traditionally, mentoring has taken the form of a one-to-one relationship, but a mentor may also work with a group. The latest innovation in this time-honored practice is Hewlett-Packard's "telementoring" program, in which mentor and mentee communicate via the Internet (Field, 1999).

WHY ADOLESCENTS NEED MENTORS

Young people growing up today, especially adolescents, have to cope with many more personal and social pressures than any previous generation. The issues they face can cause lifelong problems or trigger immediate life-threatening situations. According to *The Commonwealth Fund 1998 Survey of Adults Mentoring Young People*, eight of ten young people in mentoring relationships have one or more problems that put their health, development, or success in school at risk. The five most prevalent problems reported in the survey were the young people's negative feelings about themselves, poor relationships with family members, poor grades, associating with the wrong crowd, and getting into trouble at school (McLearn et al., 1998).

According to many parents and school counselors, today's youth face so many new and different social, psychological, and physical demands that what was once known as "normal adolescent development" may no longer exist. Any individual about to undertake the task of being a mentor must understand these problems and issues. The following brief discussion is adapted from the One to One Partnership (1996).

Peer Pressure. One of the greatest forces acting on adolescents is the power and influence of their peers. This outside influence on personal attitudes and behaviors can be either positive or negative. Mentors should recognize the power of peer pressure. Although they cannot force their own beliefs on their young mentees, they should be able to help them learn decision-making skills and practice making good choices based on their own convictions.

Substance Abuse. The temptation to experiment with alcohol, tobacco, and drugs is a constant threat to each adolescent in today's world. Mentors should set an excellent example by avoiding the use of alcohol and tobacco in the presence of mentees, encourage discussions about the issues of substance abuse, and be very observant of mentee behaviors. If there is evidence that the mentee may have a problem in this regard, the mentor should seek professional intervention by a psychiatrist, social worker, or school counselor.

Sexuality and Teenage Parenting. Young people may turn to sexual relationships for a variety of reasons. This is a sensitive issue, and mentors must take great care in any discussions related to sexuality. Professional assistance is often helpful to the mentor.

Child Abuse and Family Violence. Physical or mental abuse, within the family or in any environment, will have an immediate effect on the mentee and also create long-lasting, negative attitudes and behaviors. Most states require a school official to report suspected abuse to the proper authorities. A mentor will need to seek professional help if observations indicate that this type of abuse may be occurring.

School Safety and Violence. Many young people are exposed to bullies or to other violent behavior in the school setting. This may lead to attendance problems or diminished academic achievement. An observant mentor should discuss this with the mentee and inform the school officials about the situation, being careful not to involve the mentee in the reporting process.

Depression and Suicide. When young people are overwhelmed by issues and situations they cannot resolve, serious depression may develop. Mentors should be sensitive to this possibility. Any indications of extreme depression or suicide must be referred to the professionals involved in the program.

Nutrition and Health Care. Many young people feel they are immortal and tend to ignore good health practices. In addition to modeling a healthy lifestyle, mentors can discuss these issues, initiate visits to health-related institutions, or engage in special activities that promote good health.

Faith and Religion. This issue is usually within the domain of the family, and mentors should be sensitive to family values and practices. However, this may be an area of great concern for the mentee, or the pair may share an interest that could foster positive discussions.

Social Activities and Time Management. Young people to-day often need to juggle schoolwork, extracurricular activities, family chores, leisure activities, and other social demands. Mentors should be able to assist them with helpful discussions about time-management techniques and related decision-making skills.

Career Exploration and Part-Time Work. Because most mentors are in the workforce, career exploration is usually a natural and easy issue to address. Discussions about employment opportunities and specific job skill requirements, as well as visits to work sites, are quite common in mentoring relationships. Talking about these school-to-work issues may be a good starting point that leads naturally into related mentor-mentee activities.

STRUCTURED MENTORING PROGRAMS

Mentoring occurs in many different settings and formats. However, most mentoring relationships can benefit from a structured program of support. Structured programs enable mentors to offer mentees a variety of helpful experiences designed to improve their attitudes, behaviors, and competencies.

A structured mentoring program is generally recognized as having:

- ♦ a formal relationship between the mentor and mentee
- ♦ an established pattern for contacts
- ♦ recommended parameters for the meetings or activities
- ♦ a commitment to a time frame (usually twelve months, or not less than a school year)
- ♦ an ongoing structured training program
- ♦ monitoring and support by experienced professionals

♦ a consistent assessment and evaluation effort

Although structured mentoring programs take many forms, several have proven to be particularly practical and successful. These are the characteristics of several common mentoring models, with outstanding examples noted in parentheses:

Traditional Mentoring (school- or community-based programs such as Big Brothers/Big Sisters of America)

♦ one adult to one youth

♦ regular contact, about once a week or twice a month

♦ commitment is usually a year or a school year

♦ supported, monitored, and supervised activities

Group Mentoring or Co-Mentoring (Campus Pals; AmeriCorps chapters)

♦ one or several adults to a group of youth

♦ regular contacts could be daily for sustained period

♦ commitment to a fixed time period, usually a summer or school year

♦ supported, monitored, and supervised

Peer Mentoring (Boys and Girls Clubs; Coca-Cola Valued Youth Program)

♦ one youth to another youth (ages could vary) with adult leadership

♦ special interest such as science projects or math assistance

♦ regular contacts and commitments

♦ supported, monitored, and supervised

Team Mentoring (foster parents; faith-based programs)

♦ one or more adult(s) with multilevel youth

♦ regular contacts could be with intact family for specified period

- ◆ special interests or legal/volunteer placements
- ◆ supported, monitored, and supervised

Intergenerational Mentoring (Retired Senior Volunteer Program/RSVP; Foster Grandparents)

- ◆ interchangeable between youth and older adults as leaders
- ◆ special focus programs for youth such as homework centers
- ◆ regular contacts and commitments
- ◆ supported, monitored, and supervised

Telementoring (Hewlett-Packard Telementor Program)

- ◆ one or several adults with one or more youth
- ◆ special focus on math, science, or computer-related interests
- ◆ e-mail interaction when appropriate, with no fixed time or meeting place
- ◆ nontraditional supported evaluation procedures

GOALS AND EXPECTED BENEFITS OF MENTORING

Mentoring programs across the country have many different goals and objectives; however, most programs seek changes and benefits in the general areas of academic achievement, employment or career preparation, social or behavior modification, family and parenting skills, and social responsibilities. The specific benefits often expected include:

- ◆ improved school achievement
- ◆ increased graduation rates
- ◆ increased self-esteem
- ◆ increased school attendance
- ◆ decrease in discipline referrals
- ◆ decrease in early pregnancy rates

- increase in securing entry-level jobs
- increase in community service activities

Mentoring can be very beneficial to low-performing students and students in at-risk situations. The Mentoring Program Manual published by United Way of America (1994) lists four major tasks for which mentors are particularly valuable:

- establishing a positive personal relationship
- developing life skills
- assisting in case management of families
- increasing abilities of youth to interact with other social and cultural groups

School districts, organizations, businesses, or communities sponsoring mentor programs will vary greatly in their stated objectives and expected benefits. To cite a typical example, one successful ten-year program, the Kalamazoo Area Academic Achievement Program, aims to:

- provide the youth with a positive role model
- enhance the youth's self-esteem
- instill a sense of responsibility by allowing youth to make decisions
- develop a sense of accepting the need to improve academic performance
- participate in recreational activities and other social settings
- reinforce the efforts of the school and teachers
- create an understanding for improved social and school behaviors

THE IMPACT OF MENTORING

Regardless of the format, structure, or institutional host of the program, mentoring is a community development program.

Mentoring changes the structure and institutional boundaries of the community and the vision of the mentee. It serves as a powerful human force in a school, community, or state that can change the vision, the health, or the economic base of the community.

Mentors have the power and influence to change the negative cycles of their mentees and their families. A well-structured mentor program serves as a powerful low-cost, low-tech strategy to help rebuild the dreams of youth in at-risk situations. Mentoring is clearly an effective strategy for keeping students in school. Programs across the nation have an abundance of solid evidence supporting this fact. The most comprehensive national research evidence is from a thorough review of Big Brother/Big Sister programs (Tierney and Grossman, 1995), showing these results:

- 46 percent decrease in initiating drug use
- 27 percent decrease in initiating alcohol use
- 38 percent decrease in number of times hitting someone
- 37 percent decrease in skipped classes
- 37 percent decrease in lying to parents

Another nationwide study, the Commonwealth Fund's survey of mentoring programs (McLearn, Colasanto, and Schoen, 1998) reported similar positive results:

- 62 percent of students improved their self-esteem
- 52 percent of students skipped less school
- 48 percent of students improved their grades
- 49 percent of students got into less trouble in school
- 47 percent of students got into less trouble out of school
- 45 percent of students reduced their substance abuse
- 35 percent of students improved family relationships

Nearly all mentoring programs collect data that represent the number of relationships in place and contact hours completed by the mentor and mentee. One example of a local program reporting major accomplishments comes from California's San Luis Obispo County. During the 1998–99 school year, AmeriCorps members there provided over 52,000 hours of mentoring activities to 307 local teenagers (AmeriCorps, 2000). From these interventions, they reported the following results:

- 80 percent did not re-offend, as compared to 35–65 percent for similar offenders without mentors
- 89 percent improved or maintained a good attitude toward life with the help of their mentor
- 73 percent of juvenile offenders using alcohol or other drugs quit or decreased their use
- 71 percent of substance-abusing youth stopped or decreased their use
- 69 percent have shown improvements in school
- 96 percent began participating in positive alternatives to drug use
- 41 percent of teens who used tobacco decreased or stopped their use
- 64 percent of mentored teens made improvements in school, including a 44 percent decrease in number of times tardy and a 56 percent increase in the amount of time spent doing homework
- 38 percent of youth decreased sexual activity and 58 percent increased their use of birth control
- 85 percent of youth sought employment; of those, 56 percent obtained employment
- 58 percent of youth volunteered beyond mandated service requirements
- 71 percent of youth state that their AmeriCorps mentor helped change the direction of their life
- 62 percent of youth claim they would be in a worse place today without their mentor

KEY COMPONENTS OF A MENTORING PROGRAM

Many schools and communities across the country are initiating mentoring programs as school dropout prevention measures. The approaches vary greatly. Successful programs are based in schools, community organizations, businesses, and other institutions such as colleges and universities. Regardless of the setting, the sponsors, or the targeted youth groups, planners seeking the greatest impact on the mentees in their programs should be aware that some basic program components are critical.

The National Mentoring Partnership (1991) has developed a checklist, *Elements of Effective Practice*, to guide program planners. This nuts-and-bolts checklist identifies ten major components of successful mentor programs:

◆ a statement of purpose and long-range plan

◆ a recruitment plan for both mentors and participants

◆ an orientation for mentors and participants

◆ eligibility screening for mentors and participants

◆ a readiness and training curriculum for all mentors and participants

◆ a matching strategy

◆ a monitoring process

◆ a support, recognition, and retention component

◆ closure steps

◆ an evaluation process

For details, go to www.mentoring.org.

More recent research conducted by Public/Private Ventures (Herrera, Sipe, and McClanahan, 2000) confirmed several of these elements and provided additional guidance for program design. This research, which surveyed 722 mentoring programs nationwide, found a rapidly growing and changing field, both in traditional community-based programs and in the newer school-based programs. Despite the programs' operational and programmatic differences, the researchers identified eight factors as extremely important in the design, operations, and final impact of the program:

- engaging in social activities
- engaging in academic activities
- number of hours per month youth and mentors meet
- decision making
- pre-match training
- post-match training and support
- mentor screening
- matching
- age of the mentee

Among the many components of a structured mentoring program, the elements most critical to success are a clear statement of program purpose and goals, a recruitment and selection plan for mentors, a support and training program for mentors, and a monitoring and evaluation process for the program. Of these tasks, most program planners find designing an effective training program and developing a comprehensive evaluation process to be the most daunting. Recognizing this, the National Dropout Prevention Center recently developed and published *A Training Guide for Mentors* (Smink, 1999) to assist program planners.

Regardless of the specific program objectives, the source of mentors, or the unique target groups being served, the key to effective mentoring relationships lies in the development of trust. Recent research confirms that building that trusting relationship requires time and a significant amount of effort on the part of both mentor and mentee. In addition, Sipe (1996) reports that effective mentors are more likely to engage in certain practices:

- involve youth in deciding how the pair will spend their time together
- commit to being consistent and dependable and serve in a steady presence to the mentee

◆ take responsibility for keeping the relationship alive

◆ pay attention to the protégé's need for fun as a valuable part of the relationship

◆ respect the protégé's viewpoint

◆ seek assistance and advice from program staff when needed

PLANNING A MENTORING PROGRAM

Establishing a mentoring program for youth in at-risk situations does take some planning. Although every school and community has its own specific needs and goals, planners can benefit from past experience. The twelve-step planning program outlined below is adapted from earlier work by Crockett and Smink (1991). Based on reviews of program reports and interviews with program coordinators, the planning guide is specifically aimed at programs for students who are at risk of dropping out of school or who have already dropped out. The timeline is flexible, based on individual local needs and resources.

Establish Program Need. The program can include all students in an alternative school, or particular populations, such as all ninth- grade students. It can concentrate on academic skills, career awareness, or personal skills. The focus of a program is determined by the needs of the youth to be served. Each school and community has unique problems that must be considered in developing a mentoring program.

Secure School District Commitment. Whether the program is school-, community-, or business-based, the school district must be involved. Mentoring programs must complement, not compete with, a student's regular academic and scholastic activities. Additionally, teachers, guidance counselors, and school administrators are a prime resource in selecting students for the program, monitoring their progress in school, and locating additional help if necessary.

Identify and Select Program Staff. Many programs begin with a steering committee or other type of advisory board made up of school staff, business people, community leaders, and parents. It is helpful to assign at least one person to coordinate the program. This individual oversees the daily progress of the program and is available to both mentors and students when problems arise.

Refine Program Goals and Objectives. It is impossible to measure the success of the program without clear-cut goals and objectives. For example, if the primary objective of a program is to keep dropout-prone students in school, set goals for improvement in attendance and academic achievement.

Develop Activities and Procedures. Since a rigid schedule would inhibit the natural flow of the mentor relationship, establish guidelines for the length and frequency of mentor-student contact. Experience from existing programs suggests that contacts between mentor and student should be fairly frequent, approximately one to two hours per week but not less than one hour per month. The most common relationships span an academic school year or summer break. Short programs, spanning only a few months, do not allow time to establish the personal connection inherent to mentoring.

Identify Students in Need of Mentors. Participation by students to be mentored is, in most cases, voluntary. Teachers, guidance counselors, social workers, the court system, or their parents may refer students. Those youth who profit most from the experience will have certain qualities as well: receptivity to new ideas, commitment, ability to listen and ask questions, and enthusiasm.

Promote the Program and Recruit Mentors. Recruitment of mentors can be done both formally and informally, through flyers, posters, mailings, word of mouth, and media announcements. Some program mentors come from college campuses or from specific businesses or community groups. Overt and covert incentives, such as credit for a course or job recognition, are occasionally used. The qualities needed by mentors will, to some degree, be determined by the program's goals. But a desire to care about, understand, accept, and enjoy young people must be at the top of every list. In addition, the mentors should be perceived as trustworthy and flexible by the youth to be served. They also must have access, through their positions or socioeconomic status, to resources they can share.

Train Mentors and Students. While training may not turn a poor mentor into a good one, it can certainly be used as part of a selection process. Initial and ongoing training of mentors is vital to the success of the program. Students must also be provided with a program orientation and training opportunities so they know what is expected of them in the relationship. There is increasing evidence that lack of training is a primary cause of unsuccessful mentoring and a cause for volunteer mentors to exit a program.

Manage the Mentor-Student Matching Process. The literature on matching mentor with mentee is inconclusive. Some local coordinators say that similarity is necessary, others claim it doesn't matter. Peer mentoring, or mentoring by students just a few years older has been tried in some programs with a great deal of success. Also, similarity in personality is not necessarily a predictor of a successful match. What seems most important is the ability of the mentor to empathize with the student, identify his or her needs, and provide manageable steps to fill those needs.

Monitor the Mentoring Process. Monitoring during the program is accomplished through brief meetings, questionnaires, or telephone calls. This ensures that problems are addressed early and mismatches are reassigned. In addition, mentors must realize that they cannot resolve every one of their student's problems. Other sources of help, such as counselors and social service agencies, must be made available during the mentorship.

Evaluate Ongoing and Terminated Cases. While time and money constraints often mean that evaluations are last on the list, they are critical to the success of the program. Based in part on information gathered during the monitoring stage, evaluations measure a program's effectiveness and suggest changes and improvements for future programs and participants.

Admittedly, there are some problems with evaluating mentoring programs. Comparing participants with a control group of non-participants means that some students do not receive the benefits of a mentor. Improvements in such areas as attendance and academic achievement cannot be attributed solely to a student having a mentor. In some cases, other interventions such as parental disciplinary action or school attendance incentive programs may also affect the student.

Nevertheless, researchers and practitioners agree that some kind of evaluation is critical. Not only does evaluation provide a tool for revising and refining the program; it is also crucial to funding efforts. While the data may be imperfect, the evaluation provides a measure of whether the original goals and objectives of the program were achieved.

Revise Program and Recycle Steps. Revision of a program, based on information from mentors, students, and program staff, should be an ongoing and continuous process. As the program progresses, it may be necessary to eliminate some components and add others. The students' needs may change; if they do, the program should change to meet those needs.

Limits of and Concerns about Mentoring Programs

For all the positive aspects of mentoring programs, they have some limitations. Program coordinators who recognize these can be watchful in their program planning and mentor training programs.

Time. Goodlad (1995) notes several reasons for program failures, but by far the overwhelming deterrent is the very basic issue of time. Individuals who volunteer to be mentors naturally have other personal, family, and job-related commitments. As a result, their time is short, and often the quality of the available time is less than what it should be for each mentor-mentee activity.

Social Distance. A social distance between the mentor and mentee—differences in their socioeconomic status, culture, generation, language, or ethnic background—can present a challenge. If the mentor lacks the interest or persistence needed to bridge the gap, the relationship may falter. A more socially comfortable mentor-mentee relationship takes less effort and may get more frequent attention than the difficult relationship.

Isolation. Another problem often mentioned in mentor interviews is a feeling of isolation. Unless mentors are involved in a structured program with a strong initial and ongoing training and support program, they tend to feel alone and lacking the encouragement they need. Although time remains an issue, mentors do value training and support and are willing to participate in these efforts to the extent that time is available.

Termination. When program coordinators are aware of any of the above challenges or other problems with the relationship, they must take immediate action either to provide the needed support or to end the mentoring relationship. Not all mentor-mentee relationships are successful. Procedures must be in place to halt a relationship that is not effective or creates a disruptive atmosphere in the overall program. Most program plans do have provisions for these situations. These plans should be written and be part of the local training program and guidebook for mentors.

PROGRAM EVALUATION

The program component that usually receives the least attention from program planners is the evaluation process. Measuring the progress of the program and its impact on students is critical for many different reasons, including the need to demonstrate evidence of results for the program's sponsors. If local expertise is not available to design an evaluation model, program leaders should solicit technical assistance from local universities or from an organization such as the National Dropout Prevention Center. One prudent planning tip is to promote opportunities for providing success stories to the local media, policy makers, or sponsors who provide resources or make decisions about whether to continue the program.

EFFECTIVE PROGRAMS AND PRACTICES

In spite of the many advantages of mentoring programs, they should not be regarded as an independent intervention or offered as the only effective strategy for working with students in at-risk situations. Mentors are not miracle workers, and mentoring cannot provide an immediate cure for the problems young people face. Mentoring programs should work in conjunction with other programs, ideas, and strategies for helping youth at any stage of their development. Despite these limitations, the number of successful mentoring programs in the United States is vast. Local program planners can learn much from the programs already in place. Described below, with contact information, are several unique ideas and model programs.

Mentee Scholarships Supported by Chamber of Commerce. The Kalamazoo Area Academic Achievement Program (KAAAP) began in 1992 in five school districts, in full collaboration with the Kalamazoo County Chamber of Commerce. The program begins by matching business and community mentors with about 75 fourth grade students. After these students complete a comprehensive program of mentoring, family involvement, and work experiences and upon graduation from high school they will have earned a $4,000 grant for post-secondary education.

Since the program started, KAAAP has served more than 900 academically at-risk students and their families. Fully sponsored by Chamber of Commerce businesses and the school districts, KAAAP expects to have its first graduates in the year 2000. The W.E. Upjohn Institute for Employment Research is conducting a multi-year study of the first 300 students. The initial research results found improvements in the KAAAP students' attendance and test scores, compared to their counterparts in the control group. Working with the National Dropout Prevention Center, which provided technical assistance during the early stages of development and implementation of the project, KAAAP is making a difference.

In the 1999–2000 school year, Gayle West-Webster has initiated a new program activity utilizing older KAAAP students as mentors with the entering fourth grade students. This Jeader's Leaders program (formed in cooperation with the Turn-2 Foundation, headed by Derrick Jeader) will allow the older students serving as mentors to earn an additional $1,000 upon graduation for use in their continued education program.

For additional information:

Gayle West-Webster, Executive Director
Kalamazoo Area Academic Achievement Program
346 W. Michigan Ave.
Kalamazoo, MI 49007
616-381-4000

African-American Males. Save Our Sons (SOS) is a non-profit organization dedicated to reducing the rate of incarceration of African-American males through a series of programs, advocacy, and research. The program is sponsored mostly through contributions from local community organizations and businesses. Activities include field trips, school involvement, Saturday seminars, recreation activities, church-related activities, and other community enhancement activities. Mentoring by community volunteers is a key component. More than 100 mentoring relationships are active and involve both individual and group mentoring activities. Mentors attempt to build a strong bond with mentees and utilize many strategies, including the powers of listening and persuasion.

For additional information:

Roger G. Owens, President
Save Our Sons
P.O. Box 10706
Greenville, SC 29603
864-297-4694

Negative School Attitudes Into Post-secondary School Scholarships. The Norwalk Mentor Program began in 1986 in Norwalk, Connecticut, as a school-based mentor program for elementary and middle school students who lacked self-esteem and had negative attitudes about school. The program addresses school attendance, motivation, and the need for positive role models for students.

Mentors recruited from local businesses are given extensive initial and ongoing training in areas such as liability issues, decision making, problem solving, communicating skills, conflict resolution, and self-esteem building. Each mentor receives strategies and an age-appropriate workbook for use as a guide during the mentoring relationship. Each mentee who completes the program and graduates from high

school earns a $1,000 scholarship for use in a post-secondary educa-
tion program.

For additional information:

Donna E. Custer, Coordinator
Norwalk Mentor Program
125 East Avenue
Norwalk, CT 06852
203-854-4011

Recidivism, Substance Abuse, and Teen Pregnancy. The Ameri-
Corps Program of San Luis Obispo County, California, was developed
five years ago with community consensus and provides intensive one-
to-one mentoring services to high-risk teens. AmeriCorps members are
assigned to community agencies serving high-risk teen populations.
Staffs at these agencies provide supervision and refer appropriate youth
to members for a mentoring relationship. Two full-time administrators
oversee the program, placement and supervision of 40 to 50 AmeriCorps
members each service year. Each full-time member mentors eight to
ten teens, spending four to six hours a week with each mentee for eight
to twelve months.

The goals are to reduce recidivism, substance abuse, and teen pregnancy and increase school and life success. Specific activities include
identifying and eliminating barriers to life success, tutoring, goal setting, expanding opportunities, teaching independent living skills, helping obtain employment, helping juvenile offenders complete probation
contracts, involving youth in positive alternatives to crime and substance use, increasing parent involvement in their child's life, and acting as a guide and trusted friend. Since 1994, 160 AmeriCorps members
have provided over 160,000 hours of service to more than 1,600 teens.

Mentees include juvenile offenders (45 percent are on probation),
substance-abusing youth (57 percent have problems related to substance
use), youth living with addicted parents, teens in foster care, youth
with mental illness and behavioral issues, teen parents, and teens failing in school. Additionally, 41 percent are living in poverty, 64 percent
are living in single-parent households or foster care situations, and 42
percent are minorities.

For additional information:

Jill Lemieux, Director
AmeriCorps of San Luis Obispo County
P.O. Box 3953
San Luis Obispo, CA 93403
805-549-7890

Self-Esteem and Career Awareness. The 100 Black Men of Chicago is one of 82 chapters of the national organization that develops and fosters the dreams and aspirations of African-American youth. This chapter conducts weekly mentoring sessions with young male students from the sixth, seventh, and eight grades of Michelle Clark Middle School. The objective of the program is to help students create positive images of themselves and encourage them to begin investigating their career destinations. This comprehensive mentoring program has included activities such as an annual career day, special field trips, guest speakers, and a Heritage Bowl where Clark students square off against other students and are tested about their knowledge of African and African-American history. Other fun activities include attending basketball games, magic shows, and a visit to a downtown restaurant to congratulate the graduating mentees.

For additional information:

100 Black Men of Chicago
188 West Randolph, Suite 626
Chicago, IL 60601-2901
312-372-1262

Telementoring with Students Interested in Math and Science. The Hewlett-Packard (HP) Telementor Program is a structured, project-based program in which HP employees worldwide volunteer to telementor fifth- through twelfth-grade students in one-to-one electronic relationships. The focus of the program is to help students excel in math and science, with a particular emphasis on career explorations; students also improve their communication skills. The mentor-mentee relationships are based on regular classroom activities in which student and mentor collaborate under the supervision of a classroom teacher.

For additional information:

David Neils
International Telementor Center
3919 Benthaven Drive
Fort Collins, CO 80526
970-206-9352
davidn@telementor.org

CONCLUSION

Mentoring—a one-on-one supportive relationship based on caring and trust—can make a difference to students who are at risk of dropping out of school. The setting, format, and approach may vary, but most mentoring relationships benefit from a structured program of support. Mentoring is most effective when applied in conjunction with other strategies in a comprehensive school dropout prevention program.

REFERENCES

AmeriCorps 1998–1999 Annual Report. (2000). San Luis Obispo County, CA.

Crockett, L. and Smink, J. (1991). The Mentoring Guidebook: A Practical Manual for Designing and Managing a Mentoring Program. Clemson, SC: National Dropout Prevention Center.

Field, A. (1999, January). Tech-Mentor. In *How to Be a Great Mentor.* A guide produced by Kaplan/Newsweek/The National Mentoring Partnership. Washington, DC: Kaplan/Newsweek.

Goodlad, S. (Ed.). (1995). Students as Tutors and Mentors. London: Kogan Page.

Herrera, Carla, Sipe, C. L., and McClanahan, W. S. (2000, April). Mentoring School-Age Children: Relationship Development in Community-Based and School-Based Programs. Philadelphia: Public/Private Ventures.

Kalamazoo Area Academic Achievement Program (KAAAP). (n.d.). Mentoring Handbook. Kalamazoo, MI: Author.

McLearn, K., Colasanto, D., and Schoen, C. (1998, June). Mentoring Makes a Difference: Findings from The Commonwealth Fund 1998 Survey of Adults Mentoring Young People.

Mentoring: Elements of Effective Practice. (1991). One to One/The National Mentoring Partnership. Washington, DC.

One to One Partnership, Inc. (1996). One to One Start-Up: A Guide. Washington, DC: Author.

Sipe, C. L. (1996). Mentoring: A Synthesis of P/PV's Research: 1988-1995. Philadelphia: Public/Private Ventures.

Tierney, J. P., and Grossman, J. B. (with Resch, N. L.). (1995). Making a Difference: An Impact Study of Big Brothers/Big Sisters (Executive Summary). Philadelphia: Public/Private Ventures.

Smink, J. (1999). A Training Guide for Mentors. Clemson, SC: National Dropout Prevention Center.

8

SERVICE LEARNING

There is no royal road to learning; and what is life but learning?
Charles Dickens, *Our Mutual Friend*

INTRODUCTION

All across the country, extraordinary but true stories are emerging. America's young people are engaging in their schools and communities, applying their academic knowledge to solve community problems, and really making a difference in the lives of those around them as they also transform themselves. In one rural community, high school students conduct a needs assessment and discover that the greatest need is for a fire station—then they build that fire station. In another school district, middle school children at risk of becoming dropouts tutor first graders in reading—and improve their own reading and communication skills, raise their self-esteem, and develop a sense of belonging. Such stories are indeed good news.

The teaching methodology at work here is known as service learning. In this chapter, we explore the tremendous potential of this strategy for keeping students in school.

THE ROOTS OF SERVICE LEARNING

Service learning is a teaching and learning method that connects meaningful community service experiences with academic learning, personal growth, and civic responsibility. Students involved in service learning develop and learn through active participation in organized service that:

+ is conducted in and meets the needs of a community

+ is coordinated with an elementary school, secondary school, institution of higher education, or community service program, and with the community

+ helps foster civic responsibility

+ is integrated into and enhances the academic curriculum of the students, or the educational components of the community service program in which the participants are enrolled

+ provides structured time for the students or participants to reflect on the service experience

(Learn and Serve America, 1995).

The roots of service learning lie in the progressive educational movement led by John Dewey. Formal education, whatever the discipline, had evolved over time to become the traditional model of passing a predetermined knowledge base on to a new generation of students. The methodology is familiar: lectures, chalk and blackboards, reading, written examinations. The teacher is the source of information, and the student absorbs what he or she can.

Inspired by Dewey, a new generation of educators initiated a variety of interpretations of his theories of education, especially including experience as the teacher. Extreme versions abandoned traditional education completely, adopting totally free experiences as the vehicle of learning.

Responding to these interpretations and reiterating his own educational philosophy, Dewey emphasized that education is not an either/or proposition (*Experience and Education*, 1939). One need not, and in fact should not, choose between the two extremes. The knowledge base is important, but experience in interpreting that knowledge, testing it in current situations, and analyzing its meaning is crucial for true learning. Indeed, because a student's natural interest in a subject can be sparked only by an involvement in the subject, immediate interaction with the new knowledge in meaningful ways is needed for successful learning. The educator's task is to provide students with experiences that will be a "moving force" for real learning and understanding. One of the most effective experiential teaching methods is service learning.

What has emerged as service learning can be captured in a simple framework: preparation, action, reflection, and celebration (Duckenfield and Wright, 1995). Each of these four components adds important dimensions to this unique form of experiential education. Carefully followed, the framework assists the novice and advanced practitioner alike as they strive to produce that educational experience for their students that will have a lasting and meaningful impact.

Preparation consists of learning experiences that take place prior to the actual service. Students identify and analyze a problem, select and plan a project, and receive appropriate training and orientation.

Action is the service itself. It must have academic integrity, be meaningful to the student, provide for student ownership, have adequate supervision, and be appropriately challenging.

Reflection enables students to think critically and analytically about their service experience. Students need a structured opportunity to reflect, through discussion, reading, writing, production of products, or the arts.

Celebration recognizes students for their contributions. It also provides an opportunity for closure, which is particularly important when direct service with other people is coming to an end.

WHY SERVICE LEARNING IS EFFECTIVE

The major reasons students give for dropping out of school relate to lack of success in academics and poor social skills, including an inability to get along with peers or teachers, no sense of belonging, and disciplinary problems (U.S. Department of Education, 1992). Service learning addresses all of these areas.

IMPACT ON ACADEMICS

Several recent studies support the notion that when the teacher directly connects the service learning experience to the academic curriculum, the students involved have a greater comprehension of their learning. The "learning pyramid" graphically illustrates the concept that retention of academic learning increases in proportion to a student's involvement. The application of the learning makes it relevant; there is a reason for learning, and the age-old problem of motivation is solved (Zlotkowski, 2000).

Reviewing several research studies of service learning schools and the impact of service learning on academic learning, Shelley H. Billig found that in more than half of the high-quality service learning schools studied, students showed moderate to strong gains on achievement tests in language arts or reading, improved engagement in school, an improved sense of educational accomplishment, and better homework completion (Billig, 2000). Other studies indicated that participation in service learning was associated with higher grades and higher scores on the state test of basic skills. In one study, 83 percent of schools with service learning programs reported that the grade-point averages of participating students improved 76 percent of the time. Although much more research is needed, these early indicators show that service learning has the potential to enhance academic learning.

IMPACT ON SOCIAL SKILLS

If we look even more closely at service learning, we can begin to see how this teaching methodology packs extra power. It not only addresses academics, but also has the potential to develop the assets young people need if they are to traverse the minefields of childhood and adolescence safely and successfully: social competence, problem-solving skills, autonomy, and a sense of purpose (Benard, 1991).

- ♦ Children with *social competence* show responsiveness to others, are able to adapt to new situations and circumstances, have the capacity for empathy and caring, have good communication skills, and have a good sense of humor. These children can get along well with adults as well as their peers.

- ♦ Children with *problem-solving skills* have the ability to attempt alternative solutions to problems they confront, whether cognitive or social.

◆ Children who exhibit *autonomy* have a sense of independence, high self-esteem, an "I can do it!" attitude, and a real sense of power over their lives.

◆ Children who have a *sense of purpose* are goal-directed, success-oriented, persistent, and motivated to achieve, with high educational aspirations and a belief in a positive future.

Young people identified as at risk can develop these assets; service learning gives them the opportunity to do so. For example, students involved in a cross-age tutoring project develop *social competence*. Middle- school students may be partnered with first-grade students who have difficulty reading. Working regularly with "their" first graders, the middle-school students develop empathy for another human being. When they reflect and plan, in cooperation with the child, the child's teacher, and their peers, they build communication skills. Participating in what is really an intergenerational project, they learn to relate to others who differ from themselves.

Students involved in a community garden project that provides fresh vegetables to a local soup kitchen can develop *problem-solving skills*. Working in teams, sharing duties, and making decisions about which vegetables to plant, planting the seeds, caring for the plants, and harvesting the food, students meet and master challenges at each step.

Students who adopt a grandparent at a local nursing home, with weekly visits to provide organized recreational activities, develop oral histories, or collaborate on musical activities, can see the importance of their contribution to the lives of these senior citizens. As the students take ownership of the project planning, their sense of *autonomy* and their self-esteem grow.

The teenagers who built a fire station had a specific goal—providing fire protection to the people in their home town. This five-year project gave them a truly meaningful role in community improvement. Though they encountered a variety of obstacles, their enthusiasm, motivation, and commitment did not flag. These students' *sense of purpose* was galvanized by their service learning experience.

EFFECTIVE PROGRAMS AND PRACTICES

Service learning takes many forms. Teachers may implement a service learning project on a one-time basis, or an entire grade level or school may adopt service learning as its organizing theme. The National Service Learning Clearinghouse lists hundreds of model programs on its Web site:

http://www.nicsl.coled.umn.edu/,

and the National Dropout Prevention Center presents Program Profiles at:

www.dropoutprevention.org.

The programs described below illustrate the scope and variety of possibilities for service learning.

America's Promise: The Alliance for Youth. America's Promise occupies a unique place in America's service learning community. Developed by retired U.S. Army General Colin L. Powell, the program calls upon national and local business leaders, political figures, parents, and educators to help youth become "self-supporting and contributing members of society" by fulfilling five promises:

1. Caring adults in children's lives, as parents, mentors, tutors, coaches, with weekly face-to-face meetings and structured one-on-one biweekly scheduled interactions.

2. Safe places with structured activities in which to learn and grow, including sports programs, club activities, after-school organizations, religious and other community organizations.

3. A healthy start and healthy future, with prenatal care and parenting support, health insurance coverage, access to nutritionists and other health care providers.

4. An effective education that equips youth with marketable skills by emphasis on maintaining grade level in reading and mathematics and by providing internships, apprenticeships, and summer jobs.

5. An opportunity to give back to their communities through their own service by serving in the community/school two or more hours per week or approximately 100 hours per year.

For additional information:

http//www.americaspromise.org
1-888-55-YOUTH

Cultural Warriors. The American Youth Works Charter School in downtown Austin, Texas, targets youth that have not succeeded in mainstream schools. Cultural Warriors is a youth-centered arts program that utilizes theater to develop academic, interpersonal, and professional skills. Designed specifically for disadvantaged youth, Cultural Warriors provides a safe forum for exploring issues of crucial importance to self, family, and community, culminating in creative expression and artistic achievement.

Writing and performing their own pieces at schools and community events, Cultural Warriors address common social issues—drugs, gangs, domestic violence, sexual activity, teen pregnancy—that face today's youth. Using creative processes, Cultural Warriors develop communication, teamwork, leadership, and critical thinking skills that better equip youth to deal with these challenges effectively and appropriately. Through social commentary, Cultural Warriors share their experiences with their peers and their community, fostering a forum for constructive dialogue about how these important social issues affect us all.

For additional information:

Tashya Valdevit
American Youth Works Charter School
216 East 4th Street
Austin, TX 78701
512-472-3395

Project Spark. Project Spark is an excellent example of a districtwide approach. In Georgia, Valdosta City Schools incorporate service learning through mentoring, conflict resolution, and curricular reform. Students are an integral part of the leadership. The initial project sprang from a needs assessment showing that one of the district's top three priorities was a community service program for suspended and expelled students. Its objectives were to spark appropriate behavior, acceptance of responsibility for individual learning, interest in remaining in school, better academic performance, and service learning in order to give youth service providers opportunities to help solve the dropout problem.

At first, the primary activity of the youth service providers was tutoring elementary age students through a Study Buddy program.

However, the "spark" quickly flamed. Teachers as well as students began to envision how service learning could be integrated in a variety of ways, K–12, to enhance the school experience for all students and making school a place youth want to be, and at the same time, meet many different school and community needs.

Three years after the initial tutoring effort, service learning is thriving in all ten Valdosta City Schools. Projects have included tutoring programs, building an outdoor classroom, creating nature trails, beautifying school property, a Junior Fire Marshals program, peer mediation, conflict resolution, education about alcohol and other drugs, a Black History Museum, a Habitat House, Book Buddies, and intergenerational service programs. Strong links with the community—including AmeriCorps, Valdosta State University, and many community organizations and businesses—provide the foundation for this successful service learning program.

For additional information:

Vickie Burt
Valdosta City Schools
P.O. Box 5407
Valdosta, GA 31603
912-333-8500

A Rural School District Makes a Difference. In Gresham, South Carolina, service learning has had a significant impact on the school system and the community. Several years ago, a group of students at Britton's Neck High School conducted a needs assessment and found a rural fire department was needed. Teachers throughout the K–12 system integrated a safety curriculum into core academic courses. After securing property from a community member, the students built a fire station. As a result, nearby property has been reclassified and the cost of homeowner's insurance has dropped. The real impact, however, says Marion District Four Superintendent, Dr. Milt Marley, "is the manner in which service-learning has reconnected our youth to the community and has actively engaged our young people in the learning process."

For additional information:

Jerry Pace
Marion School District Four
Britton's Neck High School
223 Gresham Rd.
Gresham, SC 29546
843-362-3500

First Opportunity. First Opportunity is an early-intervention service learning program for eleven- to fifteen-year-old low-income youth who are at risk of dropping out of school and becoming involved in the juvenile justice system. First Opportunity addresses the issues of truancy and delinquent behavior through a holistic approach that includes community service, mentoring, life skill development, and family case management services. The overarching goals of the initiative are to develop civic responsibility and leadership skills in youth by addressing critical community needs through service learning; to support youth in school and promote positive educational experiences; to match youth with a caring adult mentor who can help them learn what they can do with their lives through role modeling and involvement; and to provide youth with the support necessary to become self-sufficient adults.

For additional information:

Sherry Glanton-Parnell
Folwell Middle School
900 20ᵗʰ Avenue, South
Minneapolis, MN 55404
612-752-8822

Learn and Serve Together II (LAST II). Learn and Serve Together II builds on a previous project that sponsored service learning at two high schools, focusing on violence and substance abuse prevention. LAST II is based on the belief that alternative school students will benefit from a service learning experience and gain new skills that can be applied throughout their adult life. The project effectively integrates two national initiatives: Learn and Serve America and Safe and Drug-Free Schools. Students at the Charlotte-Mecklenburg alternative high school, the Learning Academy, learn specific violence prevention and substance abuse prevention strategies through the health curriculum and then have opportunities to teach and model skills to their peers. Service learning provides a setting where students can apply their learning to everyday problems and situations. Emphasis is placed on reflective activities where students examine their own decision-making processes and volunteer experiences. The broad goal of the project is to promote civic responsibility and encourage students to make a commitment to volunteer service.

For additional information:

Cynthia Woods
Charlotte-Mecklenburg School District
700 East Stonewall Street
Charlotte, NC 28202
704-343-3768

CONCLUSION

Within the last decade, service learning has emerged as a positive teaching tool to engage students in community service activities that are fully integrated into their academic learning. Service learning programs across America have yielded outstanding results for students in the areas of personal and social growth, citizenship development, academic improvement, career awareness, and development of job skills. Service learning is a unique and valuable tool for meeting the myriad needs of youth in at-risk situations.

REFERENCES

Benard, B. (1991). *Fostering Resiliency in Kids: Protective Factors in the Family, School, and Community*. Portland, OR: Northwest Regional Educational Laboratory.

Billig, S.H. (2000, May). "Research on K–12 School-Based Service-Learning." *Phi Delta Kappan*, 658–664.

Dewey, J. (1939). *Experience and Education*. New York: The Macmillan Company.

Duckenfield, M., & Wright, J. (Eds.). (1995). *Pocket Guide to Service Learning*. Clemson, SC: National Dropout Prevention Center.

Learn and Serve America. (1995). Washington, DC: Corporation for National Service.

Zlotkowski, E. (2000, May 8). "Service Learning." Presentation at Clemson University, Clemson, SC.

U. S. Department of Education. (1992). *Longitudinal Study of 1988 First and Second Follow-up Surveys, 1990 and 1992*. Unpublished Data. Washington, DC: National Center for Education Statistics.

9

ALTERNATIVE SCHOOLING

O! this learning, what a thing it is.

William Shakespeare

INTRODUCTION

Alternative schooling, alternative education, alternative schools—regardless of the name, the concept is not really new to the American scene. As early as colonial America, religious groups or the wealthy offered education to the general population. More than a hundred years ago, state legislators supported many different types of schools. In South Carolina, the John de la Howe School and the Wil Lou Gray Opportunity School still serve students in at-risk situations. Other states likewise have sponsored residential schools for troubled youth. In nearly every state, governors have developed theme-based schools, usually focusing on math, science, or the performing arts. Special-interest groups have established alternative schools for special populations; examples include the Penn School in Beaufort County, South Carolina, founded in 1865 by Quakers from Pennsylvania to educate African Americans living in the low country, and the Milton Hershey School for orphaned and needy children in Hershey, Pennsylvania.

Koetke (1999) discusses other early educational opportunities and how they led to today's two basic options for alternative schooling—educational opportunities "outside the system" and those "inside the system." Alternative school opportunities outside the system include elite and costly private schools,

schools with a religious orientation, and the recently revived home schools. Alternative schools inside the system, according to Koetke, generally serve a special population, such as students with unique learning interests or disabilities, teenage parents, potential dropouts, violent individuals, or court-adjudicated youths and those in juvenile detention systems. These alternative schools will be the focus of the remainder of this chapter; they represent one of the effective strategies used to keep students in school in pursuit of a high school diploma or GED.

THE NEED FOR ALTERNATIVE SCHOOLING OPPORTUNITIES

All students can learn, and all students deserve the opportunity to achieve the quality of life they seek.

If every school board member, school administrator, teacher, parent, community and business leader believes that statement, then alternative schooling is not an option in America—it is an absolute requirement in every community. The traditional school system, and particularly the traditional high school, can no longer meet the needs of every student. Some have even suggested that students *should* drop out of traditional schools and complete their GED in alternative schools (Dynarski, 1999).

Alternative schooling that meets a variety of student and family needs enables school and community leaders to fulfill their legal responsibility to provide equal access to education for all students. The critical question is, what kind of alternative schooling should our public school systems offer? What should the alternative programs look like, and how should they be integrated with the regular school programs in each community?

State legislators have long recognized the need for alternative schooling. Many states have passed permissive legislation; California now estimates that as many as 35 percent of its public school children are in alternative schools or specialized programs of some kind. In Florida, the Dropout Prevention Act of 1986 authorizes and encourages district school boards "to establish comprehensive Dropout Prevention Programs designed to meet the needs of students who are not effectively served by traditional education programs in the public school programs." The

Act established five program categories, including educational alternatives.

In 1995, the Florida legislature amended the Dropout Prevention Act to create Second Chance Schools for students who have been disruptive or violent or who have committed serious offenses. Second Chance Schools are school district programs provided through cooperative agreements between the Department of Juvenile Justice, private providers, state or local law enforcement agencies, or other state agencies for students who have been disruptive or violent or who have committed serious offenses (Florida Department of Education, 1995). Reflecting the growing concern of political leaders as well as local school boards about violence in society and in our schools, the measure dictates a new kind of alternative school along with a new set of procedures or curriculum for troubled youth.

Mississippi passed even more aggressive legislation; Senate Bill No. 2510 (1995) amended the School Code as follows: "Beginning with the school year 1993–1994, the school districts shall establish, maintain and operate, in connection with the regular programs of the school district, an alternative school program for, but not limited to, the following categories of compulsory-school-age students . . . ." In Texas, school districts are now required to provide an alternative to expulsion, and alternative schools are springing up throughout the state. South Carolina's General Assembly passed legislation in 1999 requiring each district to establish alternative school programs to serve students who are not benefiting from the regular school program or who may be interfering with the learning of others. In Georgia, recent legislation called for alternative schools at the district level and also gave school boards the opportunity to establish charter schools.

The growing movement to establish charter schools highlights another category of alternative schooling. Led by Minnesota in 1990, followed by Arizona, California, and Colorado, more than thirty states and the District of Columbia have passed legislation permitting charter schools. An early survey by Buechler (1996) found programs ranging from traditional home study programs to cyber-schools in which students study at home via technology. The survey found that charter schools, on average, are small, serve about 100 students, and are located off the traditional school campus in community-based commercial settings. The survey also indicated that most charter schools were formed especially to serve at-risk youth.

A survey of charter schools by Molnar (1996) noted that the various state laws differ significantly in the degree of autonomy given to charter schools. "Strong" charter-school laws granted much greater autonomy, whereas "weak" laws gave charter schools little more autonomy than other public schools. In either case, about two-thirds of the schools sought to attract a cross section of students and about half were intended to serve students in at-risk situations.

According to the U.S. Department of Education's most recent review of charter schools, in school year 1997–98, a total of 1,050 charter schools served 160,000 students in 33 states and the District of Columbia (Berman et.al., 1999). The most common reasons for establishing charter schools were to realize an alternative vision of schooling and to gain autonomy from district and state regulations.

ALTERNATIVE SCHOOLING FOR STUDENTS AT RISK

The alternative schools of the 1950s and 1960s were usually designed to serve students who had already dropped out of "regular" school. These schools and programs were the primary "dropout prevention programs" of that era. However, the strategy had little effect on the dropout rate, and as district budgets began to shrink in the 1970s, many of these alternative school programs were discontinued.

The last decade has seen a resurgence of alternative schools addressing the needs of at-risk students. However, these new schools have truly emphasized dropout prevention, with special attention to a student's individual social needs and the academic requirements for a high school diploma. Many districts now offer alternative school programs at the middle school level that specifically strive to keep students in school and maximize their later opportunities to obtain a job or to pursue education beyond high school.

Magnet schools that focus on selected academic areas such as math and science or music have survived through the past several decades and remain a viable opportunity for students today. Magnet schools are most often available in larger or urban school districts, although some affluent suburbs also support such specialized schools. Perhaps the oldest and most recognized magnet school models are those in the New York City public school system. An exciting recent innovative model is the Key Elementary School in Indianapolis, whose curriculum emphasizes Howard Gardner's theory of multiple intelligences (Bolaños, 1994). Of course, the best examples of magnet schools are probably the high-profile schools supported by each state's governor, such as the Governor's Institute of the Arts (subject areas may differ by state).

The most common form of alternative school now serving youth in at-risk situations is designed as part of a school district's comprehensive dropout prevention program and usually offers middle or high school programs to students of secondary-school age. The typical student is underachieving and lacks the credits required to graduate or to stay in class with others of the same age. Some, though behind academically, want to stay in school and earn their diplomas; others have been placed in the school by the court system. In many communities, these alternative schools offer parenting programs with special opportunities for teenage mothers.

Numerous models of alternative schools have been developed to serve local needs and are operating with varied degrees of success. Rhonda Hefner-Packer (1991) identified five categories of alternative school models:

- ◆ the alternative classroom, designed as a self-contained classroom within a traditional school, simply offering varied programs in a different environment
- ◆ the school-within-a-school, housed within a traditional school, but having semi-autonomous or specialized educational programs
- ◆ the separate alternative school, physically distinct from the regular school and offering different academic and social adjustment programs
- ◆ the continuation school, developed for students no longer attending traditional schools, such as street

academies for job-related training or parenting centers

♦ the magnet school, a self-contained program offering an intensified curriculum in one or more subject areas such as math or science

In a synthesis of research for *Educational Leadership*, Mary Anne Raywid (1994) classifies popular alternative schools as schools of choice, usually magnet schools, offering different specialized learning opportunities; last-chance schools, providing continued education program options for disruptive students; and remedial schools, focusing on the student's need for academic remediation or social rehabilitation.

The National Dropout Prevention Center's database of successful dropout prevention programs contains descriptions of many alternative schools throughout the United States. Each school presents a unique combination of the students it serves, the curriculum it offers, and the way it is administered. Within the great variety of organizational structures represented in the database, however, several patterns emerge:

♦ school-within-a-school, for students needing a separate location within the traditional school, usually a separate wing with different staff, for academic or social behavior programs

♦ schools without walls, for students participating in educational and training programs delivered from various locations within the community, usually requiring flexible student schedules

♦ residential schools, for special-case students who are usually placed by the courts or the family, with special counseling and educational programs

♦ separate alternative learning centers, for students needing a special curriculum, such as parenting skills or special job skills, and a separate location from the traditional school, often in a business environment, a church, or a remodeled retail center, with excellent transportation services

♦ college-based alternative schools, for students needing high school credits; operated by public school staff,
but using a college facility to enhance the student's
self-esteem and offer other services that would benefit the student's growth

♦ summer schools, either remedial for academic credits
or to enhance a student's special interests, perhaps in
science, computers, the arts, or other fields

♦ magnet schools, focusing on selected curriculum areas with specialized teachers and with student attendance usually by choice

♦ second-chance schools, for students who are judged
to be troubled and placed in the school by the courts
or the school district as a last chance before being expelled or incarcerated

♦ charter schools, established as autonomous educational entities operating under a contract negotiated
between the state agency and the local school sponsors

BEST PRACTICES AND DESIGN RECOMMENDATIONS FOR ALTERNATIVE SCHOOLS

The National Dropout Prevention Center has working relationships with numerous alternative schools and dropout prevention projects in schools and communities across the United
States and in Canada. Many of these school partnerships have
been in place for several years, affording the Center the opportunity to review day-to-day results and determine what educational practices work best. From a review of more than 75
alternative schools, the Center has identified numerous exemplary program ideas and administrative practices in the categories of administrative structures and policies, curriculum and
instructional techniques, personal support programs, career-oriented programs, and staff development and staff relationships.

The administrative structures and policies in nearly all the
schools included a clear mission and objectives, a clear discipline code, small classes, enrollment choice by students, shared

decision making, flexible schedules, and collaboration with business/community. Curriculum and instructional techniques included an integrated curriculum, individual learning plans, active learning, accelerated learning, community and service learning, and the use of outside resources and speakers. Personal support programs included diagnostic services, family groups, parental involvement and home visits, individual and group counseling, mentoring and/or tutoring, child care and parenting training, and community support services. Career-oriented programs (found in most schools) included such practices as career days, career shadowing and internships, business partnerships, employability training, and work experience programs.

Staff development and staff relationships were key components in all schools. Best practices included a caring staff, a personalized student environment, specialized and continual staff in-service, and student incentive programs.

Most successful alternative schools share a consistent profile of educational practices that includes:

- ♦ maximum teacher/student ratio of 1:10
- ♦ a small student base not exceeding 250 students
- ♦ a clearly stated mission and discipline code
- ♦ caring faculty with continual staff development
- ♦ school staff having high expectations for student achievement
- ♦ a learning program specific to the student's expectations and learning style
- ♦ a flexible school schedule with community involvement and support
- ♦ total commitment to help each student achieve success

PROGRAM EVALUATION, STANDARDS, AND IMPACT

In general, research evaluating alternative school programs and their effect on student retention and academic achievement levels is very limited. Although some schools keep accurate records regarding attendance, discipline referrals, academic grades, and school completion, many do not. This was evident in a review by the Intercultural Development Research Association of 1,044 school districts in Texas in 1995–96. In that review, 841 districts reported that students were regularly referred to a disciplinary alternative education program; the statewide program has grown to involve more than 70,000 students. "Unfortunately, many programs collect little data on effectiveness compared to student achievement or discipline. Too often, program successes are reported through collections of anecdotes, with little or no 'hard data' collected, tabulated or analyzed" (Montecel, 1999).

With many states now requiring more accountability for all programs, including charter and alternative schools, the evaluation efforts and impact data should be improving. For example, the Florida Department of Education has recently developed an evaluation document to measure the impact of local alternative schools and dropout prevention programs. The *Proposed Quality Standards for Dropout Prevention Programs* (1999), designed for practitioners to use as a self-assessment tool for making program improvements and for reporting program results to decision makers, reflects a focus on quality and excellence. The quality standards framework comprises six major components: program climate, program resources, curriculum and instruction, transition, program planning and evaluation, and leadership. Standards for each major area define essential practices that must be in place for the program components to be effective. The third level of review specifies measurable indicators to provide evidence that the standards are being achieved.

From 1991 to 1996, the U.S. Department of Education's School Dropout Demonstration Assistance Program operated the nation's longest and largest dropout prevention program in 85 different schools and communities. The general findings from an evaluation of twenty selected programs, with data collected from more than 10,000 students, reflected very disappointing results. No program was able to improve all key outcomes examined, such as dropping out, attendance, test scores, and grades. However, the evaluation did show evidence that alternative schools are effective with at-risk students who can demonstrate their commitment to succeed. An alternative school that screened prospective students in interviews to assess their motivation and potential to succeed in school showed impacts on diploma completion rates (Dynarski, 1999).

In a research study examining a broad array of outcomes for students attending Minnesota's second-chance schools for at-risk secondary school students, a thorough review was completed for persisters (those who remained in the program) and dropouts. When all the typical indicators of student performance were examined, only the persisters showed positive directions for attendance and academic achievement in reading. The researchers did suggest that second-chance schools were providing a positive experience for these high-risk students, even though 50 percent of the students did not complete the alternative program (Lange and Lehr, 1999).

EFFECTIVE PROGRAMS AND PRACTICES

During the last decade, charter schools, second-chance schools, and a variety of other alternative schools have been able to reinvent learning opportunities and school designs. The educational scene today continues to offer numerous opportunities for creating schools that meet the needs of nearly every student, particularly the one who does not fit into traditional schools. School and community leaders seeking to plan and implement new alternative schools can learn much from the innovative and successful programs described in the rest of this chapter.

Hostos Lincoln Academy of Science. The Hostos School is a small alternative high school, one of 75 run by the New York City Board of Education, serving students who did not succeed in their previous schools. The school relies on strong interventions, including attendance at summer school and small daily family groups used to discuss all school or social issues faced by the students. Despite the fact that Hostos has 20 percent more students living below the poverty line than the average New York City school, its rate for students passing Regents exams was more than 20 percent higher than the city average. Furthermore, the school dropout rate was just 0.3 percent, compared to the citywide average of 5 percent.

For additional information:

Richard Organisciak, Superintendent
New York City Board of Education
Dropout Prevention Program
Alternative, Adult and Continuing Education
45-18 Court Square
Long Island City, NY 11101
Brooklyn NY 11201
718-752-7300

Flexible Schedules. Liberty High School, in Louisville, Kentucky, has posted equally impressive results for the past decade. The open-entry school offers three blocks of time each day in four different city locations, making attendance very convenient. Each entering student goes through a well-developed diagnostic assessment package, then follows a computer-based curriculum with supplemented materials developed by the school's staff. Students proceed through their own individualized program at their own pace. Since the program began in 1986, the school has graduated more than 5,000 students (an average of 450 each year); 72 percent of the students who enter (already at risk of school failure) complete the program, earning a high-school diploma. This graduation rate is higher than that of the regular high schools in the district.

For additional information:

Buell Snyder, Director
Jefferson County High School
Jefferson County Public Schools
911 South Brook Street
Louisville, KY 40203
502-485-7100

School-to-Work. The O.C.V.T.S. School-to-Work Enrichment Center is housed at the Career & Technical Institute located at the Lakehurst Naval Air Station, Lakehurst, NJ. The program is designed to provide a full academic program in a non-traditional format to at-risk students with a high school graduation diploma awarded to each student that successfully meets all requirements of the program. The Enrichment Center program provides each student with an opportunity to partici-pate in experiences related to the transition from school to careers through job shadowing, job internships, and employment work place-ments. The naval base provides a true partnership of these employment related experiences between the school district and the naval base facilities.

For additional information:

Thomas W. Resch. Principal
Career & Technical Institute
Ocena County Voctec Schools
P.O. Box 1125, Hangar One
Rt. 547 NAES
Lakehurst, NY 98733
732-657-4000

Staff Development. This alternative school features a concentrated basic skills program using the Jostens Learning Systems. The school closes every Wednesday afternoon from 12:00 to 3:00 p.m. for staff development activities.

For additional information:

Charlene Watson, Director
The Amelia Pride Center
Lynchburg City School Division
1200-1208 Polk Street
Lynchburg, VA 24504
804-522-3742

Alternative School for Grades One to Eight . This alternative school serves diverse students with different learning styles in grades one to eight. The school features multi-grade groups in self-contained classes. Every student has an alternative education plan.

For additional information:

Ms. Kerry Miller, Assistant Director
Education Services Commission (ESC) School at Kingston
P.O. Box 314
Huntington County, Kingston, NJ 08528
609-921-6431

Teenage Parenting Center. This school operates a Parenting Center for teenage mothers and their children as a separate facility. The school has a planned curriculum and encourages individual scheduling to accommodate the family's needs. The school collaborates with several health and social service agencies that offer on-site services as part of the program.

For additional information:

Karl Roberts, Director
The Teenage Parenting Center
Muscogee County School District
2701 11th Ave.
Columbus, GA 31904
706-641-4171

Aggression Replacement Training. The alternative high school in Elmira, New York, has an excellent student handbook that identifies specific student exit outcomes, which are reviewed by each entering student. Part of the curriculum is based on Dr. William Glasser's choice theory and reality therapy. Each staff member and student must participate in an ongoing aggression replacement training program.

For additional information:

Judy LeFever, Coordinator
SCT BOCES Alternative High School
459 Philo Road
Elmira, NY 14903
607-739-3581

Charter School in Storefronts. The Charter School of San Diego is a complex system of local programs sponsored by business partnerships in various locations, including storefronts. Started in 1991, the program places an emphasis on gaining workforce skills and credits for graduation. Transportation to the various sites is the responsibility of the student.

For additional information:

Mary Searcy-Gomez Bixby
The Charter School of San Diego
2245 San Diego Ave., Suite 127
San Diego, CA 92110
619-686-6666

Collaborative Alternative School. Rural districts in several counties of southeast Mississippi, each with the need for an alternative school, entered into a collaborative agreement to build and support an alternative school in a converted shopping center. A combination of financial resources was creatively used to initiate and maintain the school.

For additional information:

Lewis Goins, Current Director, 601-428-8080
Dewey Blackledge, First Director, 601-266-6777
(currently on staff, University of Southern Mississippi)
Pine Belt Education Service Center (Alternative School)
Southeast Mississippi Regional Alternative Education
Cooperative
923B Sawmill Road
Laurel, MS 39440
610-649-4141

High Student Expectations and Accountability Reports. A hallmark of the Academy of Creative Education is high student expectations; the accountability reports to the public and state demonstrate that these expectations are met. The school places an emphasis on staff assessments and annual program reviews. It also has an excellent public relations program.

For additional information:

Mary Jo McLaughlin, Director
The Academy of Creative Education
North East Independent School District
1033 Broadway
San Antonio, TX 78217
210-657-8970

Adult-Led Support Groups. The New York City Board of Education serves more than 100,000 students from infants to adults in 70 different types of programs ranging from theme-based schools to detention/correctional facilities. There is an emphasis on performance-based assessment of student work, with a portfolio for each student. Several schools have initiated an advisory system requiring every adult in the school to meet on a regular schedule with eight to ten students in a "family" discussion group. This support group has contributed to greater bonding to the school, increased attendance, and fewer discipline problems in the school.

For additional information:

Richard Organisciak, Superintendent
New York City Board of Education
Dropout Prevention Program
Alternative, Adult and Continuing Education
45-18 Court Square
Long Island City, NY 11101
718-752-7300

Comprehensive Learning Center Programs, K–12. The Ankeny Community School District in Ankeny, Iowa, has developed one of the nation's most comprehensive alternative schooling programs. The Ankeny Learning Program's philosophy builds on the belief that all children can learn and thrive in their school setting and that everyone learns differently. The program provides services and support to K–12 students and families in at-risk situations and allows them to develop to their fullest potential. The district's comprehensive program offers a variety of services and programs in elementary, middle, and high school environments. The learning centers are fully integrated in the life of the community; many businesses and organizations are involved in partnerships with the schools.

For additional information:

Pat Sievers, Director
Ankeny Community School District
Office of Special Programs
Box 189, 306 SW School Street
Ankeny, IA 50021
515-965-9600

CONCLUSION

Alternative schooling is enjoying a resurgence in the educational arena, partly because of legislative requirements and partly because educators see alternative schools as viable options for serving certain student populations. Alternative schools have a definite place in any comprehensive school improvement plan. Whether they offer a different instructional style, a different venue, or a second chance in a different school, alternative schools work. School and community leaders across the nation have made a difference by providing these educational opportunities, particularly to students in at-risk situations. The results show that alternative schooling is an effective strategy for dropout prevention.

REFERENCES

Berman, P. et al. (1999). The State of Charter Schools. Washington, DC: U.S. Department of Education.

Bolaños, P. (1994). From Theory to Practice. *The School Administrator, 54*(1), 30–31.

Buechler, M. (1996). Out on Their Own. *Technos, 5*(3), 30–32.

Dynarski, M. (1999). How Can We Help? Princeton, NJ: Mathematica Policy Research, Inc.

Florida Department of Education. (1995, August). *Second Chance Schools.* Tallahassee, FL: Author.

Florida Department of Education. (1999, April). *Proposed Quality Standards for Dropout Prevention Programs*, Tallahassee, FL: Author.

Hefner-Packer, R. (1991). Alternative Education Programs: A Prescription for Success. *Monographs In Education.* Athens: The University of Georgia.

Koetke, C. (1999). One Size Doesn't Fit All. TECHNOS Quarterly, Bloomington, IN: The Agency for Instructional Technology.

Lange, C., and Lehr, C. (1999). At-Risk Students Attending Second Chance Programs: Measuring Performance in Desired Outcome Domains. *Journal of Education for Students Placed at Risk, 4*(2), 173–192.

Molnar, A. (1996). Charter Schools: The Smiling Face of Disinvestment. *Educational Leadership, 54*(2), 9–15.

Montecel, M.R. (1999). Disciplinary Alternative Education Programs in Texas – What Is Known; What Is Needed. San Antonio, TX: Intercultural Development Research Association.

Raywid, M. (1994). Alternative Schools: The State of the Art. *Educational Leadership, 52*(1), 26–31.

Senate Bill No. 2510, Mississippi Legislature, Regular Session. (1995).

10

OUT-OF-SCHOOL ENHANCEMENT

A mind that is stretched by a new experience can never go back to its old dimensions.

Oliver Wendell Holmes

INTRODUCTION

The last of the four key strategies with special potential for making the most of students is out-of-school enhancement. In this chapter, we describe the pressing need for structured out-of-school experiences and the positive effects of such programs on the academic success, social behavior, and opportunities for enrichment of students in at-risk situations.

Too many students in both urban and rural environments, caught in a web of disadvantages created by family or neighborhood poverty, lack the kind of day-to-day experiences that stimulate their intellectual development (Panel on High Risk Youth, 1993). Garbarino (1995) has suggested that we are raising children in a "socially toxic environment," where the absence of adult supervision and the paucity of time spent in constructive, cooperative activities compound the effects of substance abuse, violence, criminal activity, and pressures to become sexually active.

Children spend only 20 percent of their waking hours in school (Miller, 1997). Furthermore, over 68 percent of mothers

126

with school-age children are in the labor force (Bureau of Labor Statistics, 1994). Once the traditional school day is over, and during the summer vacation months, many students spend long hours unsupervised in the home, on the street, or in the community. The gap between parents' work schedules and students' school schedules can amount to 20 to 25 hours per week (Annie E. Casey Foundation, 1998). Clearly, many children need some type of supervision during their out-of-school hours. For students in at-risk situations, programs offered by schools or community groups often provide the only quality academic support, recreation, or cultural enrichment the children experience outside of school.

Of the wide range of youth programs offered today, many are inaccessible to inner-city and rural youth. Posner and Vandell (1994) found that unless low-income children participated in an out-of-school program, enriching experiences in music and dance were not a part of their lives, nor did the children engage in team sports to any significant extent. Young people in urban, inner-city communities have fewer programs and a narrower range of activities to participate in than do young people in affluent suburbs. Adult leadership in poor, urban communities may be ineffective and disorganized, and in the absence of parental authority young people may seek protection, camaraderie, and "career opportunities" in gangs and the drug trade (Montgomery and Rossi, 1994). Although most rural areas usually lack the level of violence that characterizes some inner cities, rural schools enroll a disproportionately large share of the nation's poor. The geographic isolation, declining population, and inadequate community facilities of many rural areas intensify the problems associated with economic hardship and racial and ethnic tensions (Green and Schneider, 1990).

WHAT DOES OUT-OF-SCHOOL ENHANCEMENT DO?

This chapter focuses on structured out-of-school activities and programs for school-age youth. A review of the effectiveness of extended-day and after-school programs from the Center for Research on the Education of Students Placed at Risk (CRESPAR) distinguishes among three different types of out-of-school arrangements: daycare, after-school, and extended school day programs (Fashola, 1998).

Daycare Programs. Daycare programs provide a safe, supervised environment for children whose parents are working or otherwise engaged. They do not necessarily have an academic focus; instead, they tend to emphasize recreational and cultural activities.

After-School Programs. After-school programs are more likely to emphasize academic as well as nonacademic, recreational activities. Examples of such programs include Boys and Girls Clubs, YMCA and YWCA, Big Brothers/Big Sisters, 4-H, ASPIRA, church programs, and municipal parks and recreation programs.

School-Based Extended-Day Programs. These programs, housed in a school, are directly connected to what takes place during the school day. Most extended-day programs have an academic focus but may also include enrichment, recreational, and cultural activities.

RESEARCH ON OUT-OF-SCHOOL PROGRAMS

Research on effective out-of-school programs for students in at-risk situations is limited, and the most effective ways of implementing such programs are not well understood (Fashola, 1998). There is reason to believe, however, that out-of-school experiences have a positive effect on the academic success, social behavior, and opportunities for enrichment of students in at-risk situations.

Investigations of the effectiveness of year-round schools designed to improve students' academic success have observed positive effects (Dworkowitz, 1993; Grotjohn and Banks, 1993). Sheane (1994) identified specific outcomes achieved by year-round schools and/or districts, including decreased dropout rates; improved student achievement scores; expanded extracurricular activities; reduced absenteeism, vandalism, and/or discipline problems; and increased reentry opportunities for at-risk students. After-school tutoring and mentoring programs also have positive effects on student achievement (Benard, 1992; Floyd, 1993), and successful community-based programs offer youth in at-risk situations exceptional opportunities for enrichment (McLaughlin and Irby, 1994).

Posner and Vandell (1994) investigated the benefits of out-of-school programs for low-income minority third-grade students in four types of out-of-school situations: maternal care, informal adult supervision, self-care, and formal after-school programs. Almost 60 percent of the students qualified for free or reduced lunches, 50 percent were from single-parent homes, and none of the parents had completed college. Outcome measures included ratings of the students' behavior by the parents and children, academic ratings, report card grades, and standardized test scores.

Controlling for mother's education, child's race, and income, a student who attended after-school formal programs performed better academically and had better conduct ratings than a child who was either in maternal care or in other informal arrangements. Children in formal programs were rated as having better work habits, being more emotionally adjusted, and having better peer relations than children who were informally supervised (Posner and Vandell, 1994).

Recognizing the need for worthwhile out-of-school experiences, the U.S. Department of Education has initiated the 21st Century Community Learning Centers program, which supports school/community partnerships to keep schools open after regular school hours. Local school districts with 21st Century grants form partnerships with other community-based organizations to create after-school programs that provide safe havens, help youth develop confidence, and strengthen students' academic skills.

CHARACTERISTICS OF QUALITY OUT-OF-SCHOOL PROGRAMS

A number of studies have found that children who attend *quality* programs have better peer relations, emotional adjustment, grades, and conduct in school compared to peers who are not in such programs. Quality programs also provided students with more learning opportunities and academic or enrichment activities (Posner and Vandell, 1994; Baker and Witt, 1996). Children who were under adult supervision, whether in programs or at home, had better social skills and higher self-esteem than their peers who were unsupervised after school. In addition, students with regular attendance at after-school programs had higher grades and self-esteem than peers with lower attendance rates (Baker and Witt, 1996). Teachers and principals have reported that students who participate in after-school programs become more cooperative, learn to handle conflicts better, develop an interest in recreational reading, and receive better grades (Riley et al., 1994).

McLaughlin and Irby (1994) spent five years studying programs sponsored by urban neighborhood-based organizations such as the Boy Scouts, Girl Scouts, YMCA, church groups, libraries, museums, local parks and recreation departments, and community arts groups. The successful programs had family-like environments, established clear rules of membership, offered opportunities for active participation and real involvement, were sensitive to the interests of the youth they served, viewed youth as resources, were flexible, empowered youth to make decisions and take responsibility, and were accessible to and reached out to the neighborhood youth.

Effective out-of-school programs are capable of addressing the developmental needs—academic, recreational, and cultural—of the whole child (Fashola, 1998). High-quality programs include the following components:

Academic Component. Children's academic needs can be met through academics tied to the school curriculum, academic enrichment activities, or both. When the after-school curriculum is directly connected to what happens during the school day, it must be carefully aligned with the school's curricular objectives. Homework assistance and enrichment activities should support the regular curriculum.

Recreational Component. Out-of-school programs provide schools with an opportunity to bring recreational activities to the children who need them the most. The recreational part of a program should provide children with opportunities to develop a variety of skills and to engage in team sports.

Cultural/Social Component. The cultural component, like the recreational component, should offer students opportunities to explore and practice skills that are not taught in the classroom. Life-enhancing experiences might include such things as developing hobbies, learning to play a musical instrument, engaging in arts and crafts, and practicing a variety of positive social skills.

IMPLEMENTING EFFECTIVE OUT-OF-SCHOOL PROGRAMS

Although out-of-school programs are diverse in purpose, funding, and quality, most face a common set of issues. The following factors appear to contribute to the implementation of a good program (Fashola, 1998):

Train Staff and Volunteers. Programs that intend to change the lives of the children who participate in them have a responsibility to find qualified, caring staff and volunteers to work with the students and their families. However, if program staff and volunteers are not properly trained to implement the program, it will falter. Training should include teaching staff and volunteers how to work well with children, adapt to the needs of children of different ages, handle behavior problems, and implement program components. Training should also address the issues of supervising and monitoring staff and volunteers to make sure they are carrying out their duties and working well together.

Create a Program with Structure. When the goal of the program is to enhance academic achievement, structure is essential. Successful programs have clear goals, well-developed procedures, role assignments, and extensive professional development. Time must be provided for planning and developing procedures, staff collaboration, curriculum development, and training.

Evaluate the Program. Evaluation should be built into every program. Planners must be clear about what they expect the program to accomplish. The procedures and instruments used to collect data should be uniform across the program, and measures should be appropriate for drawing conclusions. Ideally, assessments should evaluate the effects on students who participated in the program by comparing them to a control group of students in the school or district who are similar to those in the program but who did not participate.

Include Families and Children in the Planning. Families and children should have a voice in planning the program. If activities are supposed to appeal to students, those students are the best source of information about what interests them.

Have an Advisory Board. Community support and cooperation can be fostered through an advisory board made up of community leaders. The advisory board is responsible for policy decisions and oversees the smooth running of the program.

Effective Programs and Practices

More and more school districts are implementing after-school, weekend, and summer programs to provide children, those in at-risk situations as well as others, a more structured, enriching alternative to unsupervised and sometimes dangerous out-of-school hours. For example, almost 30 percent of public schools and 50 percent of private schools offered before- and after-school care in 1993–94 (National Center for Educational Statistics, 1997). The following sections describe some of the most widely used after-school and extended-day program identified by the Center for Research on the Education of Students Placed At Risk (CRESPAR) at Johns Hopkins University (Fashola, 1998). Many of these model programs are also described in the Focus database managed by the National Dropout Prevention Center.

Language Arts After-School Programs

These programs provide remedial assistance or enrichment opportunities for students in language arts.

Junior Great Book Curriculum of Interpretive Reading, Writing, and Discussion. The Junior Great Book Curriculum of Interpretive Reading, Writing, and Discussion (JGBC) is a junior version of the Great Books Foundation program. It strives to promote cognitive processing in reading comprehension and literacy in children in grades two to twelve by emphasizing three kinds of thinking: factual, interpretive, and evaluative. Children explore these three types of information about text using a method of shared inquiry and interpretive questioning which encourages them to realize that there is more than one answer to questions asked about the text they have read. When a school chooses to engage in the JGBC program, it is provided with a two-day, ten-hour "basic leader" training course. Schools can also choose to enroll in optional one-or-two-day curriculum leader training courses. Students who participate in the programs are usually enrolled for one semester, during which they study an anthology consisting of twelve selections.

In an evaluation of JGBC that researched the effects of the program on academic achievement in reading vocabulary during the school day, 150 JGBC students were matched with 120 control students in four schools and tested on the ITBS (three schools) and CTBS (one school). This study included both urban and suburban populations. The JGBC program at each site involved a control classroom and a treatment (JGBC) classroom. Teachers were randomly assigned to a group (using a coin flip) to determine whether they would be in the control group or the experimental group. In the four schools, JGBC students outscored their control group counterparts. An additional internal evaluation of the program showed that students involved in JGBC demonstrated stronger interpretive thinking skills than students in the control group.

The Coca-Cola Valued Youth Program (CVYP). The Coca-Cola Valued Youth Program is a cross-age tutoring program designed to increase the self-esteem and school success of at-risk middle and high school students by placing them in positions of responsibility as tutors of younger elementary school students. When students agree to serve as tutors, they are required to enroll in a special tutoring class where they are paid a minimum wage stipend and work with three elementary students at a time for a total of about four hours per week. The overall goal of the program is to reduce the dropout rate of at-risk students by improving their self-concepts and academic skills. The program also emphasizes elimination of nonacademic and disciplinary factors that contribute to dropping out. For example, it attempts to develop students' sense of self-control, decrease student truancy, and reduce disciplinary referrals. It also seeks to form home-school partnerships to increase the level of support available to students.

The main evaluation of the Coca-Cola Valued Youth Program compared 63 CVYP tutors to 70 students. Two years after the program began, 12 percent of the comparison students but only one percent of the CVYP students had dropped out. Reading grades were significantly higher for the CVYP group, as were scores on a self-esteem measure and on a measure of attitude toward school.

Exemplary Center for Reading Instruction (ECRI). The goal of ECRI is to improve elementary school students' reading ability. ECRI teachers expect all students to excel. The ECRI lessons are scripted and incorporate multisensory and sequential methods and strategies of teaching. In a typical lesson, teachers introduce new concepts using at least seven methods of instruction, teaching at least one comprehension skill, one study skill, and one grammar or creative writing skill.

In an evaluation of ECRI during the regular school day, researchers investigated the effects of ECRI on students in grades two through seven in Morgan County, Tennessee, and compared them to students in a control group who were using a commercial reading program. Both schools were tested using the Stanford Achievement Test (SAT) reading and comprehension vocabulary subtests. ECRI students outperformed those in the control group, with effect sizes ranging from +.48 to +.90 in reading comprehension and from +.31 to 1.40 in vocabulary. Another evaluation of the effectiveness of ECRI with Latino bilingual students in Oceanside, California, Killeen, Texas, and Calexico, California, showed NCE gains that ranged from +6.4 to +25.7. At the end of the school year, students in both groups were tested using standardized tests, and results showed that students who had been involved in ECRI made significantly greater gains on the standardized tests than students in the control groups. ECRI is used in hundreds of schools nationwide.

ACADEMICALLY-ORIENTED AFTER-SCHOOL PROGRAMS IN OTHER FIELDS

These independent programs were developed by private organizations specifically for use in after-school settings and are currently implemented in after-school settings across the country.

Voyager Expanded Learning. Voyager Expanded Learning is an extended-school-day (before- and after-school, summer, and inter-session) program. It has a variety of academically enriching themes designed to help elementary school children in grades K–6 become active learners in mathematics, reading, science, arts, and social studies. The goal of these units is to make learning interactive and meaningful by providing a "thematic, multidisciplinary approach to instruction" that will allow students to learn "theories, facts, and concepts, while at the same time requiring them to learn higher order thinking skills by solving real-life problems." The units are divided into daily activities, with active learning projects and outcome objectives for the teachers and the students. The development of the curriculum is research-based, and the lessons for each theme are aligned with state and national standards.

Hands On Science Outreach. Hands On Science Outreach (HOSO) is an extended-school-day and after-school program developed to encourage all children, including minority, low-income, and at-risk students in pre-kindergarten to sixth grade, to have fun learning science and to learn by example and experience that anyone can engage in scientific inquiry. Hands On Science Outreach was evaluated in 1993 by Sierra Research Associates, who investigated the effects of the program on children's attitudes and understanding of Hands On Science during one eight-week session. Results of the analysis showed that the HOSO participants made statistically significant gains in their understanding compared to the control group. Hands On Science Outreach is currently active in 250 schools and sites in 26 states and the District of Columbia.

The Imaginitis Learning System. The Imaginitis Learning System is a cooperative-learning after-school language arts program created for students in grades three to twelve. The goal of the program is to expose the participants to skills needed for effective and productive learning to develop strong workplace competencies. Teachers are provided with a one-day training program that emphasizes the principles of cooperative learning. Students in the program, divided into groups by age and grade, are given the task of working together in a team to creatively construct a book that eventually becomes a portfolio exhibition. The participants work individually on their own books, as well as collectively as a team to create a finished product. The team members work together and vote on what should be included or excluded in the process and in the final product. The teachers evaluate the end products to determine improvement in the students' writing, speaking, listening, and collaborating skills, as well as the quality of the process the students went through while planning the product.

The Imaginitis Learning System program has been evaluated in four sites across the country. The evaluations given to all of the sites consisted of two parts. Students were asked to respond to two surveys that measured responses toward cooperative learning and working with others, mastering academic environments, and overall perceptions of student-teacher relationships. The second part of the evaluation measured the extent to which students reported that they would solve problems and resolve conflicts productively. When the results were gathered for all sessions, Imaginitis students reported more positive results than non-Imaginitis students. Overall, students who had been involved in Imaginitis the previous year were more likely to carry over the effects of the program the following year. This was the case in elementary schools and alternative high schools.

Mindsurf. Mindsurf is an academic K–6 after-school enrichment program created by a partnership between National Geographic and Sylvan Learning. The main goal of the program is to provide children with a safe, fun learning environment and enriching academic achievement opportunities during the after-school hours. Children are engaged in the program from 3 to 6 p.m. When children enter the Mindsurf program, in addition to working on homework and study skills, they join various "clubs" of interest (thematic units) where they work with other students and teachers. The academic content of the Mindsurf program consists of various academic enrichment themes such as Water, Blast Off, Light and Color, Awesome Animals of North America, Storytelling, Australia, North America, and Asia. These themes are explored using computers, camcorders, digital cameras, numerous software programs, and other innovative advanced technology pieces. In addition to participating in activities at learning centers, Mindsurf students receive individual kits with activities for them to engage in at home. One of the newest components of Mindsurf is directed toward helping students improve their academic achievement. Besides providing enrichment, Mindsurf attempts to provide some alignment to what happens during the day by encouraging and helping children to complete their homework. Mindsurf currently serves 400 students in four states (Maryland, Washington, Colorado, and California).

RELATED RESOURCES

A publication for the Charles Stewart Mott Foundation (1999), *Making After School Count: Expanded-Day Classes at School Can Increase Academic Achievement*, spotlights promising out-of-school programs for middle school students. The U.S. Department of Education maintains a Web site (www.ed.gov/21stcclc) that lists the programs funded under the 21st Century Community Learning Centers grants.

CONCLUSION

Given the number of mothers in the workforce, the lack of safe and enriching activities for students in at-risk situations, the dangerous and unhealthy activities that unsupervised youth too often engage in, and the need to improve the academic performance of poor, minority, and disadvantaged students, all schools and communities should set a high priority on providing safe and healthy out-of-school experiences. Although the research on extended-day and after-school programs is not extensive or rigorous enough to support firm conclusions, a number of programs give evidence of promising results. Among programs designed to improve academic achievement, those that provided greater structure, a stronger link to the school day curriculum, well-qualified and well-trained staff, and opportunities for one-to-one tutoring appeared to be particularly effective. All types of out-of-school programs appear to benefit from consistent structure, active community involvement, extensive training for staff and volunteers, and responsiveness to students' needs and interests.

Students in at-risk situations—many of whom are living in poverty, are from a traditional minority, or are limited English-language speakers—usually benefit from additional academic assistance and enrichment activities. Providing quality out-of-school experiences for such children will, in the long run, increase their ability to function well in school, graduate, and lead productive lives.

REFERENCES

Annie E. Casey Foundation. (1998). *Care for School-Age Children*. Baltimore, MD: Annie E. Casey Foundation.

Baker, D., and Witt, P. A. (1996). Evaluation of the Impact of Two After-School Recreation Programs. *Journal of Park and Recreation Administration, 14*(3), 23–44.

Benard, B. (1992). *Mentoring Programs for Urban Youth: Handle with Care*. Washington, DC: Department of Education. ERIC Document Number 349–368.

Bureau of Labor Statistics. (1994). March 1994 supplement Current Population Survey. Unpublished document.

Charles Stewart Mott Foundation. (1999). *Making After School Count: Expanded-Day Classes at Schools Can Increase Academic Achievement.* Flint, MI: Author.

Dworkowitz, B. (1993). *Pupils with Compensatory Educational Needs: Summer Program 1993.* Brooklyn, NY: New York City Board of Education. ERIC Document Number 379–377.

Fashola, O. S. (1998). *Review of Extended-Day and After-School Programs and Their Effectiveness* (CRESPAR Report No. 24). Available online: www.csos.jhu.edu/crespar/CRESPAR percent20Reports/report24entire.htm

Garbarino, J. (1995). *Raising Children in a Socially Toxic Environment.* San Francisco: Jossey-Bass.

Green, B. L., and Schneider, M. J. (1990). Threats to Funding for Rural Schools. *Journal of Education Finance, 15,* 302–318.

Grotjohn, D. K., and Banks, K. (1993). *An Evaluation Synthesis: Year-Round Schools and Achievement.* Paper presented at the annual meeting of the American Educational Research Association, Atlanta, April 1993.

National Center for Education Statistics. (1997). *School Serving Family Needs: Extended-Day Programs in Public and Private Schools.* Washington, DC: U.S. Department of Education.

Miller, B. M. (1995). *Out-of-School Time: Effects on Learning in the Primary Grades.* Action Research Paper No. 4. Wellesley, MA: National Institute on Out-of-School Time, Wellesley College.

Montgomery, A. F., and Rossi, R. J. (1994). Becoming at Risk of Failure in America's Schools. In R. J. Rossi (Ed.). *Schools and Students at Risk: Context and Framework for Positive Change.* New York: Teachers College Press.

Panel on High-Risk Youth. (1993). *Losing Generations: Adolescents in High-Risk Settings.* Commission on Behavioral and Social Sciences and Education, National Research Council. Washington, DC: National Academy Press.

Riley, D., Steinberg, J., Todd, C., Junge, S., and McClain, I. (1994). *Preventing Problem Behaviors and Raising Academic Performance in the Nation's Youth: The Impacts of 64 School Age Child Care Programs in 15 States Supported by the Cooperative Extension Service Youth-At-Risk Initiative.* Madison: University of Wisconsin.

Sheane, K. E. (1994). *Year Round Education: Breaking the Bonds of Tradition.* Tempe, AZ: Morrison Institute for Public Policy, Arizona State University. ERIC Document Number 375–518.

PART V

MAKING THE MOST OF INSTRUCTION

The next group of strategies for dropout prevention focuses on what happens in the classroom. A comprehensive effort to keep students in school must devote resources to the professional development of teachers, expand teaching methods to accommodate a range of learning styles, put modern technological resources to work in schools, and provide learning programs that are customized to meet the individual needs of each student. In the following chapters, we describe the ways in which these strategies can make the most of instruction in America's classrooms.

11

PROFESSIONAL DEVELOPMENT: AN INVESTMENT IN QUALITY

Each dollar spent on improving teachers' qualifications nets greater gains in student learning than any other use of an education dollar.

Linda Darling-Hammond, Education Commission of the States, 1998

INTRODUCTION

A push for school reform based on educational standards is sweeping the country. Articles about these standards and their impact on schools and students appear in newspapers and journals across the nation. Most writers couple the issue of higher standards with the need to assess whether students are meeting the higher standards and the need to develop ways of holding students, teachers, schools, and principals accountable for meeting the standards. Trailing behind the discussions about standards, assessment, and accountability is the recognition that effective, continual high-quality professional development must be in place to prepare teachers to help students achieve the higher standards. In this chapter, we explore the ways in which effective professional development can contribute to a comprehensive school dropout prevention effort.

LINKING TEACHER QUALITY AND STUDENT ACHIEVEMENT

Recent research has shown that "teacher expertise is one of the single most important determinants of student achievement" (Darling-Hammond, 1998). The research confirms that states and communities that choose to invest in well-qualified teachers also show gains in student achievement.

In a study by Dr. William L. Sanders of the Value-Added Research and Assessment Center at the University of Tennessee, Knoxville, researchers grouped a sample of teachers from Tennessee in quintiles based on their effects on the learning of both high- and low-achieving students. These studies revealed that the achievement of low-achieving students increased significantly—by as much as 53 percent—when they were taught by a highly effective teacher. This is in contrast to a maximum of a 14 percent increase for students taught by a less effective teacher. Students in the fifth grade were still affected by the quality of their third-grade teacher. This study also looked at the sequence of teachers to which the students were assigned. There was a noticeable impact on percentile points depending on the sequence of teachers and the teachers' effectiveness. Dr. Sanders concluded this could potentially determine the difference between a remedial label and placement in the accelerated or gifted track, and the difference between entry into a selective college and a lifetime of working at McDonalds (Haycock, 1998).

In Boston, Massachusetts, Bain and Company investigated student achievement and teacher effectiveness in mathematics and reading at the high school level. This study revealed that tenth-grade students with ineffective teachers displayed no growth in reading and math; that is, there was not a significant difference in test scores over a one-year period. In mathematics, students with the top-third teachers scored beyond the national medium on standardized tests, showing a significant improvement in math skills (Haycock, 1998).

Ferguson and Ladd (1996) reported on a study of the effects of school inputs on student test scores in Alabama. The sample consisted of a cohort of 29,544 fourth-grade students in 690 schools in 1990–91. They found that teacher test scores, teacher education, and class size affected student learning. The results of the study led the authors to conclude that teachers' skills are extremely important and exert a strong effect on student achievement.

The evidence clearly shows that there is a pressing need for highly qualified teachers in every classroom and at every level of learning. The evidence provided by these studies shows a positive relationship between teacher quality and student achievement. If standards-based reforms are to lead to an improvement in student achievement, building a foundation of teaching competency must be the states' number one priority.

HIGH-QUALITY TEACHING

How many of the nation's educators feel competent to educate tomorrow's youth using the standards that are currently in place? Four out of five teachers say they are not ready to teach in today's classrooms. Furthermore, more than one-third say they either do not have degrees in the subjects they teach or did not spend sufficient time studying content matter (McQueen, 1999). With the current system, student achievement scores nationally have decreased from average to below-average levels, partly because of inadequate teacher preparation and insufficient levels of content knowledge. In 1998, the U.S. Department of Education found that fewer than 75 percent of America's teachers could be considered fully qualified (that is, have studied child development, learning, and teaching methods, hold a degree in their subject areas, and have passed state licensing requirements).

What defines "high quality" as a characteristic of teaching? The National Board for Professional Teaching Standards (NBPTS) was established in response to a call from the Carnegie Task Force on Teaching as a Profession for an organization to define high and rigorous standards for what accomplished teachers should know and be able to do. According to NBPTS, accomplished teachers effectively enhance student learning and display high levels of knowledge, skills, abilities, and commitments. To increase the number of high-quality teachers who can meet the demand for higher student achievement, the following five characteristics must be cultivated (NBPTS, 1999):

Teachers are committed to students and their learning. A high-quality teacher knows where to find the latest resources and how to make them accessible to students, and is able to direct students in researching their academic interests. A teacher is also dedicated to knowing the student as an individual: knowing about the student's interests, abilities, skills, peer relationships, and family circumstances. With commitment to students, a teacher develops activities and strategies that foster individuality and develop the students' cognitive capacities for learning.

Teachers know the subjects they teach and how to teach those subjects to students. High-quality teachers have a rich understanding of their specialized subjects and know how this understanding links to other disciplines and real-world settings. They also know the preconceptions and background knowledge of students and present instructional materials that provide further assistance and understanding. Deep content knowledge allows teachers to create multiple paths to teaching subject matter that is practical and interesting to students.

Teachers are responsible for managing and monitoring student learning. Teachers create, enrich, maintain, and alter instructional settings to capture students' interests and know how to engage students in order to ensure a disciplined learning environment. Individual progress as well as class performance are assessed and teaching practices are modified to motivate the students based on these assessments.

Teachers think systematically about their practice and learn from experience. Accomplished teachers seek to inspire students. Characteristics such as curiosity, tolerance, honesty, fairness, respect for diversity, and appreciation of cultural differences serve as prerequisites for intellectual growth. Teachers seek to sharpen their judgment and adapt their teaching to new findings, theories, and ideas.

Teachers are members of learning communities. Accomplished teachers contribute collaboratively with other professionals to improve instructional policy, curriculum development, and staff development. Teachers are knowledgeable about community resources that can engage student involvement and help enhance student achievement.

Other organizations that have set standards to improve the caliber of teaching include the Interstate New Teacher Assessment and Support Consortium (INTASC) and the National Council for the Accreditation of Teacher Education (NCATE). The INTASC is a consortium of more than thirty states and professional associations that develops new licensing standards for teachers. These standards outline what teachers need to know and be able to do to teach students to new standards (Darling-Hammond, 1998). INTASC enables new and veteran teachers in states with a surplus of teachers to move easily to states that experience shortfalls in high-quality teachers (Darling-Hammond, 1999).

NCATE has developed new standards for teacher education and accredits all organizations that prepare teachers for the classroom. One example of NCATE at work was bringing together the college faculty of the University of Massachusetts at Amherst's secondary teacher education program (STEP) with the schools in four school districts to improve teacher education. In this program, each semester six to eight student teachers took a school-based seminar, studied pedagogy, and worked with mentor teachers (Reforms in Preservice Preparation Programs, 1999). This type of approach has made student teachers better prepared for the classrooms. These three organizations—NBPTS, INTASC, and NCATE—with their sets of closely aligned standards offer state policymakers the most powerful tools available for developing a high-quality teaching force (Darling-Hammond, 1998).

INEFFECTIVE PROFESSIONAL DEVELOPMENT PRACTICES

Although nearly all public school teachers receive some sort of professional development each year, very few participate in the kinds of activities that are effective in changing classroom practices. The content, quality, and duration of professional development programs determine their ability to improve teaching practice and affect student achievement. Most professional development in the United States today, however, is fragmented, is not focused on curriculum for students, and does not afford teachers learning opportunities related to academic content or instruction. Teachers typically engage in a variety of short-term activities that comply with state or local recertification or continuing education requirements but are rarely based on the school curriculum or on comprehensive plans to improve teaching and learning (Cohen and Hill, 1998). In many states, virtually any kind of formalized learning experience can count toward a teacher's recertification hours, even when such experiences have little relevance to content or teaching practice (Hirsch, Koppich, and Knapp, 1998).

In a policy paper designed to inform state policy for the improvement of teaching, the Center for the Study of Teacher Policy (CTP) found that while 96 percent of public school teachers reported participating in some sort of professional development activity in 1993–94, very few encountered the types of opportunities that promote significant and sustained professional learning. For example, only 30 percent of teachers participated in professional development that involved in-depth study in a specific field, and only 15 percent received nine hours or more of this type of training (Hirsch, Koppich, and Knapp, 1998).

Duration as well as type of activity appear to make a difference in how teachers perceive improvement in their classroom teaching and how well they feel prepared to accomplish certain tasks. A report from the National Center for Educational Statistics (1999), *Teacher Quality: A Report on the Preparation and Qualifications of Public School Teachers*, elicited information from teachers regarding their recent participation in professional development activities in the areas of technology, new methods of teaching, state or district curriculum or performance standards, and accommodating students from diverse linguistic or cultural backgrounds. The data indicate that teachers who spent more time in a professional development activity perceived a greater improvement than those who spent less time.

It is important to note, however, that while the amount of time spent in professional development activities is important in effecting change, the content of that activity is even more important. In a study of state efforts to reform mathematics teaching and learning in California, the Consortium for Policy Research in Education (CPRE) found that time spent in special topics/issues workshops did not have the same results in classroom practice as content-focused professional development. Spending a greater number of hours in less content-focused workshops was not associated with more of the practices called for by state reforms. In addition, the study found no relationship between student achievement scores and schools scoring high on a conventional-professional-development-practice scale. The results of the study suggest that links between instructional policy and classroom practice may be expected when teachers' learning opportunities are:

♦ grounded in the curriculum that students study
♦ connected to several elements of instruction (for example, not only curriculum but also assessment)
♦ extended in time

(Cohen and Hill, 1998).

COMPONENTS OF EFFECTIVE PROFESSIONAL DEVELOPMENT

Research studies on improving educational outcomes for students have concluded that effective instructional environments depend upon well-trained, reflective teachers who are adequately supported in terms of professional development. Recent programs have focused on fostering professional communities of learners and lifelong support programs, embedding knowledge and skill acquisition within a framework of teacher growth and development, establishing collaborative programs, and conducting interactive research within a community of learners (Rueda, 1998). In a study in Georgia, the Council for School Performance (1998) found that for professional development to have an impact on student achievement, it must involve long-term programs embedded in the school year, rather than a one-shot event; theory, demonstration, practice, and feedback, rather than a lecture on the strategy; collective study of student learning, rather than individual reflection on implementation; and a workplace structured by leadership to support ongoing collaboration about improving teaching and learning.

The U.S. Department of Education established a Professional Development Team to examine the best available research and exemplary practices related to professional development. The team developed a set of principles designed to inform practitioners and policymakers. The mission of professional development is to prepare and support educators to help all students achieve high standards of learning and development. A high-quality professional development program:

- is focused on teachers as central to student learning, yet includes all other members of the school community

- is focused on individual, collegial, and organizational improvement

- respects and nurtures the intellectual and leadership capacities of teachers, principals, and others in the school community

- reflects the best available research and practice in teaching, learning, and leadership

- enables teachers to develop further expertise in subject content, teaching strategies, uses of technologies, and other essential elements in teaching to high standards

- promotes continuous inquiry and improvement in the daily life of schools

- is planned collaboratively by those who will participate in and facilitate that development

- requires substantial time and other resources

- is driven by a coherent and long-term plan

- is evaluated ultimately on the basis of its impact on teacher effectiveness and student learning, and this assessment guides subsequent professional development efforts

(U.S. Department of Education, 1998).

EFFECTIVE PROGRAMS AND PRACTICES

In an initiative addressing results-based staff development for the middle grades, the National Staff Development Council (NSDC) identified 26 staff development efforts that enable middle-grade students and teachers to achieve high levels of learning. The programs covered a wide span of subject areas in diverse settings and provided evidence of increased student achievement. The published report contains descriptions of the programs, guidelines for selecting and/or designing professional development to improve student academic performance, and strategies for evaluating professional development programs. The author draws this conclusion:

> To face the complexities of educating middle-level students, teachers must engage in staff development that increases their knowledge and skills, challenges their beliefs and assumptions about education, provides support and coaching to develop a comfort with new practices, and engages them as active participants in the study and reform of the school culture (Killion 1999, p. 6).

Promising Practices: New Ways to Improve Teacher Quality, a publication from the U.S. Department of Education (1998), contains profiles of practices in these areas:

♦ recruiting talented and diverse people into the teaching profession

♦ improving teacher preparation

♦ raising licensing and certification standards for teachers

♦ providing professional support to beginning teachers during their initial teaching years

♦ improving professional development

♦ improving teacher accountability and incentives

The professional development programs presented in the document were nominated by regional education laboratories, reviews of research literature, and researchers for the National Commission on Teaching and America's Future. They do not, however, constitute a definitive list. Current efforts to ensure quality throughout the teaching profession are too dynamic and are happening in too many places to allow for a comprehensive evaluation (U.S. Department of Education, 1998).

In discussing professional development for teachers, *Promising Practices: New Ways to Improve Teacher Quality* presented two important tools for shaping professional development that have emerged in recent years. One is the professional development school that replaces the traditional relationship between college campuses and K–12 schools. Professional development schools are partnerships in which the school is transformed into a clinical site dedicated to best practice and professional growth, while providing university faculty with knowledge from hands-on work in the school. The second tool is teacher networking that allows teachers of like minds to get together to explore new ideas and new practices. In recent years, spurred by a foundation-funded collaborative in math and the humanities, teacher networks have become a major force for professional growth (U.S. Department of Education, 1998).

CONCLUSION

With the advent of new state academic standards, states are holding schools accountable for students' academic performance in ways they have not been in the past. Nevertheless, accountability systems as currently designed do not address the issues of teacher competencies and the school conditions that affect student achievement. Recent research has shown that teacher expertise is one of the single most important determinants of student achievement. Unfortunately, in a survey by the National Center for Educational Statistics, four out of five teachers say they are not prepared to teach in today's classrooms.

It is clear that traditional professional development practices are rarely effective in improving classroom practice. This aspect of education must be the states' number one priority if standards-based reforms are to lead to an improvement in student achievement. In order to improve educational outcomes for students, effective instructional environments must have well-trained, reflective teachers who are adequately supported in terms of professional development. It is worth repeating, "each dollar spent on improving teachers' qualifications nets greater gains in student learning than any other use of an education dollar" (Darling-Hammond, 1998).

REFERENCES

Cohen, D. K., and Kill, H. C. (1998). *State Policy and Classroom Performance: Mathematics Reform in California.* CPRE Policy Brief No. RB-27. Philadelphia: Consortium for Policy Research in Education, University of Pennsylvania.

Council for School Performance. (1998). *Staff Development and Student Achievement: Making the Connection in Georgia Schools.* Atlanta: Author, School of Policy Studies, Georgia State University. Available online: http://arcweb.gsu.edu.

Darling-Hammond, L. (1998). *Investing In Quality Teaching: State-Level Strategies 1999.* Education Commission of the States. Available online: http://www.ecs.org.

Darling-Hammond, L. (1999). *How Can We Ensure a Caring, Competent, Qualified Teacher for Every Child?* Paper presented at the AFT/NEA Conference on teacher quality, Washington, DC, September 26, 1998.

Haycock, K. (1998). *Good Teaching Matters.* Washington, DC: Education Trust.

Hirsch, E., Koppich, J. E., and Knapp, M. S. (1998). *What States Are Doing to Improve the Quality of Teaching: A Brief Review of Current Patterns and Trends.* Seattle: The Center for the Study of Teaching and Policy, University of Washington.

Killion, J. (1999). *What Works in the Middle: Results-Based Staff Development.* Oxford, OH: National Staff Development Council.

McQueen, A. (1999). *Survey: Teachers Feel Unprepared for Specialties. Star Tribune.* Available online: http://www2.startribune.com.

National Board for Professional Teaching Standards. *(1999). What Teachers Should Know and Be Able to Do.* Available online: http://nbpts.org.

National Center for Educational Statistics. (1999). *Teacher Quality: A Report on the Preparation and Qualifications of Public School Teachers.* Washington, DC: U.S. Department of Education, Office, of Educational Research and Improvement.

Reforms in Preservice Preparation Programs and Teacher Certification Standards 1999. Available online: http://www.ed.gov.

Rueda, R. (1998). *Standards for Professional Development: A Sociocultural Perspective.* CREDE Research Brief #2. Santa Cruz: Center for Research on Education, Diversity, and Excellence, University of California.

U.S. Department of Education. (1998). *Promising Practices: New Ways to Improve Teacher Quality.* Washington, DC: Author.

12

DIVERSE LEARNING STYLES AND MULTIPLE INTELLIGENCES

*An invasion of armies can be resisted, but not an
idea whose time has come.*

Victor Hugo, *Histoire d'un Crime*

INTRODUCTION

Effective teachers recognize that not all students learn in the same way. Some learn best when material is presented visually; others need to hear the information or recite it aloud. Some flourish when instruction involves hands-on manipulation; others prefer far more active pursuits. Some do well in small groups in which the students teach one another; others would rather work on their own. Some thrive on stimulation and high-energy activities; others need time for quiet reflection. The best classroom instruction includes a variety of activities and empowers all students, no matter what their learning style.

One educational theory that illuminates the subject of diverse learning styles is Howard Gardner's theory of multiple intelligences. This chapter explores that theory, describes its application in a variety of learning environments, and highlights the benefits for at-risk students when schools recognize and honor a diversity of learning styles.

THE THEORY OF MULTIPLE INTELLIGENCES

Dr. Howard Gardner of Harvard University began *Project Zero* in 1970 to investigate human potential (1983). It was from this project that he developed the theory of multiple intelligences. Gardner defines intelligence as "the ability to solve problems or to create products that are valued within one or more cultural settings." He believes that human cognitive competence is better described in terms of a set of abilities, talents, or mental skills which he calls intelligences. All normal human beings possess these eight intelligences: verbal/linguistic, logical/mathematical, musical, visual/spatial, bodily/kinesthetic, interpersonal, intrapersonal, and naturalist. Most people can develop each of the eight intelligences. The intelligences tend to work together in complex ways, and there are many ways to be smart within each intelligence. Other researchers have expanded upon the initial theory of multiple intelligences (Armstrong, 1994; Campbell, 1994; Gardner, 1991; Haggerty, 1995), and have developed useful and practical applications for classroom teachers.

THE EIGHT INTELLIGENCES

The eight intelligences are

- ◆ **verbal/linguistic**—the ability to use both oral and written language fluently to communicate effectively
- ◆ **logical/mathematical**—the ability to use abstract thought, precision, deductive/inductive reasoning, counting, organization, and logical structure to solve abstract problems and complex relationships found in mathematics and in the scientific process
- ◆ **musical**—sensitivity to pitch, rhythm, timbre, tone, color, and emotional power of music and the sounds in one's environment to perceive, discriminate, and express all aspects of music and environmental sounds
- ◆ **visual/spatial**—the capacity to perceive the world in mental images, that is, to see form, color, shape, and texture in the mind's eye

- **bodily/kinesthetic**—reliance on the whole body to express ideas and feelings and the hands to produce or transform things; components are balance, dexterity, strength, flexibility, and speed

- **interpersonal**—sensitivity to and understanding of other people's moods, feelings and points of view; ability to maintain good relationships with family, friends and people in general; ability to take leadership among other people by solving problems, influencing decisions and relationships

- **intrapersonal**—the ability to know oneself and to act adaptively to accurately assess personal strengths/ weaknesses, perceive inner moods, motivations, temperaments, and desires

- **naturalist**—the ability to recognize and classify plants, animals, and nature by their differences, patterns, configurations, and so forth

(Gardner, 1983).

According to Gardner, the eight intelligences share the following common characteristics: the potential of isolation by brain damage; the occurrence of savants, prodigies, and other exceptional people; a distinctive developmental history with a set of end-state performances; an evolutionary history that can be traced; support from psychometric findings; support from experimental psychological tasks; a core or set of operations; and the potential for encoding in a symbol system.

In Howard Gardner's most recent book, *Intelligence Reframed: Multiple Intelligence for the 21st Century*, (1999) he introduces the possibility of more intelligences. In the future, there well may be more than the eight intelligences described in this chapter.

BENEFITS OF THE THEORY OF MULTIPLE INTELLIGENCES

Applying the theory of multiple intelligences in any learning environment enriches the lives of learners and leaders by widening the range of options for both. It offers opportunities for students to take more responsibility for their own learning

FIGURE 1

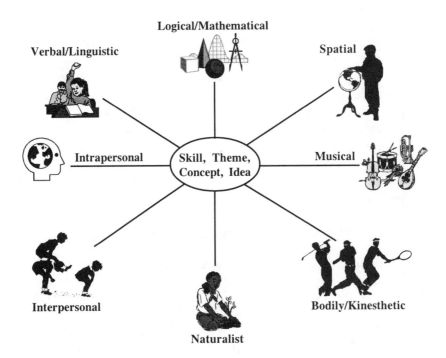

and for the teacher to become a facilitator of learning rather than the sole provider of knowledge in the classroom. In addition, implementation of this theory

- ♦ allows each learner to be recognized and rewarded for special strengths
- ♦ provides opportunities for learners to develop skills and abilities in intelligences that are less developed
- ♦ reduces the chances of boredom by offering a variety of activities
- ♦ provides a teaching/learning methodology that works for all ages

INCORPORATING THE THEORY OF MULTIPLE INTELLIGENCES INTO CLASSROOM PRACTICES

Educators new to this theory might benefit from a plan for developing a lesson or unit that exercises all of the intelligences. One method is to use a graphic organizer called a mindmap (see Figure 1). At the center of the mindmap is the unit, theme, skill, or concept to be taught. Drawing from past experience, input from colleagues, and other resources, the teacher chooses activities that call upon each of the eight intelligences.

Of course, not every concept, skill, or idea needs to be taught in eight different ways, but most activities easily integrate one or more of the intelligences. One could expand the mindmap with dotted lines to connect activities that integrate the intelligences.

EFFECTIVE PROGRAMS AND PRACTICES

Schools and educational programs have incorporated the theory of multiple intelligences into their practice in a wide variety of settings. We have selected six examples for a closer look.

Summer Stars Camp Program. In 1994, New Canaan Public Schools of Connecticut developed a Summer Stars Program based on the theory of multiple intelligences (Cantrell et al., 1997). This week-long camp encourages children aged seven to twelve to tap into their unique strengths. Campers choose materials and activities from many different topics and participate in one of three internships: the Challenger Mission at the Bridgeport Discovery Museum, the Sea Voyage at the Norwalk Maritime Center, or simulated flight training at the Sikorsky Aircraft Corporation in Stratford. Camp projects have included producing a handcrafted bound book, writing musical compositions, constructing rockets, building block structures from students' blueprints, writing and illustrating a camp newsletter, reinventing stories to tell at camp ceremonies, producing and acting in plays, designing T-shirts, and preparing astronaut food.

Camp leaders developed a pre- and post-camp survey for campers and their parents. Analysis of the surveys revealed that the camp's application of the theory of multiple intelligences

♦ positively affects children's understanding of their perceived "smarts"

♦ promotes risk taking

♦ closes the gap between parents' and students' understanding of the theory

Findings also showed that in 75 percent of the cases, both parents and children agreed on the child's best and least-developed modes of intelligence. During the first three years of camp, 99 percent of the campers were very satisfied with their course selections. Camp teachers learned that children who make their own educational choices are more highly motivated, satisfied, fulfilled, and successful. Children tended to choose courses that were directly related to their stronger intelligence.

For additional information:

Mary Lou Cantrell
South School, Gower Road
New Canaan, CT 06840
cantrellml@aol.com

Think Tank, Kent Gardens Elementary School. The Think Tank is a combination discovery room and lab at Kent Gardens Elementary School in McLean, Virginia (Knodt, 1997). All K–6 students flock to this room for up to an hour every other week. The Think Tank focuses on multiple intelligences and critical and creative thinking as a foundation for learning. Activities in the Think Tank don't occur in a vacuum; everything is fully integrated with other coursework to help students link learning in the lab to their school curriculum and home and community experiences. Projects deliberately recognize and nurture all the varied human intelligences and combinations of intelligences. Some projects use students' strengths; others encourage children to explore areas where they are weaker and may feel less comfortable. In other words, projects are designed so that intelligences are layered in creative ways. For example, students learn to make drawings (visual-spatial) by first mastering the concept of a bird's-eye view (mathematical-logical). As they create "dream home" plans, they are encouraged to label each room (verbal-linguistic). Then they brainstorm together and combine their efforts (interpersonal) before building a three-dimensional model (bodily-kinesthetic).

For additional information:

Jean Sausele Knodt
Designer and Director
Think Tank at Kent Gardens Elementary School

1717 Melbourne Drive
McLean, VA 22101

South Carolina Center for Advanced Technological Education. The South Carolina Center for Advanced Technological Education developed and piloted a curriculum for two-year technical colleges that integrates science, mathematics, engineering technology, and communications. The pilot courses used a problem-based learning approach and incorporated the theory of multiple intelligences into the instructional strategies. The evaluation report of the first year found that at the end of the course

- ◆ 84 percent of the students reported they felt capable of solving real-world problems as part of class projects
- ◆ 62 percent felt they could use mathematical knowledge to solve a science problem
- ◆ 84 percent felt they could make an oral presentation to an audience with a team of other students
- ◆ 69 percent felt they could write about the results of science or engineering projects

 (Bucci, Evans, and Choi, 1999).

Reports from students and faculty indicated that

- ◆ the curriculum pilot changed the learning environment into an active one
- ◆ students were more focused, asked better and more questions
- ◆ students had a new attitude toward learning
- ◆ students made oral team presentations of solutions to electrical problems using visuals and handouts for support
- ◆ students thought the classes were better than their other classes because they had the help of a team
- ◆ students liked the methods used in the class

For additional information:

Elaine Craft
Director, South Carolina ATE Center of Excellence
SC State Board for Technical and Comprehensive
Education

111 Executive Center Drive
Columbia, SC 29210
803-896-5410
crafte@sbt.tec.sc.us.

Lakes Elementary School. At Lakes Elementary School teachers have developed an integrated curriculum that has two goals. One goal focuses on the state's essential learning requirements; the other goal applies the theory of multiple intelligences (Meyer, 1997), with particular emphasis on the latest intelligence announced by Gardner, that of the naturalist. On some occasions students use the school grounds as their classroom. For example, sixth graders work on observation skills when mentoring their first grade buddies in special learning relationships that blossom during nature hikes, community field trips, gardening, and other outdoor activities. On other occasions, students have used the classroom to meet with a variety of professionals who are strong in the naturalist intelligence: land management personnel, fish and wildlife biologists, wastewater management specialists, parks and recreation directors, tree farmers, and logging consultants. Students have demonstrated that when they have opportunities to use their stronger intelligences and when they are having fun doing so, they become more engaged in their learning process and often teach each other.

For additional information:

Maggie Meyer
Lakes Elementary School
6211 Mullen Road
Lacey, WA 98503
meyermag@aol.com

New City School, St. Louis, MO. Tom Hoerr, Director of New City School, has seen first-hand the power of multiple intelligences since his school began implementation of this theory in the school year 1988-89. According to Dr. Hoerr,

> What began with a faculty reading program, going chapter by chapter through Dr. Gardner's *Frames of Mind*, has become a school-wide philosophy. We find MI a tool that helps us view kids through their strengths. It has had an impact on how we design our curriculum, present our instruction, assess our students, and communicate with their parents. In my mind, there is no doubt that using MI helps kids learn,

increasing their motivation and giving them different pathways to acquire information and share what they have
learned. And there's no doubt that our discipline and behavior problems have diminished since using MI. We have not
formally collected data on how our students performed before our use of MI and compared it with our MI approach.
Thus our data are anecdotal. That said, there is no question in
anyone's mind that MI offers students (and teachers) more
routes to success.

New City School's faculty has written two books about their work
with MI, *Celebrating Multiple Intelligences: Teaching for Success* and *Succeeding with Multiple Intelligence: Teaching through the Personal Intelligences*.
Dr. Hoerr also serves as Facilitator of the MI Network founded in 1991.
The Network is an informal affiliation of educators who are interested
in sharing information about implementing the theory of multiple intelligences and produces a MI newsletter, *Intelligence Connections*, three
times a year.

For additional information:

Tom Hoerr
Director of New City School
5209 Waterman Ave.
St. Louis MO 63108-1155
www.newcityschool.org

Key School, Indianapolis. The Key School in Indianapolis, Indiana, was the first multiple intelligences school in the United States.
Given a grant in 1984 to create a curriculum for gifted and talented
students at her school, Patricia Bolaños and her colleagues discovered
the idea of multiple intelligence's rather than just the verbal and spa-
tial ones emphasized in current teaching. They used this as a basis for
a curriculum for all students. Bolaños and the seven other teachers then
began the process of developing a new elementary school based on
multiple intelligences. With initial funds from Lilly Endowment, and
later from the federal magnet school program, the Key School opened
in the fall of 1987.

In addition to Gardner's theory, Key School uses Mihaly
Csikszentmihalyi's idea of "flow," a concept on intrinsic motivation.
Children at the school regularly visit a "Flow Activity Center" where
staff learns what really motivates students. On Wednesdays students
gather in the gym to hear lectures, music or demonstrations by various
community or professional groups-symphony musicians, nurses, para-

medics-about what they do in our world. These "Wednesday Programs" are conceived to be "theme related", tied into the two themes that dominate each school year and result in student projects at regular intervals.

The foundation of equal emphasis in multiple intelligences has remained firm and is reflected in the students' schedules and the staff's commitment to instruction by specialists. Many changes through the years evolved from the staff's won education and research. Progress reports have been through several revisions and class grouping patterns changes as the staff studies and learns more about student learning.

The Key School opened a middle school in 1993. The I.P.S. Key Learning Community (Key School) extended its program to the high school by opening a ninth grade in 1999. The first graduating class will be in 2003.

For additional information:

Patricia Bolaños
Principal, Key School
777 S. White River Parkway – W. Dr.
Indianapolis, IN 46221
317-226-4992

CONCLUSION

Teachers who incorporate the theory of multiple intelligences into classroom instruction choose a variety of activities for each lesson, unit, and course. Going beyond the paper-and-pencil activities, teacher lectures, and individual assignments of traditional instruction, this approach taps into the strengths of students who can succeed in other ways. Students who perform an individual musical composition, present a group skit, or create a team project or model call upon intelligences and ways of learning that are too often overlooked. Students who thrive in conventional classrooms are challenged in new and different ways; students who have difficulty with a conventional curriculum may find new dimensions of strength. When classroom instruction honors diverse learning styles and incorporates multiple intelligences, students

♦ become involved learners rather than isolated learners

♦ find new and creative ways to solve problems

♦ expand skills in their areas of weaknesses to achieve success

♦ demonstrate skills in their strengths to achieve success

♦ bond more readily to school and other fellow students

♦ become lifelong learners

These attitudes and behavior later carry over into the workplace, making today's better students tomorrow's better workers.

REFERENCES

Armstrong, T. (1994). *Multiple Intelligences in the Classroom.* Alexandria, VA: Association for Supervision and Curriculum Development.

Bucci, Paul T., Evans, W. Douglas, and Choi, Wen-Tsing. (May 1999). "The South Carolina Advanced Technological Education Fall Semester 1998 Curriculum Pilot Project: Evaluation Report," The Academy for Educational Development.

Campbell, B. (1994) *The Multiple Intelligences Handbook: Lesson Plans and More.* Stanwood, WA: Campbell and Associates, Inc.

Cantrell, M. L., Ebdon, S. A., Firlik, R., Johnson, D., Rearick, D. (1997) The Summer Stars Program. *Educational Leadership,* 55(1), 38–41.

Gardner, H. (1983). *Frames of Mind: The Theory of Multiple Intelligences.* New York: Basic Books.

Gardner, H. (1991). *The Unschooled Mind: How Children Think and How Schools Should Teach.* New York: Basic Books.

Gardner, H. (1999). *Intelligence Reframed: Multiple Intelligence for the 21st Century.* New York: Basic Books.

Haggerty, B. (1995). *Nurturing Intelligences: A Guide to Multiple Intelligences Theory and Teaching.* Menlo Park, CA: Addison-Wesley..

Knodt, J. S. (1997). A Think Tank Cultivates Kids. *Educational Leadership,* 55(1), 35–37.

Meyer, M. (1997). The Greening of Learning: Using the Eighth Intelligence. *Educational Leadership,* 55(1), 32–34.

13

INSTRUCTIONAL TECHNOLOGIES

The knowledge business is transforming the way we learn.
But will the new learning business deliver information, knowledge
and education in such different ways and vast amounts that it paral-
lels, rivals, and in some instances even displaces schools as the major
deliverer of learning? Are we ending schooling as we have know it?
. . . Will we raise and educate our children differently?

Stan Davis and Jim Botkin, *The Monster Under The Bed*

INTRODUCTION

Today's job market increasingly depends on technology, computer skills, and Internet literacy. In 1998, Assistant Secretary of Commerce for Communication and Information Larry Irving predicted that by the year 2000, 60 percent of jobs would require skills with technology (Benton Foundation, 1998). According to a U.S. Department of Labor report, "By 2006, nearly half of all U.S. workers will be employed in industries that produce or intensively use information technology products and services" (21st Century Workforce Commission, June 2000, p. 10). The Bureau of Labor Statistics projects that skilled information technology jobs will be among the fastest growing occupations in the decade ending in 2006 (U.S. Department of Commerce, 1998). This dynamic growth of technological jobs means that school

163

dropouts will be at even greater risk of unemployment than they are now.

In this chapter, we explore the need to expand the use of technology in our classrooms in ways that enhance student learning and expand opportunities for all students.

THE DIGITAL DIVIDE

Looking ahead to the twenty-first century, President Clinton challenged the nation to ensure that all children will be equipped with the skills in reading, math, science, communication, and critical thinking that are essential for enhanced learning, improved performance, and technological literacy. To promote this goal, in 1994 the White House implemented the National Information Infrastructure (II) initiative, challenging the nation's schools to connect to the Internet by the year 2000. The Education Rate (E-rate) program provided support, with the largest discounts (90 percent) going to the poorest communities and up to a 10 percent additional discount for rural communities. The program was so successful that 95 percent of all public schools were connected to the Internet by 1999 (National Center for Education Statistics, February 2000).

Simply connecting schools to the Internet, however, does not ensure technological prowess. "Almost half the money from federal education programs is going to the poorest schools in the country, but those schools continue to lack qualified teachers and technological resources." A U.S. Department of Education report found that teachers' aides, rather than qualified teachers, were teaching many students in Title I schools. The report confirmed the existence of a growing digital divide in the country's classrooms, limiting access to computers and the Internet for students from low-income families (Wong, 2000).

The digital divide is the gap between those people and communities with access to information technologies and those without it. The Department of Commerce found "that a digital divide... in many cases is actually widening over time. Minorities, low-income persons, the less educated, and children of single-parent households, particularly when they reside in rural areas or central cities, are among the groups that lack access to information resources." According to this report,

- ♦ households earning more than $75,000 are more than 20 times more likely to have home Internet access than those at the lowest income levels

- ♦ Whites are more likely to have Internet access at home than African Americans or Latinos are to have access from any location

- ♦ Latino households are still roughly half as likely to own a computer as white households and nearly 2.5 times less likely to use the Internet

- ♦ only 6.6 percent of people with an elementary school education or less use the Internet

- ♦ People with college degrees or higher are 10 times more likely to have Internet access at work than those with only some high school education (Irving, 1999).

A study by Jupiter Communications found extensive gaps in Internet use between ethnic and age groups, but the widest gap was between high-income and low-income families; about 15 million of the wealthiest households will be online in 2005, compared to 9 million of the poorest households. The study reported that 60 percent more white households than African-American households are online (Lenihan, 2000).

Increasingly, schools are being asked to bridge the digital divide. The National Center for Educational Statistics (NCES, 1998) reports that the ratio of students to computers has gone down and has almost been equalized between high- and low-minority schools and poor and rich schools. However, evidence shows that more advanced applications—programming, data bases, spreadsheets and use of the Internet to receive up-to date information—are largely the domain of white, middle- and upper-class students. Schools with a predominantly minority population or a high proportion of at-risk students tend to use computers for drill and practice exercises, rote learning, and word processing. Most economically disadvantaged youngsters cannot use school computers before or after school and do not have access to computers at home (Hancock, 1992–93).

The Potential of Technology

In the twenty-first–century classroom, technology can provide a laboratory for problem identification, systems thinking, collaboration skills, teamwork experiences, cross-cultural exchanges, and critical thinking. Technology has the potential to broaden teacher and student access to educational resources. In contrast to television and the passive learning environment of many classrooms, computers (when used properly) provide an active environment. Interactive activities allow students to make choices, view the consequences immediately, and receive timely feedback. Computers can supplement instruction, provide differentiated learning, and reach students who otherwise don't like school. Because computers are viewed as impersonal, rather than personally critical of student performance, students become less disruptive in class, change their attitude toward learning, and start to achieve (Bennett, 1999). Technology can promote positive attitudes and promote success for students who often have faced only frustration and failure.

When properly applied, educational technology can remove many barriers to learning. It can be especially helpful with at-risk students, giving students access to learning 24 hours a day and enabling teachers to customize instruction to a student's individual needs and strengths.

Forms of Technology

Educational technology can take many forms, from calculators and word processors to networked multimedia computers. One form often ignored in discussions of educational technology is the television and videocassette recorder. Television can be a powerful communications tool, helping to clarify values, teach reading and writing, improve pronunciation, and promote linguistic development. But students must be taught to view for comprehension and understanding, and watching television or videotapes must be supplemented by active learning. The Learning Technology Center (LTC) at Vanderbilt University is conducting a longitudinal study on the impact of new technologies, including video, on the improvement of literacy among at-risk children.

Technology, like television, videotapes, and computers with CD-ROM, can expand the educational horizon. Teachers can present visual images of historical persons and literary characters. Students can watch Sir Lawrence Olivier as Macbeth, at virtually no cost. History teachers, instead of merely describing recent events, can show actual footage. Art students can scroll through the paintings of Renoir or listen as a museum curator explains the dimensions of his work. Language teachers can use voice recognition programs to teach proper pronunciation. Students can download research articles (using software programs like Aportisdoc.) onto handheld devices like the Palm Pilot (which is much less expensive than a computer). Schools can purchase site licenses to download textbooks, then use software programs to have students read them, do homework, and e-mail assignments back to the teacher for grading.

RESISTANCE TO TECHNOLOGY

Educators who are reluctant to increase their use of technology cite a number of fears. The greatest inhibitors are:

- ♦ the speed at which computers and software become obsolete and the related costs of purchasing new hardware and software
- ♦ the lack of ongoing professional development relating to the proper use of technology
- ♦ the limited ability of teachers to offer differentiated learning to students with diverse learning styles (including at-risk students)
- ♦ basic infrastructure problems such as leaking roofs, limited electrical access, and poor telephone connectivity
- ♦ the anticipation that student learning in this new environment will be hard to measure with traditional tools like standardized tests
- ♦ the question of alignment of available software with state and local curricula

♦ lack of information about where to find reliable evaluations of computer software

EFFECTIVE PROGRAMS AND PRACTICES

The Buddy System Project (Indiana). The Buddy System Project, started in 1988, focuses primarily on the improvement of learning in the fourth and fifth grades. Funded by the state of Indiana through its Department of Education, the project uses technology to extend learning beyond the classroom and school day and to increase family involvement in education. Sixty elementary schools and five middle schools participate in the project.

Research has found that students using technology in the Buddy System Project show:

♦ an improvement in writing skills three times higher than that of students in comparison schools

♦ a better understanding and a broader view of math

♦ more confidence in computer skills

♦ an ability to teach others

♦ greater problem-solving and critical-thinking skills

♦ enhanced self-confidence and self-esteem (Rockman and Sloan, 1995).

For additional information:

Nancy Miller
Project Manager
INTEC Consulting, Inc.
Phone: 765-296-9257
e-mail: nasmiller@iquest.net
www.Buddyproject.org

Ombudsman Educational Services. The Ombudsman program is an alternative-education program that also uses a different delivery system—self-paced learning supported by technology. The program features small class sizes, low student-to-teacher ratios, and flexible hours. The Ombudsman Educational Services literature states that they have successfully retained between 85 and 90 percent of their high-risk student population. The program serves nearly 6,000 students at more than seventy sites in eleven states (Arizona, Colorado, Florida, Kansas,

Maryland, Missouri, Indiana, Illinois, New Hampshire, Ohio, and Texas).

For additional information:

James P. Boyle, President
Ombudsman Educational Services
1585 North Milwaukee Avenue
Libertyville, IL 60048
847-367-6383 and 800- 833-9235

Rhode Island Teachers and Technology Initiative. The Rhode Island Teachers and Technology Initiative, started in 1997, aimed to supply laptop computers and sixty hours of training to more than 2,400 teachers—approximately 25 percent of the state's teachers—by the end of the year 2000. The vision of the program is to enhance the technology skills of teachers, to make technology an essential tool in the work of teachers, and to promote the use of technology with students. The program was funded by the Rhode Island Foundation.

For additional information:

Ronald V. Gallo, President
The Rhode Island Foundation
One Union Station
Providence, RI 02903
401-274- 4564
www.rifoundation.org

CONCLUSION

In the educational arena of the twenty-first century, technology presents both a challenge and an opportunity. The challenge is to ensure that all students learn the technological skills they need. The opportunity lies in the enormous potential of technology to support and enhance learning for all students.

REFERENCES

21st Century Workforce Commission. (2000, June). A Nation of Opportunity: Building America's 21st Century Workforce. U.S. Department of Labor.

Bennett, Frederick. (1999). Computers as Tutors: Solving the Crisis in Education. Faben Inc.

Benton Foundation. (1998). *Losing Ground Bit by Bit: Low-Income Communities* in the *Information Age*, (Internet Posting) http://www.bentton.org/Library/Low-income/. Quoted in Intercultural Development Research Association's Newsletter, June–July 1999, p. 2.

Davis, S., and Botkin, J. *The Monster Under The Bed*. (1994). New York: Simon and Schuster.

Digital Divide Widens, (2000, June-July). bLink, 14.

Hancock, Vicki E. (1992–93, Dec.–Jan.) *The At-Risk Student*. Educational Leadership ASCD, 84–85.

Irving, L. (1999, Nov.). *Falling Through the Net: A report on the Telecommunications and Information Technology Gap in America*. The U.S. Department of Commerce National Telecommunication and Information Administration.

Lenihan, Rob: Income fuels digital divide. CNN-fn Internet Posting, June 20, 2000.

National Center for Education Statistics. (2000, Feb.) Internet Access in U.S. Public Schools and Classrooms: 1994–99. National Center for Education Statistics (NCES 2000-086).

Rockman, S. and Sloan, K.R. Assessing the Growth: The Buddy Project Evaluation, 1994–95, Internet posting (San Francisco, CA: Corporation for Educational Technology, 1995), quoted in Intercultural Development Research Association's Newsletter, June-July 1999, p.1.

Suda, K.E. (1999, June–July). *Educational Technology: An Update* Intercultural Development Research Association (IDRA), 1–2.

U.S. Department of Commerce. (1998, Jan.). Update: America's New Deficit, Office of Technology Policy, U.S. Department of Commerce.

Wong, Edward: "Poorest Schools Lack Teachers and Computers." *New York Times*, August 13, 2000, p. 14.

Zehr, M.A. *Screening for the Best*. (1999, Sep.). Technology Counts '99 Building the Digital Curriculum. *Education Week*

14

INDIVIDUALIZED LEARNING

*Every human being constitutes a unique combination of
countless and different factors.*

G. Allport

INTRODUCTION

In the standards-based reform that is sweeping the country,
legislatures are challenging educators to do more than parrot
the phrase "all students can learn." Most districts and schools
use this phrase as part of their vision statement, but few have
faced the hard task of making such a statement a reality. All students actually can learn—if the conditions of learning are such
that the individual needs of the students are met. Educators know
that students come from varying economic and social backgrounds, have specific learning styles, learn at different paces,
have diverse intellectual strengths, and flourish academically
in various settings. For the most part, however, few schools actually put this knowledge into practice beyond meeting the requirements for special education students.

In this chapter, we argue that individualizing the learning
experience is an effective educational strategy for all students,
and especially for students who are at risk of dropping out of
school. Individualized programs can contribute to student success in traditional classrooms, as well as in alternative school
settings.

LEARNING FROM THE IEP
(INDIVIDUALIZED EDUCATION PROGRAM)

Individualized education plans are required by law for students in special education programs. While these plans are not common in regular education programs, it is clear that large numbers of so-called normal students do not succeed in school for the primary reason that they are not treated or taught differently (Stainback and Stainback, 1992). Ignoring variations in children's learning, however, can limit opportunities for children to develop their gifts and abilities, creating further lapses in student achievement (Pugach and Warger, 1996).

Understanding what individualization means for special education students is a first step in identifying the possibilities of using it for other students in at-risk situations. The Individuals with Disabilities Education Act (IDEA) of 1997 guides the delivery of special education support and services for the student with a disability (U.S. Department of Education, 2000). It best addresses individualization through the Individualized Education Program (IEP). The IEP creates an opportunity for teachers, parents, school administrators, related services personnel, and students (when appropriate) to work together to improve educational results for children with disabilities. In special education, these plans for the student address academic and behavioral/emotional skills to be improved. By law, these records must be updated in very specific ways. This concept of individual education plans has become the basis of the individual accountability measures in place in many states for those students scoring below grade level or below standard for the grade tested.

A Guide to the Individualized Education Program (U.S. Department of Education, 2000) describes the role of the regular classroom teacher in the development and implementation of an IEP for a student with a disability. As a part of the process, the classroom teacher discusses the following components of the general education classroom with the IEP team:

+ general curriculum
+ aids, services, or changes to the education program that would help the child learn and achieve

◆ strategies to help the child with behavior, if behavior is an issue

Regular classroom teachers may also discuss with the IEP team the support from school staff needed so that the child can

◆ advance toward his or her annual goals

◆ be involved and progress in the general curriculum

◆ participate in extracurricular activities

◆ be educated with other children, both with and without disabilities (p. 11)

Imagine the potential for educational success if each child had access to an IEP. All members of the student's educational community would address the facets of individualization. Teachers, counselors, parents, and other significant adults would set aside time with a student and actually plan for the student's educational future. Progress checks would be made and adjustments in the IEP would be natural. At present, however, this individual planning only occurs for students with special needs or students in special settings such as alternative education. Unfortunately, a teacher with twenty or more students in a regular classroom would have difficulty finding the time for such intensive efforts. Limiting class size to less than twenty for at-risk students would do much to reduce the likelihood of their dropping out. Research indicates that smaller classes improve the learning environment, give students greater individual attention, and are more successful than larger classes (Lindjord, 1998, and Ellis, 1994). However, such efforts would be expensive and would divert funds from other worthy programs. Therefore, alternative means for individualizing learning experiences should be explored.

STRATEGIES FOR INDIVIDUALIZING STUDENTS' LEARNING EXPERIENCES

While it may not be feasible to use the special education model to individualize learning experiences for all students, educators can adapt and apply the lessons learned in working with special education students. Research and best practice have identified a number of effective strategies for individualizing learning that can meet the needs of students who are placed at risk for a variety of reasons. All of the following strategies provide for the differences students bring with them into the classroom:

♦ Mentoring and tutoring are cost-effective and academically effective ways of providing students with both the one-on-one attention and the academic assistance they need.

♦ Providing academic intervention when students first experience difficulties, either during the school day or through an after-school program, will help students who learn at a slower pace.

♦ Counseling and social services provide students with individualized assistance with those problems outside of school that often hinder students' learning.

♦ Teachers in the regular classroom can use a variety of instructional strategies that address the various learning styles and intelligences of their students, and teachers can adapt classroom assignments to allow students multiple experiences and choices.

♦ Alternative schools offer options for students who cannot succeed in traditional school settings.

♦ Instructional technologies—computers, in particular— provide students with opportunities to explore their own interests at their own pace.

EFFECTIVE PROGRAMS AND PRACTICES

INDIVIDUALIZATION IN THE REGULAR CLASSROOM

For the classroom teacher, curriculum development is a primary arena for individualizing the learning experience. The term *individualize* is used here in the sense of making explicit provisions for adapting the curriculum to students' particular abilities and needs (Glatthorn, 1994). Glatthorn suggests a broad list of components to be considered in this endeavor. All are vital for all students, but they are especially critical for students who are at risk of dropping out.

Content emphases. When students have a choice concerning the content to be learned, they are more motivated. In a thematic unit, individual students could be responsible for researching and presenting different content pieces.

Skills to be mastered. The curriculum should provide for a variety of skills to be mastered taking students' intellectual strengths into consideration.

Level of achievement expected. All students will not be able to succeed at the same level of achievement within the same timeframe. Teachers and curriculum developers should anticipate and plan for the differences in levels of achievement and the additional time needed by some students.

Pace of learning. All students do not learn at the same rate. Accommodations should be in place for students who can work faster, as well as for those who work at a slower pace.

Method of learning. Visual, auditory, and kinesthetic experiences should be included in the curriculum.

Learning environment. The theories of learning styles state that such variables as temperature, light, body position, and other environmental factors should be accommodated to the individual's style.

Degree of learning structure. The degree of the learning structure varies. The continuum extends from the very self-motivated learner to the one who needs constant encouragement and assistance. Some students are very comfortable with few guidelines in the learning structure; others will need greater amounts of teacher intervention.

Type and amount of feedback. Students vary in the type and amount of feedback needed. Some students want detailed feedback; others are content with quick, immediate feedback.

Means of final assessment. The key to this component is authenticity. The assessment must match the skills and content taught. Portfolio assessment works well for individualization.

Personal meaning. All learning should be relevant to the learner. The use of "real life" scenarios brings personal meaning to the learning for students. The question for the educator then becomes, "How do these areas of possible individualization translate into classroom strategies?" The answer to this question will vary from school to school and classroom to classroom. Glatthorn suggests that teachers review a number of models for individualizing learning. Models that address the components of individualization include the following (Glatthorn, 1994, pp. 105–106):

Studio or Workshop Model. Each student works on a project with teacher explanation, demonstration, and projected outcomes. Feedback is primarily individual.

Content Option Model. The teacher identifies core skills to be mastered. The student chooses between content options designed by the teacher, which encompasses the content skills.

Learning Centers Model. Students rotate through learning centers according to their needs and preferences. These centers are designed as a part of the total learning environment, but the centers will address a different learning modality or varied approach to the curriculum.

Self-Instructional Model. An assessment will determine placement of a student in sequenced curriculum. Self-instructional materials will pace the students. The most common form of self-instructional models today can be found in the instructional technology arena, better known as the computer-assisted instructional curriculum packages.

Mastery Learning Model. The teacher gives group instruction, assesses learning, and provides for individual remediation and enrichment.

Cooperative Learning Model. Students work in cooperative groups, but each individual is responsible for learning the concepts and content of the activity.

Peer Tutoring Model. Peers in the classroom provide extra assistance to students who need the remediation on an individual basis.

Teaming and Individualization. The students work together as a team to gain basic mastery and then individually for enrichment.

Learning Styles Accommodations. The teacher assesses students' learning styles and modality preferences and makes special accommodations to strengths and preferences.

EFFECTIVE PROGRAMS IN ALTERNATIVE SCHOOLS

Many successful alternative schools have included individualization as a major component of their programs. These schools draw from the concepts underlying the IEP as well as the variety of curriculum possibilities mentioned above for individualizing the learning experience.

The City-As-School Program (CAS), Buffalo, New York. In the CAS program, students become interns in many different types of work sites in the city, earning academic credit for the work they perform. For example, an internship at a local municipal court can provide credit in social studies; work at a local newspaper can provide English credit. However, the entire program for the student is tailored around the Learning Experience Activity Packet (LEAP), which is a set of goals and activities customized for each student and each internship (U.S. Department of Education, 1996). The LEAP includes the following for each student:

- weekly assignments
- final semester-long project

- monitoring by on-site supervisors
- monitoring by program teachers
- student attendance at weekly seminars

These seminars are held at City-As-School (CAS) offices, located at post-secondary institutions to allow the student in at-risk situations to be exposed to college life and campuses. The CAS program in general boasts major improvements in the students' behavior and attendance in the program. Sixty-five percent of the students have been able to maintain 100 percent attendance for as long as two years, complete all of their internships, and earn their high school diplomas (U.S. Department of Education, 1996).

Borough Academies, New York City. The Borough Academies serve students from New York City. A program called Free Options allows students to choose their schedule each day. Students can work at their own pace and earn credits as quickly as possible. Two recent classes have an 86 percent graduation rate, and many of the students in this alternative program have entered college (U.S. Department of Education, 1996).

CONCLUSION

In the current climate, as state legislatures emphasize setting standards and improving test scores, it would be easy to lose sight of individual student needs. Yet, now more than ever, schools need to plan for the individual student. A publication from the Educational Research Service, aptly titled *Ten Trends: Educating Children for a Profoundly Different Future* (Marx, 2000), advises educators to rally their communities to support education that will make it possible for all students to achieve, despite their social or economic backgrounds.

If educators accept the need for individualizing the learning experience, then the means—time, money, and effort—to support this concept must be provided, and at all levels. It may sound simple, but someone needs to notice when a student has a problem. And then teachers, counselors, or administrators must have access to programs that will make a difference. Schools need funding for appropriate personnel, time to attend to individual student needs, and strategies to address the problems.

The most effective educational strategies will be those that include individualizing learning as a significant component. Programs that address the individual needs of each student will offer the greatest opportunities for success for all students, and especially for those at risk.

REFERENCES

Ellis, T.I. (1984). *Class Size*. ERIC Clearing House On Educational Manuscripts.

Glatthorn, A. (1994). *Developing a Quality Curriculum*. Alexandria, VA: Association for Supervision and Curriculum.

Lindjord, D. (1998). *Smaller Class Size: Raising the Academic Performance of Children from Low- and Moderate-Income Families*. Journal of Early Education and Family Review: WV: Oxford Publishing Company.

Marx, G. (2000). *Ten Trends: Educating Children for a Profoundly Different Future*. Arlington, VA: Educational Research Service.

Pugach, M., and Warger, C. (Eds.). (1996). *Curriculum Trends, Special Education, and Reform*. New York: Teacher College Press.

Stainback, W., and Stainback, S. (1992). *Controversial Issues Confronting Special Education*. Boston: Allyn and Bacon.

U.S. Department of Education, Office of Special Education and Rehabilitative Services. (2000). *A Guide to the Individualized Education Program*. Available online: http://www.ed.gov.offices/OSERS

U. S. Department of Education. (1996). *Creating Safe and Drug-Free Schools: An Action Guide*. Alternative Education Programs for Expelled Students. Available online: http:www.ed.gov/offices/OESE/SDFS/actguid/altersch.html

PART VI

MAKING THE MOST OF THE WIDER SCHOOL COMMUNITY

The problems, the potential, the challenges, and the opportunities of education extend beyond the walls of the school building into the wider community. A comprehensive program for dropout prevention must link to the wider community as well. The strategies of systemic renewal and community collaboration bring educators, families, and community members together to make schools a place where all students can thrive. Career education programs prepare students to achieve success in the larger world of today's workplace. Finally, when students participate in a comprehensive program for conflict resolution and violence prevention, the community reaps the benefits many times over.

15

SYSTEMIC RENEWAL

Where there is much desire to learn, there of necessity will be much arguing, much writing, many opinions; for opinions in good men is but knowledge in the making.

John Milton

INTRODUCTION

This chapter focuses on systemic renewal—a coordinated, concerted effort to harness the forces that can bring about improvement in schools. We identify the essential components of true systemic renewal and provide examples of how stakeholders—teachers, school administrators, students, parents, and community members—can collaborate effectively to ensure that all students can achieve success in school.

THE PROBLEM

The problems inherent in educating diverse populations of students continue to confound educators and policymakers across the nation. Reforms abound, but the educational system is so constrained by traditional wisdom and vested interests that existing educational practices are difficult to replace. An effort in the 1980s to restructure the educational system through site-based management and shared decision making was pronounced a failure when positive effects on student achievement failed to materialize. Yet there was little evidence that any true changes had been made in the organization of the systems that were supposed to be restructured. To compound the problem, few educational reforms have enjoyed the financial resources necessary to actually accomplish reform objectives. In addition, most past attempts at reform have ignored the research on student learning, effective teaching, educational leadership, and implementation of benchmarking change models. As a result, educational reforms tend to be a melange of piecemeal, add-on programs, few of which are supported by data that show their effectiveness.

Two reform efforts, begun in the 1990s and continuing full-force into the 2000s, are standards-based reform and whole-school reform. The push for standards-based reform is one of the predominant issues facing today's public schools. At the 1996 National Education Summit, 44 governors and 50 corporate CEOs joined together with a commitment to the following set of priorities fundamental to achieving excellence in the nation's system of K–12 education:

♦ high academic standards and expectations for all students

♦ tests that are more rigorous and more challenging, to measure whether students are meeting those standards

♦ accountability systems that provide incentives and rewards for educators, students, and parents to work together to help students reach these standards

(Achieve, 1998).

In 1996, only 14 states had developed content standards in all four of the core curriculum areas (mathematics, English, science, and history/social studies). By 1999, 44 states had implemented academic standards in the four core areas (Quality Counts, 2000). Unfortunately, this reform is facing problems similar to those encountered by previous reforms: policies mandated without funds provided to effectively implement them, student assessments in place before teachers have been adequately trained to teach to new standards, and accountability demanded before intervention strategies have been instituted as a safety net for students (Duttweiler, 1999).

The second popular reform, whole-school reform, received its impetus from the U.S. Congress in 1994 when low-performing, high-poverty schools were allowed to use Title 1 Funds to improve the entire school. In 1997, Congress expanded the program to help low-performing schools raise student achievement by adopting research-based, schoolwide approaches (An Educators' Guide to Schoolwide Reform, 1999). To help schools identify models for whole-school reform, the U.S. Department of Education (OERI, 1998) published *Tools for Schools*, which detailed 27 school-reform models that had received support from the National Institute on the Education of At-Risk Students for development, expansion, adaptation, or evaluation. However, noting the limited evaluation data available for schools to make objective decisions on programs, five leading national educational organizations commissioned the American Institutes for Research to assess 24 whole-school reform models in terms of their effectiveness in improving student achievement in measurable ways. Of the 24 models assessed, only three met the criteria set by the publication: Direct Instruction, High Schools That Work, and Success for All (An Educators' Guide to Schoolwide Reform, 1999).

Sirotnik (1999) characterized such reforms as those discussed above as "whatever is politically fashionable . . . usually underfunded, lacking in professional development, and short-lived." There is little evidence that either of these current reforms will produce the kinds of academic achievement necessary to raise the scores of economically disadvantaged, minority students to a level reached by affluent, white students. The Education Trust issued a report—using data from the National Assessment of Educational Progress, American College Test, Scholastic Aptitude Test, college enrollment, high school graduation rates, and others—that revealed that only 5 percent of the eighth graders in high poverty schools were proficient in mathematics (Davidson and Toomer-Cook, 1998). In Massachusetts, failure rates on the state's tough new standardized exams were disappointingly high, but students in the wealthiest school districts performed best (Hart, 1998). Maryland, as well, has noted the generally lower performance of minority students and the wide gulf between students in high-poverty schools and those in more affluent schools (Maryland State Department of Education, 1998). In Connecticut, 44 percent of the eighth graders scored proficient or better on the first NAEP writing test—well ahead of the next-highest state, Maine, at 32 percent. Yet Connecticut had only 15 percent of its black students scoring at that level (Quality Counts, 2000). Furthermore, students from low-income families are three times more likely to drop out than are students from middle-income families, and more than four times more likely to drop out than are students from high-income families (NCES, 1999).

Many schools and teachers have low expectations not only for their students, but also for themselves. The Consortium for Policy Research in Education (CPRE) (Fuhrman, 1999) is studying schools in San Francisco and Chicago that are operating under severe sanctions (reconstitution and probation). CPRE found the major emphasis in these schools was on test preparation. The schools were characterized by a focus on order and control and by low expectations for student learning. These schools did not appear to be making fundamental changes in their core processes or making concerted efforts to rethink their instructional program through collective deliberation or targeted management decisions.

CPRE found many of the schools had no collective sense of responsibility for students' learning, and individual teachers were strongly influenced by what they believe their students can or cannot do. In the CPRE sample, teachers' opinions about their own capacity and that of their students determined what, if anything, was done to improve performance. These opinions were powerfully influenced by teachers' preconceptions about the individual traits of their students, the characteristics of students' families, and the communities from which the students came. Teachers identified the most powerful cause of student academic performance as those factors over which they, as teachers, had little or no control—family background. They identified the least powerful cause as those factors over which they have the greatest control—the conditions of teaching and learning in the classroom.

CPRE researchers drew the following conclusion from their investigation (Fuhrman, 1999):

The idea that a school will improve its instructional practice, and therefore the overall performance of its students, implies a capacity for collective deliberation and action that schools operating in the typical mode observed by this CPRE study did not display. (p. 8)

When asserting that "all children can learn," many practitioners add *sotto voce*, "but some not as well as others." Unfortunately, few school districts subscribe to the belief that the achievement gap between disadvantaged and advantaged students can be virtually eliminated. This is illustrated by a school improvement effort funded by the Edna McConnell Clark foundation. The Clark Foundation began working with the Jefferson County Public Schools (JCPS) in 1989. Over a six-year period, the Foundation made a series of grants to implement reforms at the three lowest-performing middle schools. When the district adopted standards-based reform in 1995, the Foundation made larger grants to the district as a whole. After a decade and millions of dollars, the three middle schools still remain at or near the bottom in achievement among the district's 24 middle schools. A wide variety of intervention efforts were implemented with disappointing results (Goodbye, Yellow Brick Road, 2000). The question is, "Why?"

The answer to the above question is complicated and, unfortunately, much too familiar. Observations by an independent research organization reporting to the Edna McConnell Clark Foundation suggest there was a lack of vision and that too many JCPS leaders believed economically disadvantaged students could not excel. There were not enough accomplished teachers, not enough principals who were leaders, not enough inspired support people and central office administrators who believed that greater gains were possible and knew how to achieve them. Although a core group of educators in the district knew what it would take to make all schools successful, they were too often stymied by powerful systemic forces resistant to the dramatic changes necessary to achieve the desired results (Goodbye, Yellow Brick Road, 2000).

THE SOLUTION: SYSTEMIC RENEWAL

An early study of the implementation of federally sponsored innovations revealed that the critical variables related to improvement, change, and effectiveness are organizational and systemic rather than individual or programmatic in nature (Berman and McLaughlin, 1978). Context does matter; reform cannot occur in an environment that is indifferent or hostile to it (Mizell, 2000). The powerful forces that mitigate against authentic change or improvement in the schools combine to form a pervasive ethos that is systemic (Duttweiler and Mutchler, 1990). Systemic renewal, therefore, is about continuous, critical inquiry into current practices; identifying innovations that might improve education; and nurturing the spiritual, affective, and intellectual connections in the lives of educators working together to understand and improve their practice (Sirotnik, 1999).

Systemic renewal strategies are based on the theory that the educational system must change to create a flexible organization that enables teachers, school administrators, students, parents, and community members to collaborate in providing within each school the experiences students need to achieve success. True systemic renewal demands:

- consistent, goal-directed policies
- administrative leadership for change
- use of data and research to inform practice
- ongoing, quality professional development
- adequate resources for schools to implement practices that ensure success for all students

(Duttweiler, 2000).

EFFECTIVE PROGRAMS AND PRACTICES

If schools are to become high-performing learning communities for all students, systemic forces need to be addressed. Evidence that this can be done is provided by Brazosport Independent School District (BISD), which has eighteen schools with an enrollment of 13,500. It serves seven distinct communities. Nine of its campuses educate a large percentage of students living below the federal poverty line. In 1991–92, half of the district's campuses had low performance on the Texas Assessment of Academic Skills (TAAS), which measures the level of student learning on Texas' academic standards. A thorough examination of the results of the TAAS showed that economically disadvantaged children, regardless of race or ethnicity, were not successful, and the gap between minority and non-Hispanic white students was too great. In the 1993–94 school year, there was a 32 percent gap between non-Hispanic white and African-American students and a 20 percent gap between non-Hispanic white and Hispanic students. By the 1998–99 school year the gap had decreased to 7 percent between non-Hispanic white and African-American students, and to 3 percent between non-Hispanic white and Hispanic students. Disadvantaged students raised their performance from 57 percent in the 1993–94 school year to 93 percent in the 1998–99 school year. Most importantly, however, all groups were performing above the 90 percent level on the TAAS (Anderson, 2000).

These amazing results were not accomplished by what former Superintendent Gerald Anderson called "drill and kill." By identifying teachers who were successfully teaching economically disadvantaged children, the district was able to develop and pilot test a process for teaching all students successfully. This required changes within the whole system, from the district office to the schools. The renewal process, which was replicated in all the districts' schools, combined elements of Total Quality Management, effective schools research, an eight-step instructional process focused on regular assessment and re-teaching to address students' learning problems, restructuring the school-day schedule to allow for tutoring and enrichment, and out-of-school opportunities for learning. Teachers received professional development in areas such as learning styles, ways to convey high expectations for all students, instructional focus modeling, interpretation of test data, Total Quality Management, and effective schools research. The process not only raised the achievement level of the disadvantaged and minority students, but the scores of non-Hispanic white students rose from 81 percent passing the TASS in 1993–94 to 98 percent passing in 1998–99 (Anderson, 2000).

CONCLUSION

The kind of accomplishments made by Brazosport can be achieved by every district where there is an organizational will to change and a renewed commitment to meet the needs of low-performing students. The effective implementation of systemic renewal means finding ways to create a collaborative mode of work to replace the existing isolation and powerlessness under the traditional system. The National Dropout Prevention Center has identified the following areas to be addressed:

♦ The educational system must be redesigned to be more congruent with the needs of those who work in it and the needs of those it serves. Congruence translates into a "goodness-of-fit" match between the characteristics, climate, and practices in the settings in which teachers teach and students learn.

♦ The technical core of the school—teaching, learning, curriculum, and instruction—must engage children in learning. Effective strategies must be adopted to meet the needs of students in at-risk circumstances.

♦ District structural elements must be redesigned to provide leadership and support to the schools and to accommodate innovations in curriculum, instruction, and the use of time and resources.

♦ Data and research must be used to assess how well the students, teachers, administrators, schools, and the district are doing. Data and research must provide the basis for assessing the effectiveness of practice, for guiding the use of resources, and ensuring a continuing process of renewal.

♦ Government, businesses, community organizations and agencies, parents, and the schools must join together to provide the social support needed to ensure resiliency in children. Addressing the problems faced by children in at-risk circumstances is the collective responsibility of everyone.

Powerful forces can also be marshaled to support change and improvement. Leadership, professional development, resources, and community support are all required to implement comprehensive approaches that provide students with opportunities to acquire the academic knowledge and skills necessary to perform to high academic standards. As educators, it is our job to create an enriching, culturally sensitive, relevant and active environment for all children. We must not just write vision statements that parrot the phrase "All children can learn"; we must shape our classrooms, our schools, and our districts so that it becomes a reality.

REFERENCES

Achieve. (1998). *Aiming Higher: 1998 Annual Report.* Cambridge, MA: Achieve, Inc. Available online: http://www.achieve.org.

An Educators' Guide to Schoolwide Reform. (1999). Arlington, VA: Educational Research Service.

Anderson, G. (2000). *Brazosport ISD: Implementation of the Quality Agenda to Ensure Excellence and Equity for ALL students.* Paper presented at the Improving Achievement Outcomes in the Middle Grades Conference sponsored by the Council of Chief State School Officers: Project to Improve Achievement in High Poverty Schools, Long Beach, CA, April 9–12, 2000.

Berman, P., and McLaughlin, M. W. (1978). *Federal Programs Supporting Educational Change, Vol. III: Implementing and Sustaining Innovations.* R-1589/8-HEW. Santa Monica, CA: The Rand Corporation.

Davidson, L., and Toomer-Cook, J. (1998, December 4). Utah Students Rank Poorly. *Deseret News.* Available online: www.deseretnews.com:80/dn/view/0 percent2C1249 percent2C20001120 percent2C00.html?.

Duttweiler, P. C. (1999). Do We Have the Cart Before the Horses? *Special Report on Standards, Assessment, Accountability, and Interventions for the Edna McConnell Clark Foundation (# 1).* Clemson, SC: National Dropout Prevention Center

Duttweiler, P. C. (2000). Do We Practice What We Preach? *Special Report on Standards, Assessment, Accountability, and Interventions for the Edna McConnell Clark Foundation (# 4).* Clemson, SC: National Dropout Prevention Center.

Duttweiler, P. C., and Mutchler, S. E. (1990). *Organizing the Educational System for Excellence: Harnessing the Energy of People.* Austin, TX: Southwest Educational Development Laboratory.

Fuhrman, S. H. (1999). *The New Accountability.* CPRE Policy Brief No. RB-27. Philadelphia: Consortium for Policy Research in Education, University of Pennsylvania.

Goodbye, Yellow Brick Road. (2000, Spring). *Changing Schools in Louisville, 3*(1), 2–15. Edna McConnell Clark Foundation.

Hart, J. (1998, Dec. 10). Test Scores Spell Out Education Weaknesses. *The Boston Globe.* Available online: www.boston.com/dailyglobe2/344/metro/.

Jenkins, L. (1997). *Improving Student Learning: Applying Deming's Quality Principles in the Classroom.* Milwaukee, WI: ASQ Press.

Maryland State Department of Education. (1998, December 16). 1998 MSPAP Results Show Across-the-Board Gains. Available Online: www.msde.state.md.us/pressreleases/19881208.html.

Mizell, H. (2000, April 5). Educators: Reform Thyselves. *Education Week,* 56:40.

NCES. (1999). *Dropout Rates in the United States: 1998.* National Center for Education Statistics, Office of Educational Research and Improvement, U.S. Department of Education.

OERI. (1998). *Tools for Schools.* Washington, DC: National Institute on the Education of At-Risk Students, Office of Educational Research and Improvement, U.S. Department of Education.

Quality Counts 2000. (2000). *Education Week, XIX* (18).

Schargel, F.P. (1994) *Transforming Education Through Total Quality Management: A Practitioner's Guide.* Larchmont, NY: Eye on Education.

Sirotnik, K. A. (1999). Making Sense of Educational Renewal. *Phi Delta Kappan, 80*(8), 606–610.

16

COMMUNITY COLLABORATION

The greatest problem with communication is the illusion that it has been accomplished.

George Bernard Shaw

INTRODUCTION

This chapter focuses on the strategy of community collaboration. We describe the values and pitfalls of collaborative efforts to bring about change, outline the key components of effective community collaboration, and provide examples of programs that have worked in a variety of settings.

COMMUNITY COLLABORATION IS A MUST

Schools do not exist in a vacuum; they never did and never will. Two or three decades ago, school administrators tended to keep the business of schools and educating our children to themselves, within the walls of the schools where administrators, counselors, and teachers were in charge of nearly everything. Starting in the 1980s and clearly in this new millennium, the business of educating children has drawn the close attention of parents, business, and community leaders, not to mention political leaders and nearly every other special-interest organization represented in the community.

This would appear to be good news—as long as all groups have a shared vision with clearly defined roles, pool their resources, contribute their efforts toward the solutions of selected issues, and do not generate barriers to reaching that end. Encouragingly, a recent survey reported by The Children's Partnership (1999) indicated that more than one in three Americans (up from one in four in a 1997 survey) believes that he or she can have a major impact on making the community a better place to live. Also encouragingly, 47 percent of African-Americans say they are more involved in setting public policy today than they were years ago.

Community change of any kind is not easy and usually does not happen on a fast track, but some changes in schools are now welcome and even encouraged. Such is the case for comprehensive school reforms and several very specific school initiatives— the School-to-Work initiative, drug abuse programs, after-school homework centers, and parental involvement programs, to name just a few. Many school leaders today actively recruit community collaborations to help study and provide solutions to a multitude of issues ranging from academic achievement to good nutrition programs for children. Community collaborations are now such a vital force in the everyday administration of schools that school and community leaders must carefully guide each of the collaborative efforts to be sure they are directed to the same unified vision of the community, avoiding duplication or wasteful efforts. For example, in just one small city with a population of 45,000 and a school enrollment of 3,000 students, eighteen different community collaborations recently focused their mission and objectives to the needs of students in at-risk situations (Wright, Smink, and Duckenfield, 1999).

WHAT ARE COMMUNITY COLLABORATIONS?

Community collaborations abound in American communities and schools today. For nearly any issue, a recognized organization is at work, with several different interest groups aligned to present a solution. For healthy school and community growth, all this energy must be focused and managed. Community collaboration is the key to success. The National Assembly of National Voluntary Health and Social Welfare Organizations, representing 35 of the nation's most recognized organizations (such as the American Red Cross, United Way, Boy Scouts, and YMCA) defines collaboration in this way:

> Collaboration is the process by which several agencies or organizations make a formal, sustained commitment to work together to accomplish a common mission. Collaboration requires a commitment to participate in shared decision-making, and allocation of resources related to activities responding to mutually identified needs. (1991, p. 1)

In the context of education, community collaborations include school-community initiatives directed at overall school renewal or a targeted issue such as improving the high school graduation rate. These collaborations or school-community initiatives arise in various ways and take a wide variety of approaches. Many collaborations spring to life in a dramatic response to a local school issue. Others are led by more focused and larger organizations, sometimes national in scope, addressing a specific issue or agenda and promoting a particular problem-solving process or solution. The Mott Foundation recently funded a review of a cross section of twenty school-community initiatives to explore the dynamics of implementing and sustaining the initiatives and to find practices that other collaborations could use to sustain their efforts (Melaville, 1998). The survey found that many of the collaborations shared similar objectives: improving the educational quality and academic outcomes for youth; gaining more efficient and effective health and social service delivery for children and families; increasing recognition of the developmental needs of young people and the importance of building on their strengths; and expanding efforts to strengthen the human, social, and economic foundations of neighborhoods and communities (Melaville, 1998). Several other findings about the initiatives should serve as guidelines for future collaborations. These are outlined below.

Ideas about Getting Started

♦ Almost half of the initiatives started in the private, nonprofit sector.

♦ Nonprofit sector leaders introduced a steady stream of new ideas and kept the initiative active.

♦ Most of the initiatives moved from planning to start-up within two years.

Ideas about Leadership

♦ Broad-based collaborative bodies, not school leaders, led overall policy development and operations.

♦ School staff led day-to-day management of initiative activities.

Ideas about Staffing Patterns

♦ All initiatives had a full-time coordinator at the broad-based community level.

♦ Almost two-thirds had a school site coordinator.

♦ Many of the initiatives had member organizations that had staff placed on a local school site either on load or at no cost.

♦ Volunteers provided a wide range of services to the initiative.

Typical Funding Patterns

♦ Most initiatives received funding from multiple sources.

♦ Most initiatives involved budgets of $100,000 or less in each site.

Typical Services Provided

♦ Most initiatives provided multiple services, which included referrals, case management, primary health care, infant and toddler programs, preschool-age childcare, before- and after-school care programs, mentoring, community service opportunities, recreation, leadership development, career development, employment and training, tutoring and literacy, community organizing, housing, economic development, and parenting.

♦ Programs had flexibility and were family-friendly.

Program Sites and Availability

♦ Activities were predominately at school sites.

♦ Most activities were offered within the normal hours of the school day.

♦ Least popular time periods were weekends.

The survey also found areas of concern; staff in most of the initiatives needed assistance in designing evaluation systems to measure results, developing long-range funding strategies, and building public support programs, among other tasks.

The Center for Mental Health in Schools (1999), in a newsletter devoted to school-community partnerships, presented a self-study survey as an aid in mapping and analyzing the current status of any collaborative. The Center suggested that the survey be completed by a team of people in the collaborative and that the results be used to clarify what resources are already available, how the resources are organized and can work together, and what procedures are in place to enhance the collaborative. More than 100 survey items were grouped in two major categories, reflecting two different types of collaborations. The first category, "Improving the School," contained several subsets: the instructional component of schooling, the governance and management of schooling, financial support of schooling, and school-based programs and services to address barriers to learning. The second category, "Improving the Neighborhood," comprised twelve main items:

♦ youth development programs

♦ youth and family recreation and enrichment opportunities

♦ physical health services

♦ mental health services

♦ programs to address psychosocial problems

♦ basic living needs services

♦ work/career programs

♦ social services

♦ crime and juvenile justice programs

♦ legal assistance

♦ support for development of neighborhood organizations

♦ economic development programs

(Center for Mental Health in Schools, 1999).

Basic Components of Community Collaborations

Community collaborations do not just happen, and the mere fact that a collaboration addresses a tremendous need or worthwhile issue in the school or community does not guarantee its success. Building a successful collaboration takes thoughtful ideas, skillful leadership, and usually a good bit of time, because changing the regular routines of people and organizations is difficult, at best. However, organizations that have passed through these trials can offer guidance to others. *The Community Collaboration Manual* (The National Assembly, 1991) offers seven key concepts for planning and implementing successful collaborations:

Shared Vision. Shared vision means that different organizations are willing to act together to meet a mutually identified need. It also implies they will trust each other and will share resources and provide assistance to carry out the common objectives.

Skilled Leadership. All collaborations need leaders who can cultivate the vision and provide the direction of the initiative.

All groups must feel a sense of selecting and contributing to the directions and leadership of the collaboration.

Process Orientation. The processes that drive each initiative are critical to its success. Therefore, each issue must be fully explored, and all parties must feel that they have participated in a fair process and can accept the final results and direction of the collaborative.

Cultural Diversity. The collaboration must not exclude any group and must be open to the richness and variety of its members and their ideas.

Membership-Driven Agenda. Groups join collaborations for varied reasons; their organizational needs must be considered in the overall mix of discussions. There must be a balance between the needs of each group and the direction of the collaborative.

Multiple Sectors. Truly successful collaboratives must include as many segments of the school and community as possible without straying from the direction of the collaborative. All advocacy groups must be represented or given an opportunity to express their concerns and recommendations. This is critical if the full community is to accept the outcomes and accomplishments of the collaborative.

Accountability. The evaluation of the collaborative processes and outcomes is vital to the overall creditability of the effort. Whether the evaluation is intended for the sponsors of the project or for the school or community members, an evaluation plan must be developed at the start and must be part of the process from beginning to end.

Designing and shaping a new community collaborative on paper is relatively easy. A crucial step is to ensure that the right mix of partners is in place from the start. A more difficult challenge is to sustain the effort—to keep the collaborative moving forward toward its mission. Of course, some barriers can be expected; astute leaders must be able to recognize these barriers, accept them as management challenges, and make the necessary adjustments. Several of the most common barriers identified by experienced organizations are:

- ◆ negative past experiences with collaborative efforts in the community
- ◆ difficult past or current relationships among possible member organizations
- ◆ competition and turf issues among potential members
- ◆ personality conflicts between representatives of these organizations
- ◆ racial or cultural polarization in the community
- ◆ differing community norms and values about cooperation

(The National Assembly, 1991).

Of course, a community collaboration may encounter many other barriers. Among these are two primary problems that impede growth and the full achievement of the collaborative objectives: the absence of a skilled leader, and the lack of a financial resource base or an aggressive plan to secure resources for sustained effort. Proactive strategies to keep community collaboration on track include such common-sense suggestions as:

- ◆ making clear communications a priority
- ◆ having clear roles for each partner
- ◆ getting to know each partner well, with attention to expectations and strengths
- ◆ making provisions to check progress and take corrective actions

When a collaboration gets bogged down in a tedious planning session, members who disagree with the direction of the discussion may simply avoid participating. Randall (1995) suggests guidelines for teams attempting to reach consensus: All participants must feel they have had sufficient opportunity to influence the decision; all group members should agree to support the decision even though it may not be everyone's first choice; everyone should commit to the decision as if it were the first choice of all group members and support that decision with his or her constituents.

IMPACT AND INFLUENCE OF COMMUNITY COLLABORATIONS

One of the true tests of a collaboration is whether it meets the objectives identified at the start. (Does a community effort that targets dropout prevention actually improve the graduation rate?) Each of the hundreds of community collaborations in America's schools and communities has its own anecdotal evidence of failures and successes; each has had an impact, one may hope more good than bad. Although reviewing the value and impact of every collaborative effort would be a vast undertaking, we can glean useful information from looking at a representative sample.

Two major programs come to mind as excellent candidates for gauging the merits of community collaborations: the full-service community-school movement initiated in many states (including Florida, Kentucky, and Washington), and the New Futures initiative launched in five cities in 1987 by the Annie E. Casey Foundation.

In a recent paper that explored whether full-service schools have had a positive impact, a notable researcher of current school reform efforts wrote, "I wish I could give an unequivocal 'yes' to this question. I have to report a strong 'maybe'" (Dryfoos, 1998). This honest response is not too far from what most other evaluation efforts have reported. However, Dryfoos did describe positive results in many different local programs, including improved reading and math performance, better attendance rates, and a decrease in suspension rates. Specifically, in Marshaltown, Iowa, the Caring Connection community school showed a reduction in the dropout rate and evidence of attracting former dropouts back into the school system.

The report *Building New Futures for At-Risk Youth* (Center for the Study of Social Policy, 1995) presents findings from the New Futures initiative, which built collaborative programs in five cities. Each of the selected cities (Dayton, Little Rock, Pittsburgh, Savannah, and Lawrence, later replaced by Bridgeport) was given $5 million to $12.5 million over five years to improve the life chances of disadvantaged youth. Communities were to form new local governance bodies, called collaboratives, made up of elected officials, businesspersons, public administrators from a wide range of agencies and organizations, parents and community representatives. Their charge was to devise new policies and practices for meeting the needs of at-risk youth while maintaining accountability for positive outcomes. The specific goals were to reduce the school dropout rate, improve students' academic performance, prevent teen pregnancies and births, and increase the number of youth who go on to a job or college.

Although the New Futures cities were unable to show definitive and quantitative improvements in any of the stated goals, they did succeed in taking some interim steps that may lead to improved outcomes for children. It is worth noting that each city:

◆ raised the awareness about the problems of at-risk youth

◆ started a new dialogue among leaders and community representatives who had not previously sat down together

◆ developed rich school-based information systems

◆ created a new body of knowledge around collaboration and local government

◆ demonstrated how to build substantive relationships between public and private sectors by combining leadership and money

◆ launched a new ongoing community-based decision-making structure

NEW AND FUTURE COMMUNITY COLLABORATIONS

New Futures and other collaboratives have taught us much about the values and pitfalls of these efforts. Such community collaborations will continue, chiefly because the educational issues and community concerns they address demand a concerted effort.

One illustration of the direction and the value of community collaborations is the 1998 Grantmaking Report of the DeWitt Wallace–Reader's Digest Fund (1999). Highlighting the previous year's work, the report lists 69 approved grants, totaling $29.8 million, that aimed to improve services to children and youth in elementary and secondary schools, in community-based organizations, and through collaborations between schools and communities. The categories of grants included new initiatives to reform the preparation of public school guidance counselors and to help public libraries develop more enriched after-school programs for school-age youth, support for programs to help schools assess the quality of instruction and improve teaching programs, and expansion of successful Fund programs that help communities develop effective systems of school-age care, reform vocational education instruction, and help young people learn about future careers.

EFFECTIVE PROGRAMS AND PRACTICES

Educational and community leaders who design and develop new community collaboratives can benefit from a look at other model programs and best practices. A few of these are described here.

Georgia Real Enterprises. In general, limited local resources and a lack of concentrated communities make it much more difficult to establish and sustain community collaboratives in rural America. For two decades, however, a nonprofit organization called Georgia Real Enterprises has provided leadership to many local communities in Georgia, nationwide, and internationally. The heart of the program creates experiential educational programs to foster entrepreneurial knowledge, skills, and enterprise development. Drawing on business leaders and other community resources, the program stresses the importance of linking education and economic development.

For additional information:

Paul F. DeLargy, Program Coordinator
Georgia Real Enterprises
1160 South Milledge Avenue, Suite 210
Athens, GA 30605
706-546-9061

The Alliance Schools Initiative. The Alliance Schools Initiative started in 1992 by The Texas Interfaith Education Alliance, and now includes more than 80 schools and communities throughout southwestern Texas. The Alliance school-community teams developed neighborhood efforts to counter gang violence, ease racial tensions, offer tutorial programs, and provide scholarships for college. These activities are provided within the regular school curriculum, in after-school centers, and in other extended-day programs.

For additional information:

Ernesto Cortez, Coordinator
Texas Interfaith Education Fund
1106 Clayton Lane, Suite 120W
Austin, TX 78723
512-459-6551

Pathways to Success. Two of the four strategic goals of the Worcester (Massachusetts) Public Schools are Ensure that all students achieve high standards and Create a community infrastructure that supports learning. Building on this approach to education, the school district and community established Pathways to Success, a program that earned the district's high school a nomination as a 21st Century High School by the U.S. Department of Education. Pathways to Success provides strong academic preparation along with a well-planned career education program featuring "articulation agreements" with community businesses and institutions of higher education.

For additional information:

Dennis Ferrante, Director
Worcester Public Schools
20 Irving Street
Worcester, MA 01609-2432
508-799-3195

Quad-County Tech Prep / School-to-Work. Another successful, national award-winning program is the Quad-County Tech Prep program, developed in response to the School-to-Work Opportunities Act of 1994. This school-to-work program is a comprehensive system that includes school-based learning, work-based learning, and related activities with business and industry in the form of articulation agreements in several technology areas. The program has reduced dropouts, improved attendance, and increased college placements.

For additional information:

Diana Rew, Coordinator
Quad-County Tech Prep/School-to-Work
Indian River Community College
3209 Virginia Avenue
Fort Pierce, FL 34981-5596
561-462-4886

CONCLUSION

Research and experience show that effective community collaborations can be powerful tools for addressing educational issues that affect the wider community—and what educational issue does not? Schools and communities embarking on collaborative efforts to address the school dropout problem can learn much from programs that have gone before them. The observations and guidelines presented in this chapter provide useful information on how to carry out a successful community collaboration.

REFERENCES

The Center for Mental Health in Schools. (1999, Winter). *Addressing Barriers to Learning: New Ways to Think, Better Ways to Link.* Los Angeles: Author.

The Center for the Study of Social Policy. (1995, May). *Building New Futures for At-Risk Youth: Findings from a Five-Year, Multi-Site Evaluation.* Washington, DC: Author.

The Children's Partnership. (1999, July). *Next Generation Special Report— Connecting Community Organizing with a Children's Agenda: The Front Lines.* Santa Monica, CA: Author.

DeWitt Wallace–Reader's Digest Fund. (1999). *1998 Grantmaking Report.* New York: Author.

Dryfoos, J. G. (1998, Feb.). *A Look at Community Schools in 1998.* Occasional Paper #2. New York: National Center for Schools and Communities.

Melaville, A. (1998). *Learning Together: A Look at 20 School-Community Initiatives.* Executive Summary. Flint, MI: Charles Stewart Mott Foundation.

The National Assembly of National Voluntary Health and Social Welfare Organizations. (1991). *The Community Collaboration Manual.* Washington, DC: Author.

Randall, M. C. (1995, Fall). Building Consensus: One Approach to Change. *NCRVE (National Center for Research in Vocational Education) CenterWork, 6,* 2.

Wright, J., Smink, J., and Duckenfield, M. (1999). *Students Serving Students.* Clemson, SC: National Dropout Prevention Center.

17

CAREER EDUCATION AND WORKFORCE READINESS

*Education and employment are two separate ends; neither
should be made subservient to the other.*

Richard J. Franke, President and CEO of
John Nuveen and Co., Inc. (1997)

INTRODUCTION

It may seem odd to open a discussion of education and employment with a blunt statement that they are two separate ends. Traditionally, to be sure, academic skills and vocational skills represented two different worlds. However, as we have seen, changes in the global economy have changed our national educational environment as well. Businesses demand high school graduates with more academic and career skills; parents call for better education to prepare their children for the twenty-first century; educators seek greater student achievement and more accountability. Almost all students will eventually enter the workforce, many embarking on multiple careers. The challenge— for leaders in education, business, and politics—is to give all students the best possible start. This means providing an appropriate blend of solid education competencies and career-based competencies. If we agree that neither education nor employment should be subservient to the other, we may also agree that both should serve our students, and serve them well.

THE NEED FOR WORKFORCE READINESS

Investments that yield high school graduates with a good basic education and career-based education are sound investments. Evidence comes from America's manufacturing workforce, where employees with less than a high school education earned less in constant dollars in 1995 than they did in 1959 (Carnevale, 1998). College graduates earned nearly one-third more (over $60,000), and that pay gap is continuing to accelerate. Urging educators to rethink how education and workforce training work together, Carnevale argued that K–12 classrooms are the front line in global economic competition and strongly recommended that communities develop a "one-stop career center" where students can receive career-based training, career education, job counseling, and placement assistance.

A recent review of the Moving Up Program operated by New York's Vocational Foundation, Inc., underscores the need for career education and supportive services tied to skill training and employment (Proscio and Elliott, 1999). This program provides career advisors who help students in at-risk situations find a job and keep it, doing "whatever it takes" to keep the young people at work and focused on additional training for advancement. The study outlined nine principles for successful job retention, including the principle that retention begins at intake. Advisors reported that when students who were determined to persevere despite their many disadvantages received guidance and assistance, they were able to stay in school and keep their jobs.

School reform initiatives during the past decade have focused on achieving excellence in several different academic areas. Only a few have been directed or clearly targeted to restructuring school counseling and guidance. However, the National Consortium of State Career Guidance Supervisors has led a "quiet reform," and in 1997 they issued *National Standards for School Counseling Programs* (Jensen, 1999). The publication outlines a three-part comprehensive effort that includes a guidance program for students; support programs for parents to advocate for the child's academic, career, and social development; and a structure for community collaboration to provide career information and workforce experiences.

NEW FORMS OF CAREER EDUCATION

Driven by the global economy, a new workplace is emerging (Clark, 1999). The traditional workplace operated under centralized control, advanced workers by seniority, and viewed workers as a cost. The emerging workplace encourages decentralized control, provides advancements by skill documentation, views workers as an investment and continues to build their educational skill levels. These developments, along with the current wave of school reform, suggest the need for a major rethinking of the design and delivery of career-oriented education and career guidance programs.

In response, the nation's high schools and community colleges are making a major transition from vocational education to school-to-work programs. The educational scene now features new forms of high school arrangements, innovative learning environments, new staffing patterns, and new alliances of organizations delivering curriculum instruction and support services. The new formats include tech prep, career academies, school-registered apprenticeships, student internships, career-oriented high schools, and school-based enterprises. Where traditional vocational education programs once targeted only a small number of young people, these new programs aim to integrate academic and career-based skills and to raise academic standards for all students. As a result, the new programs are also attracting the marginal students who once would have been assigned to the general track and were then more likely to drop out of school.

Retired AT&T executive John Metcalf, writing in the National Career Guidance News (1999), recommends that each student build a "portfolio of value." Metcalf suggests the portfolio as a tool for all students; demonstration projects monitored by the National Dropout Prevention Center indicate that the portfolio is particularly useful for students in at-risk environments. The portfolio has three essential components: academic skills, career skills, and self-investment skills. A brief description identifies academic and knowledge skills—including a solid foundation in reading and math—as paramount. The second component is evidence of marketable critical career skills, including records of experiences such as internships, apprenticeships, and job shadowing and a demonstrated capacity to continue learning. The third component is evidence of self-investment, including leadership skills and the ability to work and network with people. The National Dropout Prevention Center has developed a Student Passport (1996), similar to the portfolio of value, that includes provisions for students to illustrate other strengths and experiences such as community involvement, volunteerism, school clubs, and faith activities.

COMPREHENSIVE CAREER DEVELOPMENT PROGRAMS

The highly motivated student can probably survive in today's world of information overload, navigating the many different access points to gain a general awareness of educational paths, career patterns, or job opportunities. The average student, and particularly the student at risk, may find the effort of locating such information and then making the appropriate choices overwhelming. This student may benefit most from comprehensive career guidance and career development programs.

The National Center for Research in Vocational Education (NCRVE) has initiated a major project to help states design and implement a comprehensive career development program. NCRVE defines career development as a lifelong process that incorporates general education, occupational training, and work, as well as one's social and leisure life (Maddy-Bernstein and Matias, 1999). A comprehensive career development program addresses the needs of all students appropriately for their age group (elementary, middle, secondary, or post-secondary); the school guidance counselor is just part of a total community team that offers services to students. This comprehensive program guide should prove valuable to every guidance counselor and school-to-work coordinator in America, offering guidelines to help each school build and deliver a program specific to its local needs.

The curriculum-based recommendation most consistently offered in school reform demonstrations and other research studies is the need to integrate academic and vocational curriculum. Many local schools and organizations have addressed this issue, but NCRVE has given the task extremely high priority (Moore, 1999). NCRVE identified three approaches to integrating vocational and academic education in high schools: the academy model, the occupational clusters model, and the magnet school model. Each of these models provides greater opportunities for students who are still exploring their career options and may even hesitate to stay in school unless they have a specific career direction. Promising measures include providing more coherence and focus in the curriculum; encouraging more student-driven projects, rather than teacher-dominated classrooms; providing opportunities for more teacher collaborations; offering a range of curriculum options rather than just one general track; increasing the availability of career guidance and resources; supporting learning opportunities outside the classroom; and broadening a student's vision through expanded experiences outside the classroom.

SCHOOL-TO-WORK OPPORTUNITIES

Prompted by today's job market, with its requirement for advanced academic knowledge and workplace skills, the School-to-Work Opportunities Act of 1994 authorized the allocation of resources for initiatives that would help young people make a transition from school to work. The goal was to improve student learning, in-school retention, and transition to the workplace by improving the quality and relevance of education for all students through experiences that integrate school-based and work-based learning. The school-to-work (STW) initiatives do not mandate a single program model; rather, STW programs reflect a variety of settings and contexts. As a general rule, most STW initiatives

♦ are identified as a formal part of a secondary and/or post-secondary curriculum

♦ involve active participation of employers

♦ involve actual or simulated on-the job experiences

♦ result in formal or informal certification of skills

The national STW movement, though challenged by many national and local groups, has provided the vision for educators to work with the business community to offer relevant experiences to all students, including the "academically talented." Within the STW movement, students gain experiences in the real world in either of two types of programs: school-based learning and work-based learning. Each "delivery system" has been around for decades, but the STW movement has characterized each with specific definitions.

Work-based learning (WBL) differs from work experiences gained in regular youth jobs because WBL is intentionally structured to promote learning by linking work with school (Stasz and Stern, 1998). Work-based activities include such paid work experiences as youth apprenticeships and internships, tech prep programs, and job counseling and placement. Such programs are not really new; indeed, they resemble the cooperative education first introduced in the 1917 Smith-Hughes Act. However, work-based activities are currently a prominent part of local career-oriented programs, offering exciting opportunities to all students and greater benefits to the local businesses that participate. The potential benefits to students in at-risk situations are evident from the stated purposes of work-based learning:

+ enhancing students' motivation and academic achievement

+ increasing personal and social competence related to work in general

+ gaining a broad understanding of an occupation or industry

+ providing career exploration and planning

+ acquiring knowledge or skill related to employment in particular occupations or more generic work competencies

School-based learning (SBL) takes many different forms, often crafted by highly innovative teachers at all levels and in all curriculum areas within the school. School-based activities include career exploration, integrated academic and vocational curricula, and school-based enterprises. In school-based enterprises, high school students develop and operate their own businesses, gaining entrepreneurial experiences while still in the safety net of the school. Examples of proven SBL programs are Junior Achievement Clubs, traditional vocation-based clubs like Future Farmers of America, and other academically based clubs. More recent school-based learning opportunities include community service programs under the auspices of local service organizations like the Lions Club and service-learning projects spearheaded by the national Learn and Serve Program. The range of possible school-based programs tied to community-based service programs is virtually unlimited. Such programs provide valuable opportunities to learn and serve within the structure of a school and community collaboration.

BENEFITS FOR DROPOUT PREVENTION

In 1992, the U.S. Department of Education's Office of Vocational and Adult Education completed a three-year demonstration of exemplary dropout prevention projects across the nation, in different communities and in varied school models. The one theme that dominated the different projects was that they were customer-driven, asking "How can the school system fit the needs of our children?" rather than "How do we make these kids fit the system?" (Hamby, 1992).

The analysis of thirteen programs operated with success for three years in different environments revealed some amazing consistencies. In each case, the four main components of the curriculum included a strong emphasis on academics, a varied array of occupational studies, a varied but structured set of employability skills, and a set of life-coping skills designed to help students with the personal and social issues of daily living. The demonstration projects varied in their approach to instructional strategies, but they were consistent in regard to the types of strategies that worked best. The most successful strategies included computer-assisted instruction, multimodal technology, competency-based individualized instruction, mentoring, tutoring, on-the-job experiences, social activities, incentives, outside speakers and field trips, cooperative learning, applied academics, and curriculum integration (Hamby, 1992).

In other research, a comprehensive guidance program was found to have substantial benefits for student academic and personal development. Specific interventions such as individual and small group counseling and classroom guidance contributed directly to student success in the classroom (Jensen, 1999). Jensen reported another review, from a study in Missouri, which found that students with a more fully implemented guidance program were more likely to report that they earned higher grades and their schools had a more positive climate.

EFFECTIVE PROGRAMS AND PRACTICES

The Moving Up model, serving students between the ages of seventeen and twenty that few other programs were able to serve, yielded impressive results. Although nearly 90 percent of the people enrolled in the Moving Up program have neither a high school diploma nor a GED, the enrollees managed by VFI counselors showed a completion rate of 87 percent, and 78 percent are placed in jobs. This placement rate is well above the New York City rate of 39 percent. After one year, 62 percent were still employed, and 31 percent received salary increases within the same period (Proscio and Elliott, 1999).

Several of the thirteen model dropout prevention programs reviewed by Hamby (1992) reported a 90 percent retention and graduation rate. Contributing to these rates were exemplary educational support systems; best practices included counseling and guidance, student management and discipline, community collaboration, parental and family involvement, staff selection and development, flexible scheduling, summer school, small class size, transportation, and district commitment and support.

The STW initiatives have spawned several examples of effective teacher practices. Teachers have used new ways to assess students' knowledge and skills and to help prepare students to meet state and industry standards. Teachers and counselors have provided information about careers and school-to-work opportunities to parents and students, helping them make decisions based on students' interests and aptitude. Finally, teachers have structured classroom activities to integrate academic skills with skills required for successful employment.

Other STW effective practices are those that provide students with job-related experiences that will benefit them in the workplace—job shadowing, mentoring, internships, and opportunities for volunteering within the community. Several specific model programs deserve special mention.

Whole-School Reform. The William H. Turner Technical Arts High School, part of the Miami-Dade County School District, is a model for whole-school reform. The cornerstone of Turner Tech's instructional strategy is its integrated curriculum. Students and teachers are assigned to one of the school's seven academies (such as applied business, health, or agriscience). Students earn a high school diploma and an industry-recognized certification. In a program sponsored in part by the U.S. Department of Education and Business Week, Turner Tech achieved recognition as one of America's top ten New American High Schools.

For additional information:

Darrel P. Berteaux, Principal
William H. Turner Technical Arts High School
10151 Northwest 19 Avenue
Miami, FL 33147-1315
305-691-8324

The following career guidance programs are likewise exemplary. They have successfully demonstrated best practices in several areas, including career guidance and counseling; collaboration, articulation and communication efforts; and institutional support, leadership, and program evaluation.

For additional information:

Janice Jolly, School-to-Work Coordinator
Dorchester District Two Career Development
1101 Boone Hill Road
Summerville, SC 29477
843-832-7026

Colleen O'Reilly-Wiemerslage, Counseling Chair
La Crosse Central High School Career Center
1801 Losey Blvd. South
La Crosse, WI 54601
608-789-7900

Phyllis P. Nixon, Counselor
Rich South High School, Horizon Program
5000 Sauk Trail
Richton Park, IL 60471
708-747-5500

CONCLUSION

To meet the challenges of today's global economy, all students need a good education, sound guidance about career options, and appropriate preparation for the careers they choose.

Students who drop out of school lose these potential benefits and face a lifetime of limited opportunity. Recognizing that career education and workforce development are an investment in America's workforce, educators, business leaders, and policy makers have instituted a wide range of comprehensive guidance and career development programs. Model programs that follow best practices offer benefits for all students and are particularly effective with students in at-risk situations.

REFERENCES

Carnevale, A. P. (1998). *Education and Training for America's Future.* Washington, DC: The Manufacturing Institute.

Clark, D. (1999, April–May). What We Have Learned. *NAIEC (National Association for Industry-Education Cooperation) Newsletter, 35,* 1–2.

Franke, R. J. (1997). *Education: For Employment or for life.* Address given in Boston to company officers by Richard J. Franke, president and chief executive officer, John Nuveen and Co., Inc. Investment Bankers, Chicago, IL.

Hamby, J. V. (1992). *Vocational Education for the 21st Century.* Clemson, SC: National Dropout Prevention Center.

Jensen, L. (1999, Spring). Comprehensive Guidance Program—How Students, Parents, and the Community Benefit. *National Career Guidance News, 12,* 1, 3.

Maddy-Bernstein, C., and Matias, Z. B. (1999, Spring). Improving Career Guidance and Counseling Programs Through Professional Development. *NCRVE (National Center for Research in Vocational Education) CenterWork, 10,* 2–3.

Metcalf, J. P. (1999, Spring). Build a Value Portfolio: To Prepare for a Life of Success. *National Career Guidance News, 12,* 18–19.

Moore, D. (1999, Spring). Integrating Academic and Vocational Curriculum. *NCRVE (National Center for Research in Vocational Education) CenterWork, 10,* 1, 4.

National Dropout Prevention Center. (1996). *Service Learning Passport for Life.* (Booklet). Clemson, SC: Author.

Proscio, T., and Elliott, M. (1999). *Getting in, Staying on, Moving up: A Practitioner's Approach to Employment Retention.* New York: Public/Private Ventures.

Stasz, C., and Stern, D. (1998, Dec.). Work-Based Learning for Students in High Schools and Community Colleges. *NCRVE (National Center for Research in Vocational Education) CenterPoint, 1.*

18

VIOLENCE PREVENTION AND CONFLICT RESOLUTION

If a student has disagreements or arguments with teachers or other
students, does someone in the school intervene to mediate? . . .
A school that answers sometimes, maybe, or no has room for an
individualized approach to dropout prevention.

(Dynarski and Gleason, 1999)

INTRODUCTION

This chapter addresses the issues of violence and conflict as
factors that contribute to the school dropout problem. We list
and discuss the elements of a comprehensive program for conflict resolution and violence prevention, describe the impact and
benefits of effective models, and provide information about established programs that can serve as valuable resources for
schools and communities that seek to make their schools safe
places where all students can achieve.

THE NEED FOR VIOLENCE PREVENTION PROGRAMS

Violence has come to pervade our society. It is visible on our
televisions, in our movies, in our workplace, on tape, on CD's,
in our video games, and in sports. The violence that pervades

217

our society also pervades the public school system. According to the National Center for Education Statistics (NCES), the following instances of violence were reported in our nation's public schools during 1996–97:

♦ about 4,000 incidents of rape or other types of sexual battery

♦ about 11,000 incidents of physical attacks or fights in which weapons were used

♦ about 7,000 robberies

♦ about 190,000 fights or physical attacks not involving weapons

♦ about 115,000 thefts

♦ about 98,000 incidents of vandalism

(NCES, 1997).

Students report that they perceive more violence than teachers do; 77 percent of teachers (grades three to twelve) feel very safe in or around school, but only 50 percent of students do (Educational Development Center, 1996). Students who don't feel safe at school are likely to stay away; approximately 160,000 students miss classes each school day due to fear of physical harm (Educational Development Center, 1996). Students who do not come to school for fear of violence, students who are suspended for violent acts, and students whose classes are disrupted by violence in the school cannot learn; as a result, they often drop out (Duttweiler, 1994).

One of the most significant findings to emerge from research on dropouts is that early identification of potential dropouts is vital for effective prevention (Duttweiler and Smink, 1997). Social and task-related behavioral problems that develop into school adjustment problems can and must be identified in the lower elementary grades. There is a significant relationship between behavior in early grades and later success in school. A longitudinal study of inner-city school children found that behavior ratings in kindergarten through third grade—such as classroom disturbances, disrespect, defiance, and irrelevant responsiveness—were related to misconduct in the classroom at ages fourteen and fifteen and to school disciplinary measures. In addition, antisocial and aggressive behavior in the early grades is a strong predictor of dropping out in high school, perhaps because students who do not behave responsibly receive less one-to-one instruction from teachers and are often rejected by peers (Duttweiler and Smink, 1997).

One aspect of the relationship between violence and dropouts is the school's response to student misbehavior. The Metropolitan Life teacher survey of 1993 found that 81 percent of schools suspended students involved in violent acts. Although the strategies of suspension and expulsion are meant to give students a firm warning that their behavior will not be tolerated, these strategies can also send a harsh message of rejection that seems to "push" the student out of school, increasing the chance of eventual school dropout (Rogers, 1994).

Research suggests that some student behavioral problems arise from inappropriate curricular placement, irrelevant academic instruction, and/or inconsistent classroom management within a climate fraught with rigid behavioral demands and insensitivity to student diversity (Gable et al., 1998). We also know that children who come from violent homes are at greater risk. Reporting on research into situations that put youth at risk, Wells cited a variety of factors relating to conflict at school and at home. These included conflict between home and school culture, ineffective discipline system, negative school climate, retention and suspension, attendance or truancy, behavior and discipline problems, pregnancy, drug abuse, poor peer relationships, high incidences of criminal activities, dysfunctional home life, and child abuse or ineffective parenting (Wells, 1990).

When these problems persist, with the conflict either unresolved or mismanaged, students are at risk of eventually dropping out of school. In a 1990 NELS:88 study conducted by the National Center for Education Statistics, the reasons students gave for leaving school suggested that such conflict was a factor; 34 percent could not get along with teachers and 25 percent did not feel they belonged at school (U.S. Dept. of Education, 1990).

The need for school-based violence prevention is evident, not only for students whose situations put them at risk of dropping out, but for all students. To achieve schools where all students are safe, educators must know what to look for, know what to do, and take action—that is, they must implement a comprehensive violence prevention plan. Truly effective violence prevention means providing daily experiences—embedded in the school curriculum—that will engender and enhance in all students the positive social attitudes and effective interpersonal skills that are necessary for group living (Hamby, 1999).

VIOLENCE PREVENTION AND CONFLICT RESOLUTION

Conflict is a part of daily life in our culture. Only too often, conflict is seen as a problem that needs to be eliminated or removed, rather than a situation that can be worked through and used constructively. Faced with problems, young people often resort to confrontation (lashing out) or avoidance (suppressing anger and fear). These responses, though natural, are inappropriate and can be harmful in the long run (Rogers, 1994).

Young people must learn that disagreements are inevitable and that eliminating conflict is not a realistic goal. They need to learn how to deescalate conflict, manage it, and resolve it. All schools, at all grade levels, should teach violence prevention (VP) and conflict resolution (CR). The school's plan should incorporate prevention and intervention strategies. The process should begin with community support and needs assessment; the entire school organization, with all stakeholders, must be involved and committed.

The most significant component of the comprehensive or "whole school" approach to violence prevention is a research-based conflict resolution program. The first step is to train teachers, counselors, staff, and administrators in CR and mediation skills. Once trained, they can practice those techniques in their classrooms, on the playground, in hallways, gyms, offices, lunchrooms—throughout the whole environment of school. When CR and mediation skills are used openly and often, they become a part of the school's climate. Eventually, students begin to imitate their adult role models. As the behavior becomes a habit, they carry the skills into other arenas as well.

Conflict resolution skills begin with simple measures—active listening, effective communication without blaming or accusing, brainstorming nonviolent solutions—and extend to diversity awareness and empathy for the feelings of others. Conflict resolution seeks a solution that is satisfactory to both parties. The focus is taken away from the problem and the person and placed squarely on the solution. This strategy works well after anger has been diffused.

Another key element of a comprehensive violence prevention program is peer mediation. Students are trained in conflict resolution and mediation skills. When a mediation program is in place, students can ask peer mediators to act as neutral third parties who help resolve conflicts. Even children in elementary grades can learn how to be mediators and can successfully guide their peers through a conflict.

Conflict resolution and mediation are effective dropout prevention strategies. In a recent review of more than twenty dropout prevention programs, researchers introduced their conclusion with a question (presented at the beginning of the chapter): "If a student has disagreements or arguments with teachers or other students, does someone in the school intervene to mediate?... A school that answers sometimes, maybe, or no has room for an individualized approach to dropout prevention" (Dynarski and Gleason, 1999).

COMPONENTS OF THE STRATEGY

Programs and curricula on conflict resolution are abundant. Approximately 78 percent of public schools have adopted some form of violence prevention, anger management, or conflict resolution curriculum as part of their instructional program (U.S. Department of Education and Justice, 1998), but all too often these are delivered in piecemeal fashion by a social worker or school counselor. They generally lack an empirical evaluation of program quality and effectiveness. It is not enough merely to implement a conflict resolution program; the program must be backed with empirical evidence of its effectiveness (Wahler, Fetsch, and Silliman, 1997).

Schools that implement a comprehensive program for violence prevention and conflict resolution must act on many fronts in a coordinated effort involving a number of key elements:

- shift culture to cooperative thinking about techniques that foster conflict resolution
- meet the basic needs of students through support agencies
- actively engage adults and stakeholders
- provide a school resource officer from the local police force
- initiate a no-bullying program
- implement a conflict resolution curriculum
- teach anger management techniques
- provide peer mediation
- eliminate or control gangs
- have a crisis management plan

School personnel must look for the early warning signs of aggression and violence, then devise interventions that halt its growth. Early intervention programs can teach students how to be aware of and overcome the violence that surrounds and influences them. Children of preschool and kindergarten age can learn the conflict resolution skills of empathy, impulse control and anger management. Such programs, implemented in preschool and/or elementary school, teach nonviolent behavior, a life skill that will continue to develop in the later years of adolescence and adulthood (Duttweiler, 1995).

A conflict resolution program can be introduced at the pre-K level, year after year, and rise with those students through the school system until children of all ages, at all grade levels, are resolving their conflicts constructively. The skills of conflict resolution spread through the school district and spill over into home and family life. Eventually, the entire community reaps the benefits.

EVIDENCE OF IMPACT

The expected benefits of CR, mediation, and VP include but are not limited to higher-quality decision making, better coping skills and stress reduction skills, increased motivation; a greater sense of caring, commitment, and cohesiveness, and an increase in problem-solving skills (Johnson and Johnson, 1995). Much of the data regarding CR/VP programs are qualitative. Often students report that they feel better. Principals report the decline of office referrals and teachers often report less occurrence of conflicts.

The Committee for Children, which sponsors the Second Step Program, conducted an independent assessment of their curriculum. Twelve schools were paired to reflect similar make-ups. Random assignment placed one school in the control group and one in the experimental group. Second- and third-grade classes (four from each school), with parental consent, were targeted for participation. The Second Step curriculum was taught to teachers, who in turn taught it to students. The results showed that the Second Step curriculum led to moderate decreases in aggression and increases in neutral and pro-social behavior in school. In a North Carolina middle school, in a single school year, in-school suspension decreased 42 percent and out-of-school suspension was down 97 percent. Without the Second Step curriculum, student behavior worsened, becoming more physically and verbally aggressive over the school year (Committee for Children, 1997).

An evaluation of the program at Clark County School District of Las Vegas, Nevada, found that:

♦ peer mediators successfully resolved 86 percent of the conflicts they mediated

♦ fewer physical fights occurred on school grounds

♦ mediators had an increase in self-esteem

(Talley, 1997).

According to the Office of Juvenile Justice, the authors of a conflict resolution education fact sheet stated that by teaching young people how to manage conflict, conflict resolution education can reduce juvenile violence in juvenile facilities, schools, and communities, while providing lifelong decision-making skills (LeBoeuf and Delany-Shabazz, 1999).

The Office of Educational Research (OER) reported that reform models for low-performing schools must provide explicit

and consistent instruction in how to get along with others, resolve conflicts peacefully, and develop other life skills (Talley,
1999).

EFFECTIVE PROGRAMS AND PRACTICES

Programs abound, and many schools across the nation participate. These programs are highly successful, are research-
based, and provide excellent training. Contact program
coordinators for information about participating schools across
the nation.

The Community Board Program of San Francisco, California. This
resource and training organization has been active in the cause since
1976. The curriculum they developed is the model for all other curricula on the market today. They are proponents of the "whole school"
approach.

For additional information:

The Community Board Program
1540 Market Street, Suite 490
San Francisco, CA 94102
415- 552-1250
Fax 415-626-0595
cmbrds@conflictnet.org

Center for the Prevention of School Violence. Students Against Violence Everywhere (S.A.V.E.) is a student involvement strategy which
promotes student participation in efforts which are designed to prevent school and community violence. The message of nonviolence
dominates S.A.V.E.'s approach. Organized through the establishment
of student chapters which typically are located in schools. The membership includes students from all grade levels. Generally, middle and
high school chapters operate as extra-curricular activities while S.A.V.E.
is typically infused into ongoing school safety efforts at the elementary
level. Local chapters register with the Center for the Prevention of
School Violence which serves as S.A.V.E.'s national clearinghouse.

For additional information:

Joanne McDaniel, Interim Director
Center for the Prevention of School Violence
313 Chapanoke Road, Suite 140
Raleigh, NC 27603

800-299-6054 or 919-773-2846
Fax: 919-773-2904
Joanne_mcdaniel@ncsu.edu
http://www.nationalsave.org

Second Step Program. The Committee for Children promotes the Second Step Program, a school-based social skills curriculum for preschool through junior high that teaches children to change the attitudes and behaviors that contribute to violence. The curriculum teaches social skills to reduce impulsive and aggressive behavior in children and increase their level of social competence. Second Step school and family components are important parts of a comprehensive plan to reduce violence. Second Step teaches the same three skill units at each grade level: empathy, impulse control, and anger management.

For additional information:

Committee for Children
2203 Airport Way South, Suite 500
Seattle, WA 98134
800-634-4449
Fax: 206-343-1445
info@cfchildren.org
http://www.cfchildren.org/violence.htm

CONCLUSION

Violence and conflict are not the only reasons students drop out of school, but clearly they contribute to behavior problems, truancy, retention in grade, and other factors that place students at risk. Every school can reap the benefits of a comprehensive, research-based program for conflict resolution and violence prevention.

REFERENCES

Committee for Children. (1997). Executive Summary of Second Step Curriculum. Seattle, WA

Duttweiler, P. C. (1995). *Effective Strategies for Educating Students in At-Risk Situations.* Clemson, SC: National Dropout Prevention Center.

Duttweiler, P. C. (1994). *Is School Reform Serving the At-Risk Population?* The National Dropout Prevention Center: Journal of At-Risk Issues, Vol. 1, No. 2.

Duttweiler, P. C., and Smink, J. (1997). Critical Strategies for Effective Dropout Prevention. *School Safety Journal.* 4–9.

Dynarski, M., and Gleason, P. (1999). *How Can We Help? Lessons from Federal Dropout Prevention Programs.* Princeton, NJ: Mathematica Policy Research, Inc.

Educational Development Center, Inc. (1996, May). *Schools and Violence.* National Network of Violence Prevention Practitioners Fact Sheet, Vol. 1, No. 3. Washington DC.

Gable, P. S., Quinn, M., Rutherford, R. B., Jr., Howell, K., and Hoffman, C. (1998). *Addressing Student Problem Behavior—Part II: Conducting a Functional Assessment.* Washington, DC: Center for Effective Collaboration and Practice.

Hamby, J. V. (1999). *Developing a Comprehensive Violence Prevention Plan: A Practical Guide.* Clemson SC: National Dropout Prevention Center.

Johnson, D.W., and Johnson, R. T. (1995). *Teaching Students to Be Peacemakers* (3rd edition). Edina, MN: Interaction Book Company.

LeBoeuf, D., and Delany-Shabazz, R. V. (1997). *Conflict Resolution.* U.S. Department of Justice, Office of Juvenile Justice: Fact Sheet #55.

National Center for Education Statistics (NCES). (1996-97). *Violence and Discipline Problems in U.S. Public Schools.* U.S. Department of Education.

Rogers, M. (1994). *Resolving Conflict Through Peer Mediation.* National Dropout Prevention Center: Solutions and Strategies, No. 9.

Talley, S. (1999). *What Does It Take to Reform a Low-Performing School?* Office of Educational Research: National Institute on the Education of At-Risk Students. Baltimore, MD.

U.S. Department of Education. (1990). *National Education Longitudinal Study of 1988—First Followup Study.* National Center for Education Statistics.

U.S. Departments of Education and Justice. (1998). *Annual Report on School Safety.* NCES 98-251/NCJ 172215. Washington, DC: Author.

Wahler, J. J., Fetsch, R. J., and Silliman, B. (1997). *Research-Based, Empirically Effective Violence Prevention Curricula: A Review of Resources.* The Character Education Partnership.

Wells, S.E. (1990). *At-Risk Youth: Identification, Programs, and Recommendations.* Englewood, CO: Teacher Idea Press.

PART VII

PERSPECTIVES AND PRESCRIPTIONS

We have delved deeply into America's school dropout problem and the strategies that offer the greatest potential for addressing that problem. In the final chapters of this book, we step back for a wider perspective and then return to the challenge at hand. Countries around the world face the issue of educating children to their fullest potential. No school or community is immune from the impact of this problem. We call upon all who share our concern to become part of the solution.

19

THE GLOBAL PERSPECTIVE

In a competitive economy dominated by technology and advanced skill and competencies, high school completion may be the minimum level of education needed to have an opportunity to compete in the labour market, obtain an entry-level job, and to secure a basic standard of living. Much more education and training is required for decent jobs, incomes and life-chances. Anything less than the minimum may restrict youth to long hours, tedious jobs with little opportunity for advancement and a low quality of life.

Human Resources Development Canada
(from "High School May Not Be Enough")

INTRODUCTION

The school dropout problem is not uniquely American. Data indicate that this is a global problem with dramatic consequences. In the twenty-first century, as nations move from brawn-based to brain-based economies, education will be the key to economic success. Developed nations, with their increasingly aging populations, will be more dependent on a diminishing workforce that must be well educated and technologically prepared. Emerging nations, with their dependence on manual labor, will suffer as their workers are initially displaced and ultimately replaced by machines. The transition from an agrarian through an industrial to an intellectual economy will have enormous ramifications.

Emerging nations must move quickly to educate their populations, but most are faced with other severe problems that affect their willingness or ability to properly fund their educational programs. The Asian financial crisis and the collapse of communism slashed state funding in Eastern Europe and Central Asia. Civil wars in many parts of Africa and the destruction caused by AIDS in sub-Saharan Africa all have had a major impact on education. Some nations, for religious reasons, educate boys but not girls. Some countries are so poor that they can educate children only to the fourth or the sixth grade. Some students have their education interrupted by war or civil strife; others are pulled from school to help support their family.

This chapter will present an overview of the school dropout problem throughout the world, noting the differences by region and country and the similarities shared across borders and continents.

EUROPE

The mature economic systems of the United States, Europe, and Canada face different challenges than those in developing nations. Most developed nations offer full opportunities for attendance in primary and secondary schools up to the age of sixteen. Countries with strong vocational or apprentice programs often have a lower dropout rate than those without.

Many European nations recognize the need to revise curricula to meet the demands of today's workplace. At the same time, they must integrate growing immigrant populations into their existing school systems and address the functional illiteracy of an "educated" populace. From 10 to 30 percent of the population has difficulty with basic reading, writing, and numbering skills. This group of "hard core" underachievers fails basic skills testing in primary school, falls behind, and may drop out in secondary school. A 1999 study by the Organization of Economic Development and Cooperation (OEDC) shows that the proportion of the population that is neither in school nor in the workforce ranges from 4.3 percent in Denmark to 19.4 percent in the United Kingdom. Some schools in Europe have begun to deal with incidents of school violence and shootings. In Eastern Europe, the collapse of communism has created additional educational problems—freezing classrooms, inadequate books and supplies, and teachers waiting up to ten months for their paychecks.

European nations, like the United States, define dropouts in different ways. The chart below illustrates two different ways of determining the dropouts in Europe. The reader will notice discrepancies in the numbers reported.

Nation	Percentage Secondary School Completion Rate[1]	Dropout Statistics[2]
Austria	82	
Bulgaria	N.D.[3]	4 percent of children ages 7–16 do not attend school.
Cyprus	N.D.	No dropouts before the age of 15.
		3 percent drop out at age 15.
Czech Republic	92	No one.
Denmark	74	No one.
Finland	83	About 100 children a year.
France	74	N.D.
Germany	86	10 percent leave every year despite "compulsory education and prosecution of parents."
Hungary	80	6 percent dropout rate among native population. 30–40 percent among ethnic minorities.
Iceland	N.D.	Less than 1 percent.
Latvia	N.D.	Some children do not attend school until age 9 or 10. Dropout rate is increasing.
Netherlands	72	N.D.
Norway	N.D.	"The number of dropout is minimal."
Poland	88	2 percent in the rural areas.
Portugal	32	In 1991–92, there was a 3 percent dropout rate.

Russian Federation	N.D.	23.7 million people have an incomplete secondary school education, 4.7 million are 15–17 years old. (19.8 percent dropout rate)
Spain	50	100 percent success rate at age 14, 93.8 percent at age 15, 80.3 percent at age 16.
Sweden	87	No one. Children who do not succeed in regular program (5 percent) are sent to different educational programs.
Switzerland	87	2 percent at age 15.
Turkey	23	40 percent dropout rate in 1994-1995.
United Kingdom	87	"At present just under a third of young people drop out or fail to achieve their learning goal in full-time education."[4]

[1] Percentage of population (1996) ages 25–34 that has completed secondary school.

[2]2. Data for this chart were obtained from a variety of sources, including The Centre for Europe's Children (sponsored by a partnership with Glasgow University), Children 1st, Council of Europe, Scottish Office, UNICEF, the World Bank, the Organization for Economic Cooperation and Development, the United Nations High Commissioner for Human Rights.

[3] N.D. = No data available.

[4] David Blunkett, Secretary of State for Education and Employment, United Kingdom, "New Start in the North East," March 2000.

CANADA

Human Resources Development Canada, a division of Human Resources and Labour Canada, conducted a random sample survey of 18,000 eighteen- to twenty-year-old school leavers (dropouts) in June 1991. The impetus was "growing recognition that [high unemployment levels, the number of female lone parents and children in poverty, illiteracy, the decline in after-tax family income, reduced productivity growth, increased international competition for markets, and the effectiveness of our educational institutions] are closely interrelated. Success in the international marketplace is a function of economic productivity and technological innovation, which in turn results from the knowledge, skills and determination of a well-educated and well-paid labour force engaged in challenging and satisfying work." Forty percent of new Canadian jobs created between 1989 and 2000 will require more than sixteen years of education and training. "Most new jobs in the future will require at least high school graduation or the equivalent, and few will require less than a high school diploma" (Human Resources Development Canada, 1995).

The report found that almost 40 percent of leavers were sixteen or younger when they left school; 32 percent had completed grade nine or less. Leavers were more likely than graduates to come from single-parent or no-parent families or from families who did not think that high school completion was very important. Most came from lower socioeconomic backgrounds. The national high school non-completion rate in 1991 was in the 18–21 percent range. The report concluded, "The economic and social costs to individual Canadians and to Canadian society are too high to become complacent about a 20 percent non-completion rate" (Human Resources Development Canada, 1995).

Most Canadian school leavers were more likely than graduates to report that they

- ♦ did not enjoy school
- ♦ were dissatisfied with their courses
- ♦ disliked school rules
- ♦ had problems with teachers
- ♦ did not participate in co- and extra-curricular activities
- ♦ participated less in class than other students
- ♦ skipped classes

However the majority of dropouts were doing well in school; 37 percent of them had mainly A's and B's, while another 40 percent had C averages. Almost 50 percent, who said they left school because of personal or family-related reasons, had A or B averages (Human Resources Development Canada, 1995).

DEVELOPING NATIONS

In 1990, in Jompien, Thailand, representatives of the world's nations recognized the impact of the dropout problem and pledged education for all by the year 2000. Despite that pledge, 113 million children, two-thirds of them female, remain out of school. In April 2000, at a conference in Dakar, Senegal, delegates from 181countries reaffirmed that "Education is a fundamental human right" (Article 26 of the Declaration of Human Rights) and one of the keys to peace and economic development. Information presented at the conference included the following statistics (Education Forum, 2000):

♦ Sub-Saharan Africa spent three times as much on debt repayments as on education.

♦ India spends twice as much on arms as on education.

♦ Since 1990, government budgets to aid education have been cut by nearly 25 percent. More schools have introduced fees for books.

♦ More adults (an estimated 875 million) are illiterate today than ten years ago. The percentage of literate adults increased from 63 percent in 1970 to 80 percent in 2000; their number more than doubled, from 1.5 billion in 1970 to 3.4 billion today. The world literacy rate is projected to increase to 83 percent in 2010; this would leave one out of every six adults illiterate. Women account for around 64 percent of the world's illiterate adults. Almost 40 percent of African adults cannot read or write. In certain countries in western Africa, female illiteracy reaches 80 percent.

♦ The collapse of communism slashed public spending for education in Eastern Europe and Central Asia.

♦ AIDS in Zambia in 1999 killed more teachers than the number that graduated from all teacher colleges in that year.

♦ Every day, a teacher in Cote d'Ivoire dies of AIDS. In Uganda, 11 percent of children under 15 have been orphaned through AIDS. More than 80 percent of the world's AIDS deaths have occurred in Africa. Today, over 34 million adults and children in the world are living with HIV infection—24 million in Africa alone. Half of the 16,000 new infections each day are among people between 15 and 24 years old.

♦ In many countries in Africa, schools lack water. There are few desks; textbooks are shared. Many schools have few or no toilet facilities. Teachers are ill-equipped and poorly trained; many take pride in having students repeat work, which they erroneously believe serves as evidence of their commitment to high standards. The average class size is 37 pupils (in Mali): in Chad, as many as 70.

♦ In Zambia, less than 60 percent of all eligible pupils had a place in school; most of those in school dropped out. Of the 232,000 pupils who enter primary school every year, 50,000 drop out before grade seven and 120,000 drop out at grade seven. Only 22,000 (9.48 percent) earn a grade twelve certificate. Three quarters of the classrooms have a blackboard and chalk; only two-thirds of the children have a pencil.

♦ The E-9 (the world's nine high-population countries, representing half the world's population—Bangladesh, Brazil, China, Egypt, India, Indonesia, Mexico, Nigeria, and Pakistan) continue to account for more than three-quarters of the world's illiterate population.

♦ Primary school enrollment has increased since 1950 by a factor of more than ten in Africa, more than five in Latin America and the Caribbean, and more than four in Asia.

♦ In South Asia, a girl will spend an average of six years in school—three years less than a boy will. In rural areas, a girl is three times more likely than a boy to drop out.

ARAB NATIONS

The Arab nations have the world's highest percentage of children under fifteen. One out of four—a total of 10 million children—is out of school. The total number of adult illiterates in Arab nations is 6.7 million; the percentages range from a low of 5.5 percent in Lebanon to a high of 53 percent in Mauritania. The female literacy rate is 50 percent, while the male rate is 70 percent. This is compounded by the fact that only 33 percent of girls are in school, compared to 73 percent of boys. Most Arab countries do not consider early childhood education a government responsibility. The average percentage of countries having pre-K and kindergarten for the region is less than 15 percent (BBC News, 2000).

LATIN AMERICA AND THE CARIBBEAN

While a falling birth rate and educational reforms have had a positive effect on the Latin American economy, one out of three people in the region still lives in extreme poverty. Early childhood and other innovative programs are found mainly in middle-class urban areas. Many rural and farm communities suffer from a lack of funding and a lack of transportation to and from school. About 80 percent of three- to five-year-olds in the Caribbean attend preschool. Primary school enrollment rose from 74.3 million in 1990 to 86.8 million in 1999. By 1999, 97 percent of seven- to fourteen-year-olds were in school. Brazil achieves a 90 percent literacy rate. Mexico is approaching full primary school enrollment and 100 percent literacy (Education Forum, 2000).

However, there are widespread disparities. The literacy rate for the region as a whole is 88 percent; the range extends from 98 percent in Uruguay to 21 percent in Honduras. In Haiti and Bolivia, more than 30 percent of children are not in school. The United Nations Children's Fund (UNICEF) reports that in Haiti, only one out of four children has a seat, more than two-thirds never complete primary school, and the illiteracy rate is 55 percent—the highest in the region.

ASIA

The dropout problem in Japan is far less severe than in the United States. Like many industrialized countries, Japan is facing a rapidly aging population; indeed, Japan is graying faster than any other industrialized nation. People 65 and older will, by 2010, account for 17.2 percent of the nation's population; by 2020, that figure will rise to 26.9 percent. (The comparable figures for the United States are 12.7 percent and 16 to 17 percent, respectively.) This older population will be far more dependent on a highly trained, educated workforce. According to an article in the *New York Times*, Japan currently only requires students to complete junior high school. "Among the 10 million students of junior and senior high school age in Japan, 120,000 (1 percent) dropped out last year, a 20 percent increase from two years earlier." The author concludes that "freewheeling sex, heavy drinking and delinquency" caused the increase (French, 2000, p. A1).

The situation in South Asia is also grim. In Bhutan, poverty keeps one of four children out of school and only 56 percent of adults are literate. According to the Asian Development Bank, Cambodia's lack of an educated skilled workforce is hampering its development efforts. The Bank stated that the government did not spend enough on education and health care. "The government share of total educational expenditures is about 25 percent. As a result, about 40 percent of the population have never attended school, 32 percent are illiterate and less than one percent has had any training beyond high school," according to the Asian Development Outlook 2000 Report (Reuters, April 27, 2000).

According to *Parade Magazine* (February 27, 2000, p. 15), "At least 200 million adults in China are unable to read. Many dropped out of school because of poverty or because their parents saw work as more important than education."

Some nations have demonstrated that progress in this arena is possible. Despite modest national income and a seventeen-year-long war, Sri Lanka has kept its schools open and raised its overall literacy rate to nearly 92 percent; nearly 90 percent of its women are literate. Bangladesh doubled its educational budget and expanded its primary school enrollment and literacy. In India, enrollment in primary school stands at 71 percent (BBC News, 2000).

SOUTHWEST ASIA

Because of war, Afghanistan educates only 4–5 percent of its primary-aged children; the percentage for secondary school and higher education is even lower. In 1996, Islamic law emphasized religious education at the expense of other subjects. In Afghanistan, the law bans women from the workplace and girls from school. In Kabul and other major cities, girls' schools have been closed; women teachers, like other female workers, have been sent home.

The United Nations Children's Fund (UNICEF), whose mission is to protect the world's children, has published the following statistics:

- More than 130 million children of primary school age in developing countries, including 73 million girls, are growing up without access to basic education. That means that about 40 percent of children of elementary school age either never enter school or drop out before attaining even a basic education. Millions of others attend substandard schools where little learning takes place.

- At the end of 1999, an estimated 855 million people (more than one-sixth of the world's population) were functionally illiterate. Two-thirds of the world's illiterate are women who are unable to read a book or sign their names.

- The higher the number of years attending school, the lower the death rate of infants and mothers in childbirth.

- Achieving 100 percent attendance in school for all children would require the expenditure of an additional $7 billion per year over the next ten years—"less than is annually spent on cosmetics in the United States or on ice cream in Europe."

- A developing nation that lacks an educated workforce is less attractive to the global business community than a nation that has maximized its human resources through education.

- The number of people living in poverty has grown to more than 1.2 billion—one out of five— including more than 600 million children.

♦ According to estimates by the International Labor Organization (ILO), workers in developing countries include some 250 million children between the ages of five and fourteen.

♦ In parts of Latin America, the poorest 20 percent of people share less than 3 percent of national income.

♦ "A quality education has the power to transform societies in a single generation." (UNICEF, State of the World's Children, 1999).

CONCLUSION

Developed industrialized nations usually have the resources, educational infrastructure, and alignment of educational, business, and political structures to address the problem of school dropouts. Developing nations usually do not. Too often, a country's leaders sacrifice future national growth by under-funding education while pouring money into developing their military might.

Today's uneducated children become tomorrow's illiterate adults. In the globally competitive marketplace of the twenty-first century, education is an essential resource. Its potential benefits extend beyond the individual, the family, the local community, and transcend state and national boundaries. The world cannot afford to deny its children this fundamental human right.

REFERENCES

Asian Development Outlook 2000 Report: Cambodia Development Hurt by Low Education. Reuters, April 27, 2000.

BBC News, April 26, 2000 online; www.news.bbc.couk/hi/english/world/from-our-own-correspondent/newsid-726000/726727.stm

Blunkett, David. (2000, March). "New Start in the North East."

Education at a Glance - OECD Indicators. (1998).

Education Forum. (2000). Newsletter of the World Education Forum in Dakar.

French, Howard W. (2000). Dropouts' Career in Japan: Painting the Town. *New York Times*, March 5, 2000, p. A1.

Human Resources Development Canada. (1995). "High School May Not Be Enough."

Parade Magazine, February 27, 2000, p. 15.

United Nations Children's Emergency Fund (UNICEF). (1999). State of the World's Children.

20

A PRESCRIPTION FOR AMERICA

It was the best of times; it was the worst of times.

Charles Dickens, *A Tale of Two Cities*

INTRODUCTION

Schools hold within their walls tomorrow's adults. If those adults are to be responsible citizens, they must have a knowledge of history and government. If they are to cherish the world's cultural heritage, they must understand and appreciate art, music, and literature. If they are to contribute to society in a positive way, they must learn to resolve conflict peaceably. If they are to be productive workers, they must master a broad array of academic and technical skills. A child who is to thrive in the world tomorrow must thrive in school today.

No one can project a complete picture of the future, but its outlines show a clear correlation between education and opportunity. As a society, we cannot afford to let a significant number of students drop out of school. How can America prosper if we waste our human resources? Our schools must graduate young people who are ready for jobs—including jobs that haven't been invented yet, and careers in companies manufacturing products that haven't been imagined yet. Although training workers is not the sole function of schools, they do bear responsibility for ensuring that everyone is prepared for the workforce.

241

Maintaining global competitiveness may well require raising educational standards. However, simply raising standards is futile unless we provide the means for all students to reach them. Economists at Cornell University and the University of Michigan found that increasing the number of course credits required for graduation would increase the dropout rate between 3 percent and 7 percent a year. This would mean that an additional 26,000 to 65,000 students would drop out annually (*Teacher Magazine*, May 2000). The potential results for those students include poorer job prospects and lower lifetime earnings (Olson, 2000, p. 6).

Conversely, lowering standards only hurts those whom we claim to be helping. In the short run, it may seem that placing underachieving students in less demanding courses will build their self-esteem. In the long run, such courses leave students unprepared for higher education or future employment. True achievement is the only solid foundation for self-esteem.

America's schools spend huge amounts on remediation of students who fail. For most students, however, remediation simply means repeating a grade or attending summer school—returning to the same system that failed to educate them in the first place, tackling the same material in the same way. Not surprisingly, many give up and drop out.

If America is to flourish in the twenty-first century, we must do a better job of educating all our children. As a first step, we must reject the notions that some children can achieve and others cannot, that some students deserve to graduate and others do not. Dropping out is non-discriminatory; its problems do not start or stop at the city line, the poverty line, or the color line. As long as we accept the myth that dropouts are inevitable, students will fall by the wayside. We must replace this long-ingrained myth with the new conviction that dropping out is unacceptable—an insidious disease that affects not only students, but parents, teachers, and communities—and we must act on that conviction.

An increasing number of non-high-school graduates are using the General Educational Development certificate (GED) to obtain high school certification. In 1998, half a million Americans obtained a GED degree, more than double the number who

received it in 1971. These examinations cover mathematics, reading, social studies, science, and writing. Since 1988, it has included an open-ended writing component as well as multiple-choice questions. One-seventh of all graduates are actually GED recipients (*Education Week*, 2000).

In this chapter, we offer bold prescriptions for action. We demand changes in the way schools work and in the way we treat students. We propose higher expectations for parents, for teachers, and for those who train and support our teachers. We challenge local, state, and federal leaders to set new priorities to match new educational standards and goals. We call on the business community and the media to promote student achievement. All of us must do our part. America's children deserve no less.

SCHOOLS

Schools should be as customer-driven as any successful business. Outside the school, today's young people are active—engaged in sports, at the computer, at work, and at play. Schools must be equally engaging, exciting, and intellectually stimulating. Children are naturally motivated to learn, and most start school as active learners. But often as they progress through the system the responsibility for learning shifts, until by high school it is the teacher who is the worker. Too many high schools resemble factories where knowledge is poured into students like coal into a furnace or molten steel into a mold. Schools must treat students not as passive recipients of content, but as active participants in their own learning.

As educators, we need to show students the relevance of what they learn. We need to stop teaching bits and piece of information and start teaching how facts are connected to produce a coherent body of knowledge. We need to stop teaching "what to think" and start teaching "how to think"—how to solve problems, how to think creatively and analytically, how to work on teams.

There is no shortage of creative, innovative ideas for school reform. We must choose the programs that work; we must implement the strategies that have proven their effectiveness.

♦ *Early education is effective.* We must fund pre-school programs fully and make them available to all.

♦ *Mentoring is effective.* We must offer students personal direction in structured and supportive relationships.

♦ *Alternative education is effective.* We must implement programs that are open to a diversity of learning styles.

♦ *Professional development is effective.* We must train our teachers in the techniques they need to promote student achievement at a high level.

♦ *Individualized learning is effective.* We must provide flexible learning opportunities for those who learn at a different pace.

♦ *Instructional technology is effective.* We must find ways to weave technology seamlessly into the teaching and learning process.

♦ *Community collaboration is effective.* We must link schools with partners outside the classroom that support the learning process.

♦ *Conflict resolution is effective.* We must provide a safe, supportive, and nurturing school environment. We must recognize that many students bring problems to school, and help them deal with those problems.

These strategies and others—service learning, out-of-school enhancement, career education—are familiar from earlier chapters. In those chapters, we highlighted a number of model programs that implement these strategies effectively. Of course, there is ample room for other creative ideas. Why not pay senior citizens a stipend to teach young children to read, or serve as mentors to teens? Why not link their computers to those in students' homes for after-school help with homework? Why not establish high schools that are open into the evening hours, so that students who must hold down paying jobs can continue their education? This will allow students to work, if they must, and attend school as well. In short—why not find ways to make school work for all students?

Students

Too often, we speak of "at-risk" children as if they were solely responsible for the problems they face. We assume that our time-honored teaching methods must be correct; therefore, the students these methods fail to reach must be at fault. Students who struggle against the constraints of "one size fits all" education are identified as "at risk," with all the stigma the label implies.

But the educational system doesn't fit all students; it never did! This often comes as a surprise to people who were a good match for the system as students (many of whom return to the system as teachers). Now that we know better, however, we must change our approach to the students in our schools.

Students and student learning must be at the center of what happens in school. For any task involving students, we must ask, "Does this add value to student learning?" (Frequent classroom interruptions don't add value. Physical education classes in which instructors throw balls to the assembled masses don't add value. Teachers who daily hand out unexplained worksheets do not add value. Unsupervised, unstructured study halls—though they may serve the school's scheduling program—don't add value.) Tasks that don't add value to student learning have no place in schools.

Schools must use a variety of techniques to find out what students know and can do. Assessment of student work must be valid, authentic and continuous.

Students should no longer compete for grades against their peers. Instead, each student's academic growth should be measured against meaningful and relevant standards.

Students must have a voice in the decision-making processes that affect their education. Confining students for six hours a day in a place where they do not want to be is ultimately a prescription for failure.

Parents

In most cases, parents are their children's first and most significant teachers. They bear the primary responsibility for nurturing and guiding their sons and daughters from infancy through adolescence. Although they entrust schools with the education of their children, parents can certainly make a difference—after all, children spend 91 percent of their time under the influence of their parents and only 9 percent in school. We must teach parents how to encourage and support the learning process.

Statistics indicate that parental involvement diminishes as a child progresses through the educational system. Just when students need more support to overcome peer pressure, gangs, drugs, and the media, parents become less involved. We must draw parents back into the school setting—and not merely as spectators or fundraisers. In this effort, schools must recognize the constraints on a parent's time. It makes little sense, for example, to schedule parent-teacher meetings at a time when parents have to be at work or tend to younger siblings.

TEACHERS

In the twenty-first century, information, knowledge, and technology will rule. Teachers continue to be purveyors of information, but because the amount of existing information now doubles every five years, teachers must also become enablers, giving students the techniques and tools to find information for themselves and the power to transform that information into knowledge.

Teachers must impart to students the skills of investigation and analysis, writing, mathematical reasoning, problem solving, and conflict resolution. They must develop confident and independent learners who can work alone or in groups to gather information, order it, manipulate it, and apply it. And they must do this throughout the school, not just in the classrooms of innovative educators.

Teachers must embrace new methods. In too many of today's classrooms, nobody sees a student's written work except the teacher. Why not present an excellent paper to the class as a model of quality work?

Too often, teachers are evaluated on their teaching styles and techniques, rather than on what students have learned. Why not change the emphasis and direction to place greater value on improved learning?

Too often, we send untrained and inexperienced teachers into schools with a high percentage of at-risk students. We—that is, governors, mayors, school districts, superintendents, and schools of education—must do better. We must develop training materials and programs specifically geared toward identifying such students early and responding appropriately. We must find mechanisms and direct funds to place our most innovative and experienced teachers in our schools with a high at-risk population.

We must change the way we educate educators. Too often, academicians without any recent classroom experience—and some who have never been in an American public school at all—are teaching our future teachers. The deans of our schools of education need to meet with those in our K-12 system and jointly design programs to help *all* children to learn. We need to create a seamless educational system from pre-K through the university which fosters lifelong learning.

Doctors, dentists and other professionals continually upgrade their skills. Teachers should do no less. The teaching profession suffers from the common misperception that teachers only work when they are in front of a class. A professional teacher's workday must include time to collaborate with colleagues and explore new teaching methods. We must value lifelong learning as much for teachers as for students.

Finally, we must coordinate our efforts. Too often, teachers, schools, and community organizations operate in virtual isolation. Educators from pre-kindergarten to college must recognize that we all belong to the same educational system. We must learn to work together for the benefit of all our students.

GOVERNMENT LEADERS

Today's American society is enraptured with novelty. In many cases, this leads to grasping at straws—untried, untested and non-replicable models to "fix" our educational system. Politicians look for expedient answers that will not cost additional money and will be measured only after they have left office, or settle for short-term "solutions" that arise from shortsighted thinking.

America's leaders must give education the high priority it deserves. This means spending money. We must stop trimming school funding from local, state, and federal budgets. Schools cannot be expected to achieve the same or better results with less funding; children should not have to compete with municipal services for scarce community resources.

Education reform must move to the top of our national agenda. The federal government should join states in setting goals, developing performance standards, evaluating existing programs, and disseminating results from successful schools and replicable model programs. This too will cost money.

Within the next decade, schools across America will need to replace most of their teacher and administrative staff. If these schools are to hire qualified people, they must be able to pay them salaries commensurate with their responsibilities and their education. (Astonishingly, some communities pay their sanitation workers more than they pay their educators.)

Our nation's educational infrastructure—buildings and grounds, electrical systems, plumbing, heating—also demand attention. Many of our schools were built in the early part of the last century. Some have only recently converted from coal heating. Our government leaders need to find the money to upgrade these systems before a tragedy involving the death of children and teachers forces them to do so.

Some states already spend more money on prisons than on education. Data indicate that more than three-quarters of those in prison dropped out of school. When a society has the resources to incarcerate its young people but not to educate them, something is wrong. Education is a one-time cost; ignorance is a lifetime expense. If we can find the money for prisons, we can find the money for schools.

THE BUSINESS COMMUNITY

Schools and businesses share a deep common interest in keeping students in school until they graduate. Students who drop out of school will have difficulty getting a job or sustaining a career. Too often, their options shrink to two socially costly and unproductive choices—crime or welfare. Conversely, businesses need active and intelligent employees who achieve to their maximum ability. When students fail to master the skills the workplace demands, the options of American businesses are limited. They can move elsewhere—an expensive proposition. They can "dumb down" their activities. Or they can work to improve the schools.

The business community needs to assume a more active role in schools. Although many business leaders lament the quality of workers schools produce, most never work closely with schools to define the skills they seek. Closer consultation, perhaps coupled with long-term hiring relationships, could benefit both schools and businesses. Business managers could bring the world of work into the school, introducing students to real-world skills like writing a résumé or conducting a job interview.

Some businesspeople have concluded that there needs to be a better correlation between grades and success in the business world. Few businesses ask for school transcripts or consult school officials about a prospective employee's attendance, tardiness, or academic achievement. This must change.

Education will be the cornerstone of economic success in the twenty-first century. If American business is to thrive in the world marketplace, it must focus on creating a world-class public education system. Many foreign students compete to attend America's highly acclaimed colleges and universities. Few, if any, come to this country expressly to attend our public schools. Primary and secondary schools serve far more students than colleges and universities do, and spending money on the early grades is by far the most cost-effective way to raise student achievement levels. Yet businesses, foundations, and other organizations lavish funds on college and universities while ignoring the needs of the public schools that underpin our nation's educational system.

The business community has much to gain when public schools thrive. Too often, educators have one agenda, politicians another, and businesspeople yet a third. We challenge America's educational and business organizations—the National Education Association, the American Federation of Teachers, the American Society for Quality, the National Alliance for Business, the AFL/CIO, and the National Association of Manufacturing, to name a few—to form a coalition to address the essential task of strengthening public education.

THE MEDIA

Today's media largely promote values that are in many ways contrary to the values of families, schools, and society in general. Television, radio, Hollywood, the music industry, and the world of professional sports glorify instant gratification, material possessions, glamour, beauty, wealth, celebrity, entertainment, drugs, alcohol, and violence, while giving scant attention to education, community service, conflict resolution, respect for diversity, commitment, hard work, and responsibility. Against this vast and relentless current, schools must exert an enormous effort if they are to maintain the principles and values that support educational achievement for all. We call on the media to acknowledge a greater responsibility for forming the character of America's young people in a way that benefits our society. They must be as dedicated to this as they are to making a profit.

THE REST OF US

We must overcome complacency about our schools. Our own children may have good teachers; our own community may have good schools; our own state may have good standards and good accountability. But that is not enough. We must work to ensure that **all** our nation's children have good teachers, **all** communities have good schools, **all** states have good standards and good accountability. We must insist that full education and high achievement are goals that **all** can reach.

The key to economic development is public education. If you look at the problems facing America—welfare, health costs, taxes, crime—you find, at the very core, education. You cannot solve any of these other societal problems without starting at the core, and by improving education you begin the process of reforming the other systems.

As we have seen, education is also an economic issue. We must measure our schools against the world's best. Our nation's workforce competes in a global marketplace. At the top of the scale, American businesses demand well-trained, technologically prepared employees. If they cannot find them at home, they will look elsewhere. Likewise, the world is full of low-skilled, low-wage workers. The job market for young people who drop out of school today is limited at best. To maximize the potential of our nation's human resources, we must work to ensure that all our students stay in school—and all succeed.

Educational change is inevitable. We must not tolerate a public school system that does not function as it should. The question is not whether to reform our public schools, but how? And who will be the driving force behind this change? Parents, businesspeople, political leaders, and educators all have a stake in school reform. All of us must rise to the challenge.

One thing is abundantly clear—America will never reach the maximum of its capabilities so long as it tolerates a public school system that is not functioning to its fullest potential. We, all of us, have a moral, social, and economic reason not to permit students to drop out of school.

Education is America's great equalizer. It allows for a shrinking of the economic stratification in American society by allowing people means of moving up in society. The ability of children to get a better education than their parents has always paved the way toward upward mobility. The key to a vibrant economic future is to improve our entire educational system.

The fifteen effective strategies place an enormous burden on all the schools, the educators, the parents, colleges, schools of education, politicians, and businesspeople as well. But it is a burden, which can be borne more easily, if all those who have an interest in the success of our schools share it.

In this book, we have shown that solving the school dropout problem is an essential component of school reform. We have outlined fifteen effective strategies for dropout prevention, ranging from early education and family involvement, through professional development and individualized instruction, to community collaboration and career education. We have described individual programs that have implemented these strategies with noteworthy success. Each strategy can make a difference on its own; applied in a concerted effort, the fifteen strategies are a powerful force.

Explore these strategies; put them to work. Start somewhere, and start soon. America's future depends on each of us.

REFERENCES

Olson, Lynn. (2000). Study Links Dropout Rate with Course Requirements. *Education Week*, March 29, 2000, p. 6.

Teacher Magazine. (2000, May). Findings.